# PYGMALION IN THE CLASSROOM

# PYGMALION IN THE CLASSROOM

## Teacher Expectation and Pupils' Intellectual Development

**Robert Rosenthal**
HARVARD UNIVERSITY

**Lenore Jacobson**
SOUTH SAN FRANCISCO
UNIFIED SCHOOL DISTRICT

**Holt, Rinehart and Winston, Inc.**
NEW YORK     CHICAGO     SAN FRANCISCO     ATLANTA
DALLAS     MONTREAL     TORONTO     LONDON

Cover photograph courtesy of IBM

To Annette, Mary Lu, Roberta, David, and Virginia,

who fulfill our expectations.

# PREFACE

People, more often than not, do what is expected of them. Much of our behavior is governed by widely shared norms or expectations that make it possible to prophesy how a person will behave in a given situation, even if we have never met that person and know little of how he differs from others. At the same time, however, there is considerable variability of behavior so that often we can more accurately prophesy the behavior of a person we know well than we can prophecy the behavior of a stranger. To a great extent, our expectations for another person's behavior are accurate because we know his past behavior. But there is now good reason to believe that another factor increases our accuracy of interpersonal predictions or prophecies. Our prediction or prophecy may in itself be a factor in determining the behavior of other people. When we are led to expect that we are about to meet a pleasant person, our treatment of him at first meeting may, in fact, make him a more pleasant person. If we are led to expect that we shall encounter an unpleasant person, we may approach him so defensively that we make him into an unpleasant person. That, in general, is the concern of this book. It is about interpersonal self-fulfilling prophecies: *how one person's expectation for another person's behavior can quite unwittingly become a more accurate prediction simply for its having been made.*

The existing evidence for the effects of these interpersonal self-fulfilling prophecies will be summarized and, in greater detail, new evidence will be presented. This new evidence is from an educational context, and it is addressed to the question of whether a teacher's expectation for her pupils' intellectual competence can come to serve as an educational self-fulfilling prophecy.

To anticipate briefly the nature of this new evidence it is enough to say that 20 percent of the children in a certain elementary school were reported to their teachers as showing unusual potential for intellectual growth. The names of these 20 percent of the children were drawn by means of a table of random numbers, which is to say that the names were drawn out of a hat. Eight months later these unusual or "magic" children showed significantly greater gains in IQ than did the remaining children who had not been singled out for the teachers' attention. The change in the teachers' expectations regarding the intellectual performance of these allegedly "special" children had led to an actual change in the intellectual performance of these randomly selected children.

There are many determinants of a teacher's expectation of her pupils' intellectual ability. Even before a teacher has seen a pupil deal with academic tasks she is likely to have some expectation for his behavior. If she is to teach a "slow group," or children of darker skin color, or children whose mothers are "on welfare," she will have different expectations for her pupils' performance than if she is to teach a "fast group," or children of an upper-middle-class community. Before she has seen a child perform, she may have seen his score on an achievement or ability test or his last year's grades, or she may have access to the less formal information that constitutes the child's reputation. There have been theoretical formulations, and there has been some evidence, most of it anecdotal, that the teacher's expectation, however derived, can come to serve as an educational self-fulfilling prophecy. After a consideration of the new experimental evidence bearing on these formulations, the implications for educational research and practice will be considered.

This book is intended for students of education and of the behavioral sciences, generally, and for research investigators in these fields. Because it is our hope that the book may reach those students who are undergraduates, as well as those who are seasoned educators and research investigators, we have intentionally run the risk of displeasing both ends of that rather broad range. There may be a few things that seem overly technical or detailed to the undergraduate, and some that seem too oversimplified, too nontechnical to the experienced behavioral scientist. There may be too many tables in the text for the undergraduate or for the intelligent layman. There may be not quite enough tables for those scientists and educators who want to know all. As one compromise, there is an extensive series of tables in the Appendix; here, more technical data may be found by those who would utilize them. (When in the text, reference is made to these tables of the Appendix, the table number is preceded by the letter "A.") In addition to the Appendix, there is a series of footnotes, some of them longer and more technical for the more technically oriented reader.

Throughout the text, references are freely made to such statistics as $\chi^2$, $t$, and $F$. These statistics are usually given after some assertion has been made in the text, and they indicate to the more technical reader how the assertion was tested for validity. Following such symbols there often will be a letter $p$ with some decimal value, usually .05 or .01 or .001. These decimals give the probability that the finding reported could have occurred by chance. For example, in comparing two groups the statistical significance of the difference in scores may be reported as $t = 2.50$, $p < .01$, one-tail. This means that the likelihood was less than 1 in 100 that the difference found could have occurred by chance. "One-tail" means that the direction of the difference was predicted in advance of the analysis. Other commonly reported statistics are the correlations $r$ and rho. Both these statistics can take values from .00 to $+1.00$ or .00 to $-1.00$. The closer such a correlation value comes to $+1.00$ or $-1.00$, the more the two variables under discussion vary together or are predictable from each other. For these correlations, too, $p$ values are reported that tell the likelihood that the degree of association found could have occurred as a chance variation from a .00 correlation. For the statistics given, "$df$" are often reported. That symbol tells approximately on how many cases or subjects the statistic given has been based. The $df$ is almost, but not quite, the same as the exact number of cases employed. If all this is forgotten, the reader can still do nicely with just the recollection of the meaning of $p$. A $p$ of .10 means that once in ten times the result obtained could have occurred by chance. The reader must attach his own interpretation to the plausibility of a given assertion associated with a given $p$ value. Psychologists often, and statisticians sometimes, behave as though a $p$ value of .05 or .01 (or even smaller) should be obtained before it is claimed that a finding is worth talking about; but basically that is a matter of personal taste. Professor E. G. Boring called to our attention Polanyi's (1961) comment that Enrico Fermi regarded anything that happened with a probability ($p$) less than .10 as a miracle, though R. A. Fisher was thought by some to have wanted at least a $p$ of .05 before he would call it a miracle.

The research program on the effects of interpersonal self-fulfilling prophecies has been in operation for over ten years, and it was from this program that the educational research reported in this volume developed. For most of its history, that research program has been supported by the Division of Social Sciences of the National Science Foundation (G-17685, G-24826, GS-177, GS-714, and GS-1741). Without this support, little of the research reported, and none of the educational research reported here fully for the first time, could have been carried out. For their support we are very grateful.

The administrative support and confidence of Dr. Paul Nielsen, Superintendent, South San Francisco Unified School District, were also indispensable to the conduct of our educational experiment. We want to thank him for making this study possible. The assistance of Mae Evans and other members of Dr. Nielsen's staff is also acknowledged with gratitude. Our debt to the teachers and children of "Oak" School is considerable, and we acknowledge their help gratefully.

Many people assisted in the analysis of our data and in the preparation of our manuscript. We received valuable advice from Nate Gage, Jerome Kagan, David Marlowe, and Jerome Singer. Very special thanks are also due Bruce Biddle who read the entire manuscript and made many valuable suggestions for the improvement of many aspects of the book. Computational and statistical assistance were provided by Sean Edwards, John Laszlo, David Reichard, Jan Rudy, and especially by George Smiltens. Typing of the various drafts of the manuscript was expertly undertaken by Mari Tavitian and Mary Lu Rosenthal.

Finally, we want to thank the two people who participated most intensively in the conception of the idea of the Oak School Experiment and who served as constant consultants throughout every stage of the experiment and of this manuscript, Annette Insel and Mary Lu Rosenthal.

*Cambridge, Massachusetts*  R.R.
*South San Francisco, California*  L.J.
*February 1968*

# CONTENTS

# PYGMALION IN THE CLASSROOM

# PART 1

# THE SELF-FULFILLING PROPHECY ෧

# 1

# Everyday Life

The story was well-told by Robert Merton (1948). On a Wednesday morning in 1932, Cartwright Millingville comes to work. His place of business is the Last National Bank, and the office he occupies is that of its president. The tellers' windows, he notes, are rather busy for a Wednesday. Long lines of depositors are unusual for midweek, so far from payday. Millingville hopes sympathetically that they have not been laid off, and he begins his presidential chores.

The Last National Bank is a sound and solvent institution. Its president knows that, its stockholders know that, and we know that. But the people in those lines before the tellers' cages don't know that. They, in fact, believe that the bank is foundering, that if they do not quickly withdraw their deposits there will be none to withdraw, and so they are lined up now, waiting to withdraw their savings. Until they believed that and acted on their belief, they were quite wrong. But once they believed it and acted upon it, they "knew" a truth or reality unknown to Cartwright Millingville, unknown to the stockholders, and unknown to us. They knew that truth or reality because they caused that truth or reality. Their expectation, their prophecy, led to its own fulfillment. The bank failed.

Not only the collapse of economic institutions has been attributed to the operation of the self-fulfilling prophecy. Merton also pointed out the importance of such expectations in the relations among races and the behavior of minority groups generally. Inferiority of scholastic achievement among Negroes of a given state may indeed have become a reality when that state spent less than one fifth as much in the education of its Negro youth compared to the education of its white youth. Rose (1956) goes further, in a sense, by saying that both whites and Negroes expect the Negro to fail, a double expectation that "keeps the Negro from trying."

There is nothing in the concept of the self-fulfilling prophecy that makes it go in only one direction, however. That is nicely illustrated in the case of race relations by a particular self-fulfilling prophecy called "Sweeney's miracle" (*Look* Editorial Board, 1965).

James Sweeney taught industrial management and psychiatry at

Tulane University where he was responsible for the operation of the Biomedical Computer Center. It was Sweeney's expectation that he could make even a poorly educated Negro into a computer operator. The poorly educated Negro chosen was George Johnson, a former hospital porter who became janitor at the computer center. In the morning he swept and cleaned, and in the afternoon he learned about computers. He was learning a great deal about computers when word circulated that to be a computer operator one had to earn a certain score on an IQ test. Johnson took the test, which showed that he should not even be able to learn to type, much less operate a computer. But Sweeney was not convinced. He went to the administration and threatened: no Johnson, no Sweeney. Both stayed; Sweeney still runs the Computer Center, and Johnson now runs the main computer room in which position he is responsible for the training of new employees.

Another major theorist to employ the concept of the self-fulfilling prophecy was Gordon Allport (1950). His application was to the field of international tension and war. It was likely, Allport suggested, that nations that expect to go to war, go to war. The expectation to wage war is communicated to the opponent-to-be who reacts by preparing for war, an act which confirms the first nation's expectation, strengthens it, leads to greater preparations for war, and so on, in a mutually reinforcing system of positive feedback loops. Nations expecting to remain out of wars sometimes seem to manage to avoid entering into them.

More prosaic but no less interesting than the analysis of large-scale social and economic phenomena is the analysis of the way a man golfs or bowls in relation to what is expected of him. As a participant observer, William Whyte (1943) studied the bowling behavior of a group of young men, members of Whyte's famous street-corner gang. That group, and especially its leaders, "knew" how well a man should bowl. On a given evening, the group "knew" that a given member would bowl well, and so he did. On another evening, the group "knew" that some member would bowl poorly, and so he did, even if he had bowled well the evening before. The group's expectancy of the members' performance seemed to be determining that performance. Perhaps the morale-building banter and encouragement given him who was expected to do well helped him to do so by increasing his motivation and by decreasing his anxiety with its interfering effects. The communication, to a member of the group, of the group's expectation that he would bowl poorly may have reduced his motivation and increased his anxiety to a point where it interfered with his performance.

Although not dealing specifically with the effects of one person's expectancy on another's behavior, some observations by Jastrow (1900) are relevant. He wrote of the athlete who so fears his failure that his coordination is impaired and he does fail. ". . . the entertainment of the notion of a possible failure to reach the mark lessens the intensity of one's effort, and prevents the accomplishment of one's best" (p. 301). In his examples, Jastrow did not specify that the expectancy of failure came from another person. The example provided by Whyte, however, does suggest that such expectancies often do come from other people.

The effects on a person's behavior of the expectancies others have of that behavior is further illustrated by the learning theorist E. R. Guthrie (1938). A shy and socially inept young lady became self-confident and relaxed in social contacts by having been systematically treated as a social favorite. A helpful group of college men had arranged the expectancies of those who met her so that socially adept behavior was expected of her. The expected adeptness was duly evoked by the expectation for it. In the more serious area of reactions to disaster, Goldstein (1962) notes Drayer's (1956) observation of the importance of the expectations of the rescue workers. In both civilian and military disasters, the victims seem to respond in accordance with the response expected of them by the rescue workers. Psychiatric experience in the United States Army seems to suggest that the more clearly a psychiatric casualty is treated as such, the less likely it is that he can return to duty (Bushard, 1957). In the more everyday experience of driving an automobile, Shor (1964) has pointed out that one driver's expectation of another's automotive behavior can serve as self-fulfilling prophecy.

Jastrow (1900) gives details of a well-documented case of self-fulfilling prophecies in the world of work. The year was 1890 and the Hollerith tabulating machine had just been installed at the United States Census Bureau. The machine, something like a typewriter, required the clerks to learn a new skill which the inventor, Hollerith, regarded as quite demanding. He expected that a trained worker could punch about 550 cards per day. After two weeks the workers were adequately trained and began to produce about 550 cards per day. After a while the clerks began to exceed the expected performance but only at great emotional cost. Workers became so tense trying to beat the expected limit that the Secretary of the Interior forbade the establishment of any minimum performance criterion. This was seen as a step necessary to preserve the mental health of the establishment.

Then, a new group of some 200 clerks was brought in to augment the Hollerith machine work force. These clerks knew nothing of the work, had no prior training, and had never even seen the machine. No one had told these workers what the emotional cost of the work might be nor of the upper limit of production that could be achieved. This lack of information turned out to be their greatest asset. Within three days this new group was performing at the level which was reached only after seven weeks by the earlier, "more properly" indoctrinated, group. Whereas clerks from the initial group were exhausted after producing 700 cards per day, members of the new group began turning out three times that number and without ill effects.

Some seventy-five years after the Census Bureau adopted the Hollerith system and provided us with an industrial example of the self-fulfilling prophecy, Bavelas (1965) described a more formal test of the proposition in an industrial setting. In a large industrial concern, a large number of female applicants for employment underwent an evaluation procedure. Each applicant was administered tests of intelligence and of finger dexterity. The foremen who were to supervise these employees were led to believe that certain of these women had scored high on the tests and that certain of these women had scored low. What the foremen were told bore no relationship, of course, to the actual performance of the applicants. Some time later, the foremen's evaluations of their workers and the workers' actual production records were obtained. It turned out that foremen evaluated more favorably those workers who were believed to be superior on the basis of their alleged test scores. This much could be attributed to a simple "halo" effect in which the perception of the foremen was affected by their expectation. Not so simply interpreted was the finding that the objective production record of the workers was superior if the foremen had expected superior performance. This result could not be attributed to a simple halo effect, but rather to another case of an interpersonally self-fulfilling prophecy. Interestingly, the workers' actual test scores showed no relationship to either the foremen's subsequent evaluation or to the objective production record.

The cases of self-fulfilling prophecy presented so far serve only to illustrate the concept, not to establish the reality, utility, or generality of the phenomenon. With the exception of the research by Bavelas, the examples given provide at best a kind of anecdotal evidence. While they are not, therefore, worthless, they are also inconclusive. Assuming for the moment only that people make prophecies about future events, or hold expectancies about them, we may examine a typology of possible relationships existing between prophecies of events and the events as they subsequently occur.

**Table 1-1**  Typology of Relationships
between Prophecies
and Subsequent Events

TYPE I  NO RELATIONSHIP BETWEEN PROPHECY AND EVENT
Case 1  A.  And no relationship is claimed
Case 2  B.  But a relationship is claimed

TYPE II  SOME RELATIONSHIP BETWEEN PROPHECY AND EVENT

A.  The relationship is negative
Case 3  1.  But not due to the prophecy
Case 4  2.  And due to the prophecy

B.  The relationship is positive
        1.  But not due to the prophecy
Case 5  a.  coincidental
Case 6  b.  prophecy is due to related past events
Case 7  2.  And due to the prophecy

## SOME POSSIBLE RELATIONSHIPS
## BETWEEN PROPHECIES AND EVENTS

Table 1-1 shows some of the more likely relationships between
prophecies and the events as they subsequently occur. In Case 1 there
is no relationship between the prophecy and the event prophesied, and
no such relationship is claimed. (That would be the situation of the
statistically sophisticated roulette player: Granting a fair roulette
wheel, there should be no relationship between the bet and the
particular color or number which wins.) In Case 2 no relationship is
found between prophecy and event, but the prophet thinks otherwise.
(A roulette player who wins consistently, an infrequent but quite
possible occurrence, even with a fair wheel, may come to believe
his prophecies affect the turning wheel.) That not only the unsophisti-
cated perceive relationships where none exist has been amply docu-
mented by Chapman and Chapman (1967).

The Type II relationships have in common that some relationship
really does exist between prophecy and subsequent event, but the
nature of the relationship may be positive or negative, and the relationship may or may not be due to the prophecy itself. Thus, in Cases
3 and 4 we have an antiself-fulfilling prophecy. The prophecy accurately predicts its own opposite, a state of affairs Merton (1948) has
called the "suicidal prophecy." The worried physician who prophesies
his patient's early demise, and therefore takes extraordinarily good

care of him, serves as example. He serves also to illustrate that subtype (Case 4) of negative relationship between prophecy and event in which the relationship is due to the prophecy itself. It is also possible, however, that the prophecy itself is not the effective variable but rather some correlated attribute of the prophet. Thus, worried physicians may also have professional competencies such that their patients live longer, and the fact of their worried nature may be irrelevant though it leads to a spurious negative correlation between worry over patients' health and patient longevity (Case 3).

Similarly in Cases 5–7, the self-fulfilling prophecy is not always really self-fulfilling. The prophecy may be related to the subsequent event without having been responsible for it (Cases 5 and 6). Thus, an optimistic teacher who prophesies good achievement for an educationally difficult child may obtain good achievement from him, not because she prophesied it, but because of the personality correlates of her optimism (Case 5). Sometimes a prophecy seems to lead to the event prophesied when actually the reverse is true. The observation of related events in the past shapes the prophecy which turns out simply to be an accurate prediction not affecting the event prophesied (Case 6).

Finally, there is that type of relationship between prophecy and subsequent event in which the prophecy is not incidental but instrumental in its own fulfillment (Case 7). That is the relationship in which we are most interested, but it is not always so easy in practice to distinguish it from other types. In Chapter 3 this problem will be taken up more rigorously, and a stronger kind of evidence will be presented to demonstrate the reality and generality of the phenomenon. To proceed now, somewhat on faith, the question must be asked: Assuming the operation of self-fulfilling prophecies, what makes them happen? Are there some general principles that would explain the prophecy's role in its own fulfillment regardless of the nature of the specific prophecy?

## MOTIVATION FOR
## PROPHECY FULFILLMENT

It is unpleasant to have one's expectations disconfirmed though a windfall does not ordinarily lead to psychological depression. But, by and large, people do not like to be wrong. This common-sense assertion is supported by experimental evidence, evidence that is desirable because from common sense alone we "know" too many things that are not true. Carlsmith and Aronson (1963) showed that when subjects were expecting to taste a bitter substance but were given a sweet substance instead, the sweet tasted less sweet. When they were expecting to taste a sweet substance but were given the bitter, the bitter was judged more bitter than usual. The everyday analogue of this experiment is that occasional experience when one misperceives one delicate morsel for another. An unpleasant gustatory experience results from ingesting an unexpected food item even when it would normally rank high in one's hierarchy of food preferences. Sampson and Sibley (1965) at least partially confirmed the Carlsmith and Aronson findings.

Aronson, Carlsmith, and Darley (1963) provided further evidence by showing that subjects sometimes prefer an objectively more unpleasant task over one which is more pleasant but unexpected. Subjects also seem to be more satisfied with their task performance when they have done about as expected. Aronson and Carlsmith (1962) showed that subjects who performed poorly but expected to do so seemed more satisfied than even those subjects who performed well but had not expected to.

Consistent with these findings is an experiment by Harvey and Clapp (1965), which found that when subjects expected others to say nice things about them they reacted more favorably to hearing nice than not-nice evaluations. This finding was not surprising. But, when subjects expected to hear unpleasant things said about them and subsequently did hear them said, they reacted more favorably than when they expected unpleasant evaluations but received pleasant ones instead. It appears from these and other studies, though there are also studies not supporting the idea (McGuire, 1966), that there may indeed be a measure of pain in nature's unpredictability, even when nature's response has been cordial; and that nature's unkindnesses may be far easier to bear when they have been prophesied. There may be an evolutionary advantage to this state of affairs. If, in the long run, man does not like surprises too well, that may foster the enterprise of gaining greater understanding and therefore greater control of nature. That enterprise includes magic and religion and science, and the last of these permits more or less quantitative statements of the amount of reduction of potential surprise in nature. A greater understanding of nature gives greater power to control it or adapt to it, and then the potential surprises can be reduced still more. If man has been able to survive better for having been more accurate in his prophecies, then it seems reasonable to think that man has a vested interest in predictive accuracy. Reassurance of such accuracy may be more rewarding to man than some minor unpredictable boon of nature. In any case, whether we employ biological concepts like "survival value" or not, it is agreed by many theorists that man wants at least a minimal stability, consistency, order, or predictability in his world (Allport, 1950; Festinger, 1957; Kelly, 1955; Potter, 1964; Rotter, 1954; Tolman, 1932).

# 2

# The
# Healing
# Professions

When, in the last chapter, illustrations were given of the self-fulfilling prophecy, the prophets involved were not charged with the task of changing the people or institutions about which they made their prophecies. In most of the examples given, there was no intent on the part of the prophet to affect the events prophesied. This chapter considers those prophets who are charged by society to bring about beneficial changes in the people about whom they must make professional prophecies. In this sense the healing professions of clinical psychology, psychiatry, medicine, and rehabilitation are like the educational professions. Indeed, at times it becomes difficult to make a clear distinction between the healing and educational professions. Where shall we place the school counselor, for example, the director of special education, or the pupil-personnel specialist? A consideration, then, of self-fulfilling prophecies in the healing professions may enlighten our subsequent consideration of self-fulfilling prophecies in educational contexts.

## HYPNOSIS

Though it was the sociologist Merton (1948) who drew heavily upon and contributed greatly to the concept of the self-fulfilling prophecy, and particularly for the analysis of such large-scale social and economic phenomena as racial and religious prejudice (and the failure of banks), the concept was applied half a century earlier in a clinical context. Albert Moll (1898) spoke specifically of clinical phenomena in which "the prophecy causes its own fulfillment" (p. 244). He mentioned hysterical paralyses cured at the time it was believed they could be cured. He told of insomnia, nausea, impotence, and stammering all coming about when their advent was most expected. But his particular interest was in the phenomenon of hypnosis. It was his belief that subjects behaved as they believed they were expected to behave.

Much later, Martin Orne (1959) showed clearly and dramatically that Moll was right. Two matched classes in introductory psychology were each given a lecture on the subject of hypnosis. As part of the lecture there was a demonstration. In one of the classes the hypnotic demonstration included three subjects' showing catalepsy or rigidity of their dominant hand. If the subject was right-handed the demonstration would show rigidity of his right hand; if left-handed, then the rigidity would seize the left. The other classroom received essentially all the same information about hypnosis, but there was no mention made, nor any demonstration, of the dominant-hand catalepsy. Subsequently, nine subjects from each of the two classes were hypnotized by an experimenter who did not know which lecture the subjects had attended. Among the subjects who did not expect catalepsy of the dominant hand, none showed catalepsy of the dominant hand alone. However, among the subjects who had learned that "hypnosis implies dominant-hand catalepsy" most of the subjects showed just that. There is further evidence to show that Moll was right (Barber and Calverley, 1964) though Levitt and Brady (1964) showed that the subject's expectation did not always lead to a confirming performance.

In the studies just now cited we were not dealing specifically with the hypnotist's expectancy as an unintended determinant of the subject's response. It was more a case of the subject's expectancy as a determinant of his own response. As yet there have been no reports of studies in which different hypnotists were led to have different expectations about their subjects' performance. That is the kind of study needed to establish the effects of the hypnotist's expectation on his subject's response. Kramer and Brennan (1964) do have an interpretation of some data which fits the model of the self-fulfilling prophecy. They worked with schizophrenic patients and found them to be as susceptible to hypnosis as college undergraduates. In the past, schizophrenics had been thought far less susceptible to hypnosis. Their interpretation suggested that, relative to the older studies, their own approach to the schizophrenic patients communicated to them the investigators' expectancy that the patients could be hypnotized.

## PSYCHOTHERAPY

In the area of psychotherapy, a number of workers have been impressed by the effects of the self-fulfilling prophecy. One of the best-known of these was Frieda Fromm-Reichmann (1950), who spoke, as other clinicians have, of iatrogenic psychiatric incurabilities. The therapist's own belief about the patient's prognosis might be a determinant of that prognosis. Strupp and Luborsky (1962) and Shapiro

(1964) have also made this point, and Karl Menninger (1964), commenting on an earlier time, said "mental illness was incurable because psychiatrists and others had lost their faith and hope . . . [later] . . . the mentally ill were once more regarded as curable, and so proved to be" (p. 275). These clinical impressions are supported to some extent by a few more formal investigations. Heine and Trosman (1960) did not find the patient's initial expectation of help to be related to his continuance in treatment. They did find, however, that when the therapist and patient had congruent expectations that patients continued longer in treatment. Experimental procedures to help ensure such congruence have been described by Jerome Frank and have met with considerable success (Frank, 1965). Briefly put, prospective patients are given psychotherapy lessons; they learn what to expect and what will be expected of them.

Goldstein (1960) found no client-perceived personality change to be related to the therapist's expectancy of such change. However, the therapist's expectancy was related to duration of psychotherapy. Additionally, Heller and Goldstein (1961) found the therapist's expectation of client improvement significantly correlated (.62) with a change in the client's attraction to the therapist. These workers also found that after fifteen sessions, the clients' behavior was no more independent than before, but that their self descriptions were of more independent behavior. The therapists employed in this study generally were favorable to increased independence and tended to expect successful cases to show this decrease in dependency. Clients may well have learned from their therapists that independent-sounding verbalizations were desired and thereby served to fulfill their therapist's expectancy. The most complete discussion of the general importance to the psychotherapeutic interaction of the expectancy or prophecy variable is that by Goldstein (1962). But hypnosis and psychotherapy are not the only realms of clinical practice in which the clinician's expectancy may determine the outcome.

## FATALITY RATES

The fatality rates of delirium tremens have recently not exceeded about 15 percent. However, from time to time new treatments of greatly varying sorts are reported to reduce this figure almost to zero. Gunne's work in Sweden summarized by the staff of the *Quarterly Journal of Studies on Alcohol* (1959) showed that *any* change in therapy led to a drop in mortality rate. One interpretation of this finding is that the innovator of the new treatment expects a decrease in mortality rate, an expectancy which leads to subtle differential patient care over and above the specific treatment under investigation. A prophecy again may have been self-fulfilled. Similarly, in an analysis of suicidal behavior, Kobler and Stotland (1964) eloquently suggest that families' and healers' expectations for a patient's suicide may be communicated to the patient with a resulting increase in the likelihood that the patient will fulfill the prophecy. "In our view, those who actually commit suicide respond to the expectation that they will kill themselves" (p. 262).

Professor H. Péquignot, writing in a noted French medical magazine (1966), has pointed out the self-fulfilling nature of many medical prognoses. An approximate translation tells us:

> A whole series of symptoms can actually permit the prediction of approaching death. But only in the case where one does nothing to fight them. We have too many examples before our eyes of situations considered irreversible and which became that way because this diagnosis had been given. . . . The havoc of a pessimistic prognosis in medicine is no longer taken into account. A pessimistic prognosis acquires by the discouragement it carries with it on the part of the doctor, the family, the people looking after the patient and of the sick person, a potential of automatic verification which renders it formidable. (p. 10)

Greenblatt (1964) described a patient suffering from advanced cancer who was admitted to the hospital virtually dying. He had been exposed to the information that Krebiozen might be a wonder drug, and it was administered to him. The improvement was dramatic and he was discharged to his home for several months. Then came exposure to the information that Krebiozen was probably ineffective. He relapsed and was readmitted to the hospital. There, his faith in Krebiozen was restored though the injections he received were of saline solution rather than of Krebiozen. Once again he was sufficiently improved to be discharged. Finally, he was exposed to the information that the American Medical Association denied completely the value of Krebiozen. The patient then lost all hope and was readmitted to the hospital, this time for the last time; he died within forty-eight hours.

Gordon Allport (1964) described another patient, one dying of an unknown illness. The attending physicians told him quite frankly that he could not expect to be cured since the diagnosis was unknown. The only hope they offered him was that a distinguished diagnostician had been called in and was soon to give his expert opinion. The specialist arrived but needed only a little time to reach his conclusion. To the physicians in attendance and almost out of the patient's earshot he pronounced: "moribundus." After some years, our patient, who did not die, called on the specialist to report on his good health and to thank the physician for saving his life. The ex-patient explained how the medical staff had told him that he could be cured only if the disease could be diagnosed. Therefore, he explained, he knew that he would recover as soon as he heard the consultant's diagnosis of "moribundus."

In Allport's anecdote we see something of a paradox. The staff and the patient expected that if a diagnosis could be made that the patient could be cured. The "diagnosis" was made and the patient was cured although the diagnosis was itself a prophecy for incurability. Presumably, had our patient known the true nature of the prophecy the outcome of his illness might have been less favorable. Such anecdotes as we have told, by themselves cannot be regarded as strong evidence for the operation of expectancy effects or of prophecies self-fulfilled. Such anecdotes and others (Beecher, 1962) are, however, supported by the results of more formal investigations into the effects of the placebo in medical practice.

## PLACEBO

Arthur Shapiro (1960), in his excellent review of the history of the placebo effect, points out that until very recently, perhaps the late nineteenth century, virtually all medical treatment was treatment by placebo. Treatments worked, though, as evidenced by the high esteem in which even physicians of long ago were held. Shapiro tells how well they worked. In 1794, Professor Ranieri Gerbi of Pisa devised a cure for toothache guaranteed to prevent recurrence for a full year. A particular worm was required, *curculio antiodontaligious* by name, which was crushed between the thumb and forefinger of the right hand. The fingers were then applied to the painful tooth. In order to establish the scientific validity of this cure, an investigatory body was convened in order to assess the efficacy of the treatment. The commission's inquiry revealed that 68.5 percent of the hundreds of toothaches investigated yielded immediately to the power of the worm (Shapiro, 1960).

Modern medicine is vastly more sophisticated though it has been observed that new drugs always seem most efficacious early in their career, losing some of their therapeutic potency with the passage of time. This phenomenon, like the operation of placebo effects in general, can be partially understood in terms of the healer's expectation for the efficacy of the preparation. In the absence of firmer data we can only conjecture about the physician's expectation and its communication to the patient at various points in time (Sheard, 1963). When a new drug comes onto the market, its advantages and efficacy well-publicized, the doctor might say to a patient: "Here is a new drug, one not available yesterday, which has been shown to be effective for just your medical condition." The voice in which this is said is enthusiastic.

Meanwhile, at the medical schools, the medical researchers are subjecting the new drug to more rigorous test. Not only are patients administered the drug, but other, equivalent patients are not administered the drug. Still more rigorously, another group of patients may receive a placebo, but they and perhaps their physician are led to think that the placebo is the new drug. If 60 percent of the patients given the real drug are improved, perhaps 30 percent who are given nothing are also improved, and 50 percent of those given the dummy drug may be improved. Careful studies of this sort then find their way into the medical literature. The conscientious physician we met earlier as an enthusiastic prophet reads the new and careful research performed, and, out of respect to his scientific training, changes his view of the new drug.

The next patient for whom the now not-so-new drug would be indicated is also given the drug. But this time the physician, perhaps in a more matter-of-fact, even tentative, tone of voice, says: "Here is a fairly new drug which has been sometimes useful in the treatment of your condition." While speaking, he may have in mind the research, which shows most of the efficacy of the new drug to be in the mind of the patient and, perhaps, in the mind of the physician. This knowledge may materially reduce the efficacy of the drug. It would seem to be quite likely that the earlier-seen patient would be more benefited than the later-seen patient.

Some credibility accrues to our fantasy from the research by Fisher, Cole, Rickels, and Uhlenhuth (1964). In their study of the effects of meprobamate, they trained some physicians to play a "treatment-oriented" role while other physicians were trained to play a "research-oriented" role. The treatment-oriented role called for the physician's communicating to his patients great confidence in the drug. The research-oriented role called for the physician's communicating to his patients grave doubts about the efficacy of the drug. The more confident, enthusiastic physicians, it turned out, were considerably more successful in keeping their patients in treatment than were the research-oriented physicians. Such a result is consistent with our hunch that drugs become less effective over time because the healer's doubts about the drug increase. These doubts, which are communicated to the patient, tend to increase as less favorable research reports become available.

Sometimes it is not therapeutic potency that is lost with time but rather nontherapeutic potency, or "undesirable side effects." That seems to be the case with the use of oral contraceptives. Early in their usage there is a large number of complaints of undesirable side effects which drop out with the passage of time. Gregory Pincus of the Worcester Foundation for Experimental Biology gives the details and also shows that these reported side effects are probably placebo effects (1966). He employed three groups of women. One group was given the oral contraceptive with the usual warnings that there might be undesirable side effects. A second group was given a placebo instead of the real contraceptive but was also given the usual warnings. These two groups of women were asked to continue using their usual mode of contraception throughout the course of the experiment. The third group of women was given the oral contraceptive but was not given the usual warnings to watch for undesirable side effects. Reactions of nausea, vomiting, headache, vertigo, gastralgia, and malaise occurred about 6 percent of the time among the women who had not been led to expect side effects. In both groups in which the women had been warned about side effects they occurred about three times that often. The women who received the placebo with warning showed about the same degree of side effects as the women who received the real drug with warning. When the symptom considered was amenorrhea, the side effect occurred three times more often when the placebo was administered than when the drug was administered with the usual warning. When the drug was administered without the usual cautions, amenorrhea did not occur at all.

Oral contraceptives are "real" chemicals that no doubt perform their functions without much assistance from the expectation of the patient or of the physician. But, as we have learned from Pincus' research, the alleged side effects can hardly be attributed to the specific effects of the drug. There is considerable additional evidence to show that an almost limitless number of side effects can be found when only the pharmacologically inactive placebo has been prescribed. These reactions include dryness of the mouth, nausea, sensation of heaviness, headache, difficulty concentrating, drowsiness, warm glow, relaxation, fatigue, sleep, skin rash, palpitation, and constriction of the pupils (Beecher, 1955). In the light of these "drug effects" from nondrugs, it should not surprise us that the colorful effects of LSD25 have also been reported from the ingestion of placebo by a subject who thought he might be given a "psychotomimetic" drug (Reed and Witt, 1965).

The effectiveness of placebo drugs is not so surprising even to the man in the street who shows us his sophistication by having adopted the term "sugar pill" for everyday talk. What might be surprising to to him, as it is even to many behavioral scientists, is the effectiveness of placebo surgery. We turn to Beecher (1961) for the details. An operation (ligation of the internal mammary arteries) was developed for the relief of angina pectoris; the results were spectacular. But the benefits of the operation had nothing to do with the operation itself; the benefits were the results "of what happened in the minds of the patients and the surgeons involved" (Beecher, 1961, p. 1103). The benefits of this surgical procedure were not equitably distributed among surgeons, however. Those who were enthusiastic about the procedure brought relief to their patients nearly four times as often as did the more skeptical surgeons. In carefully controlled experiments, it turned out that simply making skin incisions was just as effective in treating the angina pectoris as performing the specific operation. Understandably, the popularity of this particular surgery waned quickly. We might guess that if it were used it would now be less effective than formerly unless perhaps performed by a surgeon un-acquainted with Beecher's work.

The research dealing with placebo effects suggests the wisdom of that physician who admonished: "Treat as many patients as possible with the new drugs while they still have the power to heal" (Shapiro, 1960, p. 114), an admonition that might be seconded by other con-temporary investigators (for example, Honigfeld, 1964; Lesse, 1964; Schofield, 1964).

The hypothesis that the healer's self-fulfilling prophecy may be an important component of the placebo effect will require additional, direct experimental test. But the hypothesis is fairly well-supported by still further work of Beecher.

In the investigation of moderate levels of experimentally induced pain, Beecher (1966) compared the effects of morphine to the effects of placebo in the control of pain. Morphine was no better than the saline solution placebo. The "trouble" was that Beecher had employed a double-blind design in which neither the subject nor the investigator knew when morphine had been administered and when the placebo had been administered. Other investigators did not have Beecher's "trouble." They obtained beautiful data differentiating morphine's effect from placebo's effect. They, however, always knew when the mor-phine was being administered and when the placebo. That made the self-fulfilling prophecy possible. Beecher's double-blind method did not permit the operation of self-fulfilling prophecies. When the investigator does not know what to expect, he cannot "communicate subtly" to the subject how he ought to respond. It should be mentioned that morphine *is* effective in the control of "real" pain and even of experimentally induced pain as long as the level of that pain is severe (Beecher, 1966).

## COLLECTIVE PROPHECIES

In most of the discussion so far the emphasis has been on a single prophet, the hypnotist, the psychotherapist, the physician. Sometimes it is less easy and less useful to think of the prophecy of a specific healer when many healers are involved, as in the treatment or rehabilitation of a given patient. In the field of vocational rehabilitation, researchers of the Human Interaction Research Institute concluded that the expectancies or prophecies of the project staff seemed to lead to commensurate client performance. The researchers evaluated a project that attempted to demonstrate that a mentally retarded young man could learn to be gainfully employed. "The staff found that when they expected him to assume some personal responsibility, he was able to do so" (Coffey, Dorcus, Glaser, Greening, Marks, and Sarason, 1964, p. 11).

There is an experiment in which the entire staff of a hospital was led to believe that a new tranquilizer and a new energizing drug were being introduced into the hospital (Loranger, Prout, and White, 1961). Actually both the new drugs were placebos, but only the hospital director and the authors were aware of that. According to staff assessment, the drugs were found very effective in patient treatment with about 70 percent of the patients helped at least a little. When more controlled observations of patient improvement were employed, the benefits of the energizer placebo disappeared, but the benefits of the pseudotranquillizer remained statistically significant. At the very least, staff prophecies or expectancies can affect their perception of patient improvement; very likely staff prophecies can also affect patients' actual improvement (Goffman, 1961; Stanton and Schwartz, 1954; Zusman, 1967).

An experiment by Taylor (1966) is relevant here. For ten psychiatrically hospitalized patients Taylor obtained measures of their degree of maladjustment. For an arbitrarily selected six of the patients, the attendants and nurses were told that a new instrument, developed at Harvard, predicted that these patients would show surprising improvement. About the other four patients, the control group, nothing was said. The favorable expectancies or prophecies were successfully induced in the staff as judged by the staff's rating the special-prognosis patients more favorably than the control patients. The ten patients were then followed up until the time of their leaving the hospital. A number of dispositions were possible, and six psychologists and social workers ranked the favorableness of the various dispositions from (1) most favorable, to (6) least favorable. The mean ranks of outcome favorability ranged from 1.2 for outright discharge to 5.2 for discharge against medical advice. Table 2-1 based on raw data obtained from Taylor's report, shows the mean ranks of favorableness of dispositions for the male and female patients of the experimental and control groups. The lower ranks represent the more favorable dispositions, so we see that female patients receive more favorable discharges than male patients and that, especially among female patients, those who are expected to improve more are given more favorable discharges. With a total of only ten patients it is difficult for even a large effect to achieve a conventional level of statistical significance. It was, therefore, of special interest to note that the differences between the experimental and control patients could have occurred by chance from only two to thirteen times in a hundred. (Taylor employed three different statistical tests, yielding $p$ levels of .02, .06, and .13.)

| Table 2-1 | Favorableness of Results of Hospitalization | | |
|---|---|---|---|
| SEX OF PATIENT | EXPERIMENTAL | CONTROL | DIFFERENCE |
| Male | 3.5 | 4.7 | +1.2 |
| Female | 1.2 | 3.5 | +2.3 |
| MEAN | 2.3 | 4.1 | +1.8 |

All patients had been pretested for general level of adjustment before the experiment began. The pre-experimental level of psychopathology was no better (and possibly a little worse) in predicting quality of discharge than was the expectation of the hospital staff.

The investigator in this study, a graduate student, had encountered considerable hostility to her research on the part of ward personnel. They seemed to resent the extra work necessitated by the study, and at times appeared not to understand the procedures required. In view of these difficulties, Taylor was quite surprised by her findings and concluded that expectations or prophecies about other people's future behavior may be much more malleable than is generally supposed.

# 3

# Behavioral
# Science

B ehavioral scientists are said to be so self-conscious
about their science making that one day there may
be a science of those scientists who study scientists. For the most part,
that is in the future; but there is, in the present, a developing science
of the behavioral scientist as he conducts his research.

The social situation that comes about when a behavioral scientist
meets his research subject is a situation of general and unique importance. The general importance derives from the fact that the
interaction of investigator and subject, like any other two-party interaction, can be investigated empirically so that we may learn more
about two-party interactions in general. The unique importance derives from the fact that the interaction of investigator and subject,
quite unlike any other two-party interaction, is the source of so much
of what we know about human behavior. To the extent that we hope
for dependable knowledge about human behavior, we must have
dependable knowledge about the interaction between the behavioral
scientist and his research subject.

Several aspects of the interaction between investigator and subject
have been examined, and a summary of many of the findings is available elsewhere (Rosenthal, 1966). Here we shall be concerned with
only one aspect of the investigator-subject interaction, the effect on his
subject's behavior of the investigator's hypothesis or prophecy about
the subject's behavior. Some such hypothesis or prophecy about the
subject's behavior is virtually guaranteed. Behavioral scientists, like
other scientists, would not conduct research at all if they did not have
some expectation or prophecy about the result. Even in those more
loosely planned investigations sometimes called "fishing expeditions"
or, more elegantly, "heuristic searches," the expectations or prophecies
of the scientist are reflected in the selection of the entire pool of
variables chosen for study. Scientific "fishing expeditions," like real
ones, do not take place in randomly selected pools.

## SURVEY RESEARCH

The literature dealing with the self-fulfilling prophecy in survey
research is a venerable one, and one of its most venerable examples

is the study by Stuart Rice (1929). He told how some 2000 applicants for charity were interviewed by a group of 12 skilled interviewers. Interviewers talked individually with their respondents who had been assigned in a wholly nonselected manner. Respondents ascribed their dependent status to factors predictable from a knowledge of the interviewers' expectancies. Thus, one of the interviewers, a staunch prohibitionist, obtained three times as many responses implicating Demon Rum than did another interviewer regarded as a socialist who, in turn, obtained half again as many responses implicating industrial factors than did the prohibitionist interviewer. Rice concluded that the expectancy of the interviewer was somehow communicated to the respondent who then replied as prophesied. Hyman, Cobb, Feldman, Hart, and Stember (1954) disagreed with Rice's interpretation. They preferred to ascribe his remarkable results to errors of recording or of coding. What the correct interpretation is, we cannot say, for the effects, if of observation or of prophecy, were private ones. In either case, of course, the results of the research were strikingly affected by the expectancy of the data collector.

One of the earliest studies deliberately creating differential expectancies in interviewers was that conducted by Harvey (1938). Each of six boys was interviewed by each of five young postgraduates. The boys were to report to the interviewers on a story they had been given to read, and the interviewers were to use these reports to form impressions of the boys' character. Each interviewer was given some contrived information about the boys' reliability, sociability, and stability, but told not to regard these data in assessing the boys. The results of standardized questions asked of the interviewers at the conclusion of the study suggested that biases of assessment occurred even without interviewers' awareness and despite conscious resistance to bias. Harvey felt that the interviewers' bias evoked a certain attitude toward the boys which in turn determined the behavior to be expected as well as the interpretation given to that behavior. Again, we cannot be sure that subjects' responses were actually altered by interviewer expectancies. The possibility, however, is too provocative to overlook.

Wyatt and Campbell (1950) trained over 200 student interviewers for a public opinion survey dealing with the 1948 United States presidential campaign. Before collecting their data, the interviewers prophesied the percentage distribution of responses they would obtain to each of five questions. For four of the five questions asked, interviewers tended to obtain more answers in the direction of their expectancy although the effect was significant statistically in the case of only one question. More recent evidence for the self-fulfilling effects of prophecies in surveys and related research comes from the work of Hanson and Marks (1958), and Schwab (1965), and a very thorough discussion can be found in Hyman *et al.* (1954).

## EXPERIMENTAL PSYCHOLOGY

A comparison of the literatures of experimental psychology and of survey research suggests that experimental psychology has been the less avid in the pursuit of information about its data collectors' unintended effects on subjects' behavior. There are three possible reasons. The first is logistic, and it has to do with the fact that survey research data collectors are more numerous per investigation than are psychological experimenters and are, therefore, more available for study. The second reason is methodological, and it has to do with the greater standardization of procedure possible in the laboratory than in the field, a fact which may seem to make it less necessary to worry about laboratory experimenter effects than about field interviewer effects. The third reason is psychological, and it has to do with the fact that the laboratory experimenter is more often the responsible investigator in a research enterprise than is the field interviewer who is more often a "hired hand." Such unintended effects of the data collector as the operation of self-fulfilling prophecies are psychologically easier to investigate in one's hired hands than in one's research assistants, or in one's doctoral students, or in oneself. But in spite of these difficulties there are studies of the self-fulfilling effects of the laboratory experimenter's prophecies though some of them come more from the tradition of survey research than from experimental psychology.

There is, for example, an analysis of 168 studies which had been conducted to establish the validity of the Rorschach ink-blot technique of personality assessment. Levy and Orr (1959) categorized each of these studies on each of the following dimensions: (1) whether the affiliation of the author was academic or nonacademic; (2) whether the study was designed to assess construct (indirect) or criterion (direct) validity; and (3) whether the outcome of the study was favorable or unfavorable to the hypothesis of Rorschach validity. Results showed that academicians, more interested in construct validity, obtained outcomes relatively more favorable to construct validation and less favorable to criterion validation. We cannot be sure that the reported findings can be considered as another case of expectancy or prophecy effect; it might have been that the choice of specific hypotheses for testing or the choice of research designs or procedures for testing them determined the apparently biased outcomes. At the very least, however, this study accomplished its task of calling attention to the potential self-fulfilling effects of experimenters' prophecies.

Perhaps the earliest study which employed a straightforward experimental task and also probably varied the prophecy of the experimenter was that of Stanton and Baker (1942). In their study, 12 nonsense geometric figures were presented to a group of 200 undergraduate subjects. After several days, retention of these figures was measured by five experienced workers. The experimenters were supplied with a key of "correct" responses, some of which really were correct, and some of which were not. Experimenters were explicitly warned to guard against any bias associated with their having the keys before them and thereby unintentionally influencing their subjects to guess correctly. Experimenters obtained results in accordance with their "knowledge" of what the results should be. When the item on the key was correct, the subject's response was more likely to be correct than when the key was incorrect.

In a careful replication of this study, Lindzey (1951) emphasized to his experimenters the importance of keeping the keys out of the subjects' view. This study failed to confirm the Stanton and Baker findings. Another replication by Friedman (1942) also failed to obtain the statistical significance obtained in the original. Nonetheless, significant results of this sort, even when occurring only in one out of three experiments, cannot be dismissed lightly. Stanton (1942) himself presented further evidence which strengthened his conclusions. He employed a set of nonsense materials, ten of which had been presented to subjects, and ten of which had not. Experimenters were divided into three groups. One group was correctly informed as to which ten materials had been exposed, another group was incorrectly informed, while the third group was told nothing. The results of this study also indicated that the materials which the experimenters expected to be more often chosen were, in fact, more often chosen.

An experiment analogous to those just described was conducted in a psychophysical laboratory by Warner and Raible (1937) who interpreted their study within the framework of parapsychological phenomena. The study involved the judgment of weights by subjects who could not see the experimenter. The latter kept his lips tightly closed to prevent unconscious whispering (Kennedy, 1938). In half the experimental trials, the experimenter knew the correct response and in half he did not. Of the seventeen subjects, six showed a large discrepancy from a chance distribution of errors, and all six of these subjects made fewer errors on trials on which the experimenter knew which weight was the lighter or heavier. At least for those six subjects who were more affected by the experimenter's knowledge of the correct response, the authors' conclusion seems justified ($p = .03$). As an alternative to the interpretation of these results as ESP phenomena, they suggested the possibility of some form of auditory cue transmission to subjects.

Among the most recent relevant studies in the area of ESP are those by Schmeidler and McConnell (1958). These workers found that subjects who believed ESP possible ("sheep") performed better at ESP tasks than did subjects not believing ESP possible ("goats"). These workers suggested that an experimenter, by his presentation, might affect subjects' self-classification, thereby increasing or decreasing the likelihood of successful ESP performance. Similarly, Anderson and White (1958) found that teachers' and pupils' attitudes toward each other might influence performance in classroom ESP experiments. The mechanism operating here might also have been one of certain teachers' expectancies being communicated to the children whose self-classification as "sheep" or "goats" might thereby be affected.

Most of the evidence presented to show the occurrence of interpersonal, self-fulfilling prophecies has so far been anecdotal or only a little stronger. The industrial experiment by Bavelas was a notable exception in that it was a well-controlled experiment in which different prophecies were experimentally created in the minds of the foremen employed. The same may probably be said of the series of experiments begun by Stanton and Baker (1942) in which the experimenters were led to expect different replies from their subjects. Such experiments provide stronger evidence than most of the research presented so far. In most of that research what was shown was that an interpersonal prophecy about another's behavior was accurate. But, as was suggested earlier in Chapter 1, such accuracy could come about in different ways. To show that a prophecy is accurate does not necessarily show that the prophecy led to its own accuracy. The prophecy that the sun will rise is not the effective agent in bringing on the dawn. When a prophecy is based on the prior observation of the event prophesied, the prophecy is, in a sense, "contaminated by reality." The prophecy itself may or may not play a role in its own fulfillment.

When a physician predicts a patient's improvement, we cannot say whether the doctor is giving a sophisticated prognosis or whether the patient's improvement is based in part on the optimism engendered by the physician's prophecy. If school children who perform poorly are those expected by their teachers to perform poorly, it might be that the teachers' prophecy is accurate because it is based on knowledge of past performance, or it might be accurate because it is self-fulfilling. In order to disentangle the self-fulfilling nature of a prophecy from its nonself-fulfilling but accurate nature, experiments are required in which only the prophecy is varied experimentally, uncontaminated by the past observation of the events prophesied. That was the intent of the experiments to be described next. They were part of a research program specifically designed to investigate the self-fulfilling effects of a psychological experimenter's hypothesis or prophecy.

## RECENT STUDIES

In the first experiment in the current series (Rosenthal, 1966), ten advanced undergraduates and graduate students of psychology served as experimenters. All were enrolled in an advanced course in experimental psychology and were, therefore, already involved in conducting research. Each student-experimenter was assigned as his subjects a group of about twenty students of introductory psychology. The experimental procedure was for the experimenter to show a series of ten photographs of people's faces to each of his subjects individually. The subject was to rate the degree of success or failure shown in the face of each person pictured in the photos. Each face could be rated as any value from —10 to +10 with —10 meaning extreme failure and +10 meaning extreme success. The ten photos had been selected so that, on the average, they would be seen as neither successful nor unsuccessful, but quite neutral, with an average numerical score of zero.

All experimenters were given identical instructions on how to show the photographs to their subjects; all were given identical instructions to read to their subjects, and all were cautioned not to deviate from these instructions. The purpose of their participation, it was explained to all experimenters, was to see how well they could duplicate experimental results which were already well-established. Half the experimenters were told that the "well-established" finding was that people generally rated the photos as successful (ratings of +5), and half the experimenters were told that people generally rated the photos as unsuccessful (ratings of —5). Then the experimenters conducted their research.

The results were clear. Every experimenter who had been led to expect ratings of people as successful obtained a higher average rating of success than did any experimenter expecting ratings of people as less successful. Such clear-cut results are not common in behavioral research, so two replications were conducted. Both these subsequent experiments gave the same result; experimenters tended to obtain the data they expected to obtain. Table 3-1 summarizes the numerical results of all three experiments. Other workers in other laboratories have also been able to show that the experimenter's expectation may affect the results of his research though the details cannot be given here (Rosenthal, 1966). In fairness, too, we must add that there are also studies to show that the experimenter's expectation does not always affect the results of his research (Rosenthal, 1964; in press).

| Table 3-1 | Mean Photo Ratings Obtained by Experimenters with Different Prophecies | | | |
|---|---|---|---|---|
| EXPERIMENT | PROPHECY | | DIFFERENCE | $p$ |
| | +5 | −5 | | |
| First | +0.4 | −0.1 | +0.5 | .007 |
| Second | +2.3 | +0.5 | +1.8 | .0003 |
| Third | +0.7 | −0.6 | +1.3 | .005 |
| MEAN | +1.1 | −0.1 | +1.2 | .000001 |

Subsequent experiments in the program of research described here were designed not so much to demonstrate the self-fulfilling effects of the psychologist's prophecy as to learn something about the conditions which increase, decrease, or otherwise modify these effects. It was learned, for example, that the subject's expectations about what would constitute behavior appropriate to the role of "experimental subject" could alter the extent to which they were influenced by the effects of the experimenter's hypothesis (Rosenthal, 1966).

Through the employment of accomplices, serving as the first few subjects, it was learned that when the responses of the first few subjects fulfilled the experimenter's prophecy, his behavior toward his subsequent subjects was affected in such a way that these subjects tended to fulfill further the experimenter's hypothesis. When accomplices, serving as the first few subjects, intentionally disconfirmed the expectation of the experimenter, the bonafide subjects subsequently contacted were affected by a change in the experimenter's behavior and also disconfirmed his experimental hypothesis. It seems possible, then, that the results of behavioral research can, by virtue of the early data returns, be determined by the performance of just the first few subjects (Rosenthal, 1966).

In some of the experiments conducted, it was found that when experimenters were offered a too-large and too-obvious incentive to affect the results of their research, the effects of prophecies or hypotheses tended to diminish. It speaks well for the integrity of our student-experimenters that when they felt bribed to obtain the data we led them to expect, they seemed to oppose us actively. There was a tendency for these experimenters to "bend over backward" to avoid the biasing effects of their prophecy, and bend so far backward that the results of their experiment tended to be significantly opposite to the results they had been led to expect (Rosenthal, 1966).

### Prophecy Communication
Individual differences among experimenters in the degree to which they obtain results consistent with their hypothesis have been discovered. The evidence comes both from additional experiments and from the analysis of sound motion pictures of experimenters interacting with their experimental subjects (Rosenthal, 1966). Those experimenters who show greater self-fulfilling effects of prophecies tend to be of higher status in the eyes of their subjects, and they conduct their experiments in a more professional, more competent manner. They are more likeable and more relaxed, particularly in their movement patterns, while avoiding an overly personal tone of voice that might interfere with the business at hand. It is interesting to note that though the influence of an experimenter's expectancy is quite unintentional, the characteristics of the more successful influencer are very much the same ones associated with more effective influencers when the influence is intentional. The more successful agent of social influence may be the same person whether the influence be as overt and intentional as in the case of outright persuasion attempts, or as covert and unintentional as in the case of the experimenter's subtly communicating his expectancy or prophecy to his research subject.

We know that the process whereby the experimenter communicates his expectancy to his subject is a subtle one. We know that it is subtle because for five years we have tried to find in sound films the unintended cues the experimenter gives the subject—and for five years we have failed, at least partly. But there are some things about the unintentional communication of expectancies that we have learned.

We know that if a screen is placed between experimenter and subject that there will be a reduction of the expectancy effect so that visual cues from the experimenter are probably important. But the interposed screen does not eliminate expectancy effects completely so that auditory cues also seem important (Fode, 1960). Just how important auditory cues may be has been dramatically demonstrated by the work of Adair and Epstein (1967). They first conducted a study which was essentially a replication of the basic experiment on the self-fulfilling effects of experimenters' prophecies. Results showed that, just as in the original studies, experimenters who prophesied the perception of success by their subjects fulfilled their prophecies as did the experimenters who had prophesied the perception of failure by their subjects.

During the conduct of this replication experiment, Adair and Epstein tape-recorded the experimenters' instructions to their subjects. The second experiment was then conducted not by experimenters at all, but by tape recordings of experimenters' voices reading standard instructions to their subjects. When the tape-recorded instructions had originally been read by experimenters prophesying success perception by their subjects, the tape recordings evoked greater success perceptions from their subjects. When the tape-recorded instructions had originally been read by experimenters prophesying failure perception by their subjects, the tape recordings evoked greater failure perceptions from their subjects. Self-fulfilling prophecies, it seems, can come about as a result of the prophet's voice alone. Since, in the experiment described, all prophets read standard instructions, self-fulfillment of prophecies may be brought about by the tone in which the prophet prophesies.

Early in the history of the research program on self-fulfilling prophecies in the behavioral sciences it had been thought that a process of operant conditioning might be responsible for their operation (Rosenthal, 1966). It was thought that perhaps every time the subject gave a response consistent with the experimenter's prophecy, the experimenter might look more pleasant, or smile, or glance at the subject approvingly, even without the experimenter's being aware of his own reinforcing responses. The experimenter, in other words, might unwittingly have taught the subject what responses were the desired ones. Several experiments were analyzed to see whether this hypothesis of operant conditioning might apply. If it did apply, we would expect that the subjects' responses gradually would become more like those prophesied by the experimenter—that there would be a learning curve for subjects, but no learning curve was found. On the contrary, it turned out that the subjects' very first responses were about as much affected by their experimenters' expectancies as were their very last responses. Since the very first response, by definition, cannot follow any unwitting reinforcement by the experimenter, the mechanism of operant conditioning can be ruled out as necessary to the communication of experimenters' prophecies.

True, there was no learning curve for subjects, but there seemed to be a learning curve for experimenters. Several studies showed that prophesied results became more likely as more subjects were contacted by each experimenter (Rosenthal, 1966). In fact, there was very little expectancy effect in evidence for just the very first-seen subjects. If the experimenter were indeed learning to increase the unintended influence of his prophecy, who would be the teacher? Probably the subject. It seems reasonable to think of a subject's responding in the direction of the experimenter's hypothesis as a reinforcing event. Therefore, whatever the covert communicative behavior of the experimenter that preceded the subject's reinforcement, it will be more likely to recur. Subjects, then, may quite unintentionally shape the experimenter's unintended communicative behavior. Not only does the experimenter influence his subjects to respond in the expected manner, but his subjects may well evoke just that unintended behavior that will lead them to respond increasingly as prophesied. Probably neither subject nor experimenter "knows" just exactly what the unintended communication behavior is, and neither do we.

# 4

# Behavioral Science: Intellectual Performance and Learning

In the last chapter some indication was given of the growing literature which shows that in the interaction between experimenter and subject, the hypothesis held by the experimenter may function as a self-fulfilling prophecy. In the studies described so far, however, that behavior of the subject which was affected by the experimenter's hypothesis was not specifically related to the subject's intellectual performance. Because the central proposition of this book is that one person's prophecy of another's intellectual performance can come to determine that other's intellectual performance, it becomes especially important to examine those cases of interpersonal, self-fulfilling prophecies in which the prophecy concerns intellectually relevant behavior. That is the purpose of the present chapter. First we shall consider the evidence that comes from experiments in which the subjects were humans. Then we shall consider the evidence that comes from experiments in which the subjects were animals.

## HUMAN BEHAVIOR

### Interpretation of Inkblots

The ability to produce a large number of alternative interpretations of a set of inkblots is a correlate of intellectual ability as defined by standard tests of intelligence (Sommer, 1958; Wysocki, 1957). Some research, in fact, shows that the number of percepts given in response to inkblots is related to ordinary IQ scores almost as much as two

IQ scores based on different tests are related to each other. A recent experiment by Marwit and Marcia (1967) was designed to test the hypothesis that the number of responses given by a subject to a series of inkblots was a function of the examiner's expectation. Thirty-six undergraduate students enrolled in a course in experimental psychology served as the examiners. Their task was to administer an inkblot test to a total of fifty-three students enrolled in an introductory psychology course. Some of the examiners prophesied many responses from their subjects either on the basis of their own hypotheses or because of the principal investigators' hypothesis. The remaining examiners prophesied few responses from their subjects either because that was their own hypothesis or because that was the principal investigator's hypothesis. The results showed that the source of the hypothesis made no difference. Examiners prophesying greater response productivity obtained 54 percent more responses than did examiners prophesying fewer responses, ($p < .0003$). Both in terms of the statistical significance and in terms of the magnitude of the effect, it seems safe to conclude that an examiner's prophecy may be a significant determinant of his subjects' productivity in responding to an inkblot stimulus.

Not only the total number of responses to an inkblot but also the number and proportion of responses which involve human percepts have been related to scores on standard tests of intelligence (Sommer, 1958; Wysocki, 1957). In a recently reported experiment, Masling (1965) led half his examiners to believe that relatively more human than animal percepts should be obtained from their subjects in inkblot tests. The remaining examiners were led to believe that relatively more animal than human percepts should be obtained from their subjects. This latter group, it turned out, obtained a ratio of animal to human percepts which was 33 percent higher than that obtained by examiners looking for relatively more human percepts in their subjects' responses, ($p = .04$). From the two experiments described, it seems that at least the interpretation of inkblots can be determined in part by the expectancy of the examiner who administers the task, though Strauss (1967) found no effect of examiner expectancy on the ratio of movement to color responses given by subjects.

### Performance of Intellectual Tasks
In the experiments described below, the subjects' response was even more directly related to one type or another of intellectual competence. Wartenberg-Ekren (1962) employed eight examiners who each administered the "Block Design" subtest of the Wechsler Adult Intelli-

gence Scale to four subjects. Two of the four subjects seen by each examiner were alleged to be earning higher grades in school than the other two subjects. In spite of the fact that all the examiners expected superior performance from the subjects alleged to be earning higher grades as indicated by a postexperimental questionnaire, there were no differences obtained in the performance of the two "types" of subjects. These negative findings may have been due in part to the special efforts of the examiners to remain unaffected by their expectations. Thus, one of the eight examiners, on his own initiative, instituted a "blind procedure" by not looking at the code sheet which told which "type" of subject was coming in next. A second experimenter was blind to the status of half his subjects although not intentionally so.

A secondary analysis of subjects' ratings of their examiner's behavior showed that when examiners were contacting subjects alleged to be earning higher grades they behaved in a more friendly, likeable, interested, encouraging manner, showed a more expressive face and used more hand gestures (Rosenthal, 1964). Though we might expect these warmer behaviors to affect the performance of the subjects, they did not appear to in the study described. That was surprising because Gordon and Durea (1948) found that when the examiners behaved more warmly toward their eighth-grade subjects, the IQ scores obtained were over six points higher than when they behaved more coolly toward their adolescent subjects. More recently, Crow (1964) found that even with college-age subjects, those who were treated more warmly performed better at a coding task which was very similar to one of the subtests ("Digit Symbol") of the Wechsler Adult Intelligence Scale. There is an experiment by Ware, Kowal, and Baker (1963) in which the performance required was that of detecting signals. The subjects of the experiment were all in military service. Results found the subjects significantly more alert in the detection of signals when the experimenter was warmer, and less alert when the experimenter was cooler toward the subjects. Finally, there are the dramatic results reported by Sacks (1952) in which more warmly treated nursery school children showed a net profit of nearly ten IQ points relative to more indifferently treated children.

The agreement among the studies reported is the more impressive for the variety of subjects employed. It does seem generally to be the case that intellectually more competent performance is obtained by warmer rather than cooler examiners. Yet warmth seemed to make no difference in the Wartenberg-Ekren experiment, and we are in no position to say why not. Her basic finding that prophecies about intelligence test scores are not necessarily self-fulfilled has also received recent support in work described by Ray Mulry in a personal communication (1966). Getter, Mulry, Holland, and Walker (1967) had ten examiners administer the entire Wechsler Adult Intelligence Scale to over sixty college students. For one third of the subjects, examiners were led to expect superior performance; for one third of the subjects, examiners were led to expect inferior performance; and for one third of the subjects, examiners were given no expectancies. The results showed no difference in subjects' intellectual performance that could be attributed to the expectancy of the examiner.

To our knowledge, there is only one other investigation of the self-fulfilling effects of an examiner's prophecy when the task is a standardized test of intelligence. That was an ingenious experiment by Larrabee and Kleinsasser (1967) in which they had five examiners administer the Wechsler Intelligence Scale for Children (WISC) to twelve sixth graders of average intelligence. Each subject was tested by two different examiners; one examiner administering the even-numbered items and the other examiner administering the odd-numbered items. For each subject, one of the examiners was told the child was of above-average intelligence while the other examiner was told the child was of below-average intelligence. When the child's examiner expected superior performance the total IQ earned was 7.5 points higher on the average than when the child's examiner expected inferior performance. This difference could have occurred by chance, however, 9 times out of 100. When only the performance subtests of the WISC were considered, the advantage to the children of having been expected to do well was less than three IQ points and could easily have occurred by chance. When only the verbal subtests of the WISC were considered, the advantage of having been expected to do well, however, exceeded ten IQ points ($p < .05$). The particular subtest most affected by examiners' expectancies was information for which the probability of the expectancy advantage having been due to chance was about 1 in 2000. It appears, then, that when the subjects are children, examiners' prophecies may be self-fulfilling although the two studies described earlier suggest this to be less likely when the subjects are adults.

In another recent experiment, by Hurwitz and Jenkins (1966), the tasks were not standardized tests of intelligence, but rather two standard laboratory tests of learning. Three male experimenters administered a rote verbal learning task and a mathematical reasoning task to a total of twenty female subjects. From half their subjects the experimenters were led to expect superior performance; from half they were led to expect inferior performance.

In the rote learning task, subjects were shown a list of pairs of nonsense syllables and were asked to remember one of the pair members from a presentation of the other pair member. Subjects were given six trials to learn the syllable pairs. Somewhat greater learning occurred on the part of the subjects contacted by the experimenters believing subjects to be brighter although the difference was not significant statistically nor large numerically; subjects alleged to be brighter learned 11 percent more syllables. The curves of learning of the paired nonsense syllables, however, did show a difference between subjects alleged to be brighter and those alleged to be duller. Among "brighter" subjects, learning increased significantly more monotonically or increasingly over the course of the six trials than was the case for "duller" subjects. (The coefficient of rank correlation between accurate recall and trial number was .71 for the "bright" subjects and .50 for the "dull" subjects ($p$ of difference $<$ .02).

In the mathematical reasoning task, subjects had to learn to use three sizes of water jars in order to obtain exactly some specified amount of water. On the critical trials the correct solution could be obtained by a longer and more routine procedure which was scored for partial credit, or by a shorter but more novel procedure which was given full credit. Those subjects whose experimenters prophesied superior performance earned higher scores than did those subjects whose experimenters prophesied inferior performance ($p = $ .08). Among these latter subjects, only 40 percent ever achieved a novel solution, while among the allegedly superior subjects 88 percent achieved 1 or more novel solutions. Subjects prophesied to be dull made 57 percent again as many errors as did subjects prophesied to be bright.

To summarize the research reported so far, it would seem that at least sometimes a subject's performance of an intellectual task may be unintentionally determined by the prophecy of the examiner. Perhaps it is appropriate to stress the unintentional aspect of the self-fulfilling prophecy since in several of the experiments described, the examiners and experimenters tried hard to avoid having their prophecies affect their subjects' performance.

## ANIMAL BEHAVIOR

There is a tradition in the behavioral and biomedical sciences that animal subjects be employed in experiments even though the organism in which the ultimate interest resides is man. Sometimes this choice of the animal model for man is dictated by the greater convenience of using animals and sometimes by the nature of the experimental procedure which may be too dangerous to try on man without animal pretests. Sometimes, though, there is the positive advantage that animal subjects are less likely to try to guess the purpose of the experiment and then try to "help it along" or even "foul it up" (Orne, 1962). It would, therefore, constitute a powerful source of evidence if it could be shown that even the behavior of animal subjects could be the result of the experimenter's, trainer's, or teacher's expectation or prophecy. Pavlov thought it might be.

Not all who know the name Pavlov know of his interest in the Lamarckian theory of the inheritance of acquired characteristics. He had, in fact, gathered evidence to show that the transmission of modifications occurred in the case of the learning ability of mice. In 1929, however, at the meeting of the 13th International Physiological Congress, Pavlov made an informal statement to the effect that a closer check on his experiments showed no increased learning ability on the part of his mice. What the check did show was an increased teaching ability on the part of the research assistant who probably expected to obtain the increased learning ability for which he seemed responsible (Gruenberg, 1929).

Much earlier than Pavlov's Lamarckian experiments, in 1904, there was a case of self-fulfilling prophecies involving the behavior of a horse known as Clever Hans (Rosenthal, 1965). By means of tapping his hoof Hans could add, subtract, multiply, and divide. He could spell, read, solve problems of musical harmony, and answer personal questions. His owner, Mr. von Osten, a German mathematics teacher, unlike the owners of other clever animals of the time, did not profit financially from his horse's talents, and it seemed unlikely that he had any fraudulent intent. He was quite willing to let others question Hans even in his absence so that cues from the owner could be ruled out as the reaon for the horse's abilities. In a brilliant series of experiments Pfungst (1911) discovered that Hans could answer questions only if the questioner himself knew the answer and was visible to the horse during his foot-tapping of the answer. Finally, it was discovered that whenever people asked Hans a question, they leaned forward very slightly the better to see Hans' hoof. That, it turned out, was the unintentional signal for Hans to begin tapping. Then, as Hans approached the number of hooftaps representing the correct answer, the questioners would typically show a tiny head movement. That almost imperceptible cue was the signal for Hans to stop tapping, and Hans was right again. The questioner, by expecting Hans to stop at the right answer was actually "telling" Hans the right answer and thereby fulfilling his own prophecy. Pfungst did not learn all of this so easily. It took a long and elegant series of experiments to learn the secret of Hans' success. Pfungst summarized eloquently the difficulties in discovering Hans' talents. He and others too long had been misled by, and we paraphrase, "looking for, in the pupil, what should have been sought in the teacher."

**Learning in Mazes**

The purpose of the experiment was to test the hypothesis of the self-fulfilling prophecy with a larger number of animals than one horse (Rosenthal and Fode, 1963). A class in experimental psychology had been performing experiments with human subjects for most of a semester. Now they were asked to perform one more experiment, the last in the course, and the first employing animal subjects. The experimenters were told of studies that had shown that maze-brightness and maze-dullness could be developed in strains of rats by successive inbreeding of the well- and the poorly performing maze-runners. There were sixty perfectly ordinary laboratory rats available, and they were equitably divided among the twelve experimenters. But half the experimenters were told that their rats were maze-bright while the other half were told their rats were maze-dull. The animal's task was to learn to run to the darker of two arms of an elevated T-shaped maze. The two arms of the maze, one white and one gray, were interchangeable; and the "correct" or rewarded arm was equally often on the right as on the left. Whenever an animal ran to the correct side he obtained a bit of food. Each rat was given ten chances each day for five days to learn that the darker side of the maze was the one which led to food.

| Table 4-1 | Average Number of Correct Responses on Each of Five Days | | |
|---|---|---|---|
| DAY | BELIEF ABOUT SUBJECT | | $p$ |
| | DISADVANTAGED | GIFTED | |
| First | 0.73 | 1.33 | .03 |
| Second | 1.10 | 1.60 | —— |
| Third | 2.23 | 2.60 | —— |
| Fourth | 1.83 | 2.83 | .05 |
| Fifth | 1.83 | 3.26 | .03 |
| MEAN | 1.54 | 2.32 | .01 |

From Table 4-1 we learn that beginning with the first day and continuing on through the experiment, animals believed to be better performers became better performers ($p = .01$). Animals believed to be brighter showed a daily improvement in their performance while those believed to be dull improved only to the third day and then showed a worsening of performance. Sometimes an animal refused to budge from his starting position. This happened 11 percent of the time among the allegedly bright rats; but among allegedly dull rats it happened 29 percent of the time. This difference in reluctance rates was significant at the .001 level. When animals did respond and correctly so, those believed to be brighter ran faster to the rewarded side of the maze than did even the correctly responding rats believed to be dull ($p < .02$).

When the experiment was over, all experimenters made ratings of their rats and of their own attitudes and behavior *vis-à-vis* their animals. Those experimenters who had been led to expect better performance viewed their animals as brighter, more pleasant, and more likeable. These same experimenters felt more relaxed in their contacts with the animals and described their behavior toward them as more pleasant, friendly, enthusiastic, and less talkative. They also stated that they handled their rats more and also more gently than did the experimenters expecting poor performance.

### Learning in Skinner Boxes

The next experiment to be described also employed rat subjects, using this time not mazes but Skinner boxes (Rosenthal and Lawson, 1964). Because the experimenters (thirty-nine) outnumbered the subjects (sixteen), experimenters worked in teams of two or three. Once again about half the experimenters were led to believe that their subjects had been specially bred for excellence of performance. The experimenters who had been assigned the remaining rats were led to believe that their animals were genetically inferior.

The learning required of the animals in this experiment was more complex than that required in the maze-learning study. This time the rats had to learn in sequence and over a period of a full academic quarter the following behavior: to run to the food dispenser whenever a clicking sound occurred; to press a bar for a food reward; to learn that the feeder could be turned off and that sometimes it did not pay to press the bar; to learn new responses with only the clicking sound as a reinforcer (rather than the food); to bar-press only in the presence of a light and not in the absence of the light; and, finally, to pull on a loop which was followed by a light which informed the animal that a bar-press would be followed by a bit of food.

Each team of experimenters conducted experiments in one of five laboratories. Table 4-2 shows separately for each laboratory the mean (standardized) rank of performance for the allegedly bright and the allegedly dull rats. A lower rank means a superior performance. In all five laboratories animals showed superior performance if their experimenters prophesied superior performance.

| Table 4-2 | Average Ranks of Operant Learning in Five Laboratories | | |
|---|---|---|---|
| LABORATORY | BELIEF ABOUT SUBJECT | | $p$ |
| | DISADVANTAGED | GIFTED | |
| I | 5.3 | 4.3 | —— |
| II | 6.5 | 4.9 | —— |
| III | 5.8 | 5.1 | —— |
| IV | 4.6 | 3.7 | —— |
| V | 6.0 | 4.1 | —— |
| MEAN | 5.6 | 4.4 | .02 |

Just as in the maze-learning experiment, the experimenters of the present study were asked to rate their animals and their own attitudes and behaviors toward them. Once again those experimenters who had expected excellence of performance judged their animals to be brighter, more pleasant, and more likeable. Once again these "teachers" of the allegedly gifted described their own behavior as more pleasant, friendly, enthusiastic, and less talkative. Compared to the "teachers" of the "genetically deprived" subjects, those assigned the "well-endoweds" tended to watch their animals more closely, to handle them more, and to talk to them *less*. One wonders what was said to the animals by those experimenters who believed their rats to be inferior.

The absolute amount of handling of animals in this Skinner-box experiment was considerably less than the handling of animals in the maze-learning experiment. Nonetheless, those experimenters who believed their animals to be Skinner-box bright handled them relatively more, or said they did, than did experimenters believing their animals to be dull. The extra handling of animals believed to be brighter may have contributed in both experiments to the superior learning shown by these animals.

In addition to the differences in handling reported by the experimenters of the Skinner-box study as a function of their beliefs about their subjects, there were differences in the reported intentness of their observation of their animals. Animals believed to be brighter were watched more carefully, and more careful observation of the rat's Skinner-box behavior may very well have led to more rapid and appropriate reinforcement of the desired response. Thus, closer observation, perhaps due to the belief that there would be more promising responses to be seen, may have made more effective teachers of the experimenters expecting good performance.

## Learning in Troughs

Ever since Thompson and McConnell (1955) showed the possibility that classical conditioning could occur in the lowly aquatic worm, planarian, considerable theoretical interest and research activity has been invested in that organism. The planarian earns this interest because it is the lowest organism phylogenetically to show what might be considered a rudimentary brain. Part of the research activity revolving around this worm has dealt with the problem of various possible artifacts that might be confounding experimental results. It has been shown, for example, that different experimenters obtain significantly different results in their studies of the learning of turning in worms, though the reasons for these differences are not clear (Rosenthal and Halas, 1962).

The study of worm behavior that is of greatest interest to us here is one by Cordaro and Ison (1963). They employed seventeen experimenters to conduct a conditioning experiment with thirty-four planaria. Five of the experimenters were led to expect that their worms (two apiece) had already been taught to make many turning and contracting responses. Five of the experimenters were led to expect that their worms (also two apiece) had not yet been taught to make many responses and that in "only 100 trials" little turning and contracting could be expected. The seven experimenters of the third group were each given both these opposite expectancies, one for each of their two worms. Behavior of the worms was observed by the experimenters looking down into a narrow (½ inch) and shallow (¼ inch) V-shaped trough into which each worm was placed.

| Table 4-3 | Number of Planaria Responses Obtained under Four Conditions of Experimenter Expectancy | | |
|---|---|---|---|
| EXPERIMENTER EXPECTANCY | RESPONSES | | MEAN |
| | CONTRACTIONS | TURNS | |
| Pure high | 18 | 47 | 33 |
| Mixed high | 15 | 30 | 23 |
| Mixed low | 5 | 15 | 10 |
| Pure low | 1 | 10 | 5 |

The results of the Cordaro and Ison experiment are summarized in Table 4-3. Regardless of whether the experimenter prophesied the same results for both his worms or prophesied opposite results for his two worms, when the experimenter expected more turning and contracting he obtained more turning and contracting ($p < .005$). From these results (and from some of the others reported earlier), we cannot be sure whether it was only the experimenter's perception of the behavior of the animal that was affected or if the animal's behavior was directly affected by the prophecy of the experimenter. However, Mulry (personal communication, 1966) has suggested that when stimulation of planaria is not automated, the experimenter could unintentionally increase the responsiveness of the worms by systematic variation of his procedure. Still more intriguing is the possibility that changes in the respiration and body temperature of the experimenter might lead to changes in the responsiveness of the worms. Stanley Ratner, in a personal communication (1967) has suggested that such effects are not entirely implausible.

**Replication**

Essentially the same design pioneered by Cordaro and Ison was employed in the important research of Ingraham and Harrington (1966). They, too, employed a conditioning task, but for their choice of subjects they ranged up the phylogenetic scale back to rat subjects as were employed in the experiments described earlier.

Experimenters in the Ingraham and Harrington study were cautioned to give their subjects equal amounts of handling, a caution that should have served to reduce the possibility that experimenters' prophecies could be self-fulfilled by virtue of differences in handling of animals believed to be bright or dull. In the earlier studies employing rat subjects, the expectancies of the experimenters were varied by their being told that their animals had been specially bred for brightness and dullness. In the Cordaro and Ison study, expectancies were varied by experimenters being told that their worms had or had not been pretaught to show many responses. In the Ingraham and Harrington study, expectancies were varied more subtly and less decisively by experimenters being told that there *might* be genetic differences in the rats' ability, but that these alleged differences were, in fact, being investigated by their own experiments.

In spite of the differences in instructions about handling and in the mode of creating expectations, Ingraham and Harrington also found superior performance among rats whose experimenters expected superior performance, though the level of statistical significance was less impressive ($p = .08$). Table 4-4 shows the results of their study in the form analogous to that employed in the presentation of the Cordaro and Ison findings. Comparison of Table 4-3 with 4-4 shows that the rank ordering of performances for the four conditions are in perfect agreement (rho $= 1.00$). In addition, the difference between the pure high and low groups in both studies is between two and three times greater than the difference between the mixed high and low groups.

| Table 4-4 | Average Performance of Rats Obtained under Four Conditions of Experimenter Expectancy |
|---|---|
| EXPERIMENTER EXPECTANCY | PERFORMANCE |
| Pure high | 54 |
| Mixed high | 53 |
| Mixed low | 45 |
| Pure low | 33 |

Direct comparison of the Ingraham and Harrington results with the results of the earlier reported studies employing rats for subjects is difficult because of differences mentioned above and because of differences in the task and in the units of measurement employed. Nevertheless, a crude comparison is possible between their results and those obtained in the maze learning experiment already described. Both experiments lasted over a five-day period. For each of these five days and for the entire experiment, Table 4-5 shows the percentage of superiority of performance of the animals believed to be superior over the performance of the animals believed to be inferior. In each experiment considered as a whole, animals for whom superior performance was prophesied performed 55 percent again as well as did the animals for whom inferior performance was prophesied. Consideration of the results on a day-by-day basis, however, shows that the effect of experimenters' expectancies varied somewhat differently over time in the two studies. On the first day the results for the two studies were very similar but beginning with the second day, Ingraham and Harrington found a steady decrease in the magnitude of the expectancy effect. In the Rosenthal and Fode study, on the other hand, there was a decrease from the first to the third day after which the effect began to increase progressively through the end of the experiment. In the Ingraham and Harrington study the tendency for expectancy effects to decrease with time was statistically significant

($p < .02$) and in the Rosenthal and Fode study the tendency to curvilinearity of expectancy effects was also statistically significant ($p < .002$). Only further research can help us to understand the differences.

| Table 4-5 | Percentage of Performance Superiority of Prophesied Superior over Prophesied Inferior Rats | |
|---|---|---|
| DAY | EXPERIMENT | |
| | INGRAHAM-HARRINGTON | ROSENTHAL-FODE |
| First | 78% | 82% |
| Second | 95% | 45% |
| Third | 69% | 17% |
| Fourth | 31% | 55% |
| Fifth | 00% | 78% |
| MEAN | 55% | 55% |
| $p$ | .08 | .01 |
| N OF SUBJECTS PER GROUP | 27 | 30 |

### Learning in Lesioned Rats

To our knowledge, there is just one more reported study of the effects of experimenters' expectancy on animal learning, an ingenious experiment by Burnham (1966). He had twenty-three experimenters each run one rat in a T-maze discrimination problem. About half the rats had been brain-lesioned by removal of the cortex and the remaining rats had received sham surgery which involved cutting through the skull to the brain but without removing any brain tissue. The purpose of the study was explained to the experimenters as an attempt to learn the effects of lesions on discrimination learning. Experimenters' expectancies were manipulated by labeling each rat as either lesioned or nonlesioned (sham surgery). Some of the really lesioned rats were labeled accurately as lesioned but some were labeled as unlesioned. Some of the really unlesioned rats were labeled accurately as unlesioned but some were labeled as lesioned. Table 4-6 shows the median ranks of learning ability in each of the four conditions. A lower rank indicates superior performance. Not surprisingly, the best performance was obtained from the intact animals who were believed to be intact. The difference between their performance and that of all other animals was significant at the .02 level. Also not surprisingly, experimenter expectancy made no difference when rats were actually lesioned. Regardless of what the experimenter believed, the lesioned animals did not learn well. What was somewhat surprising, was that the intact animals who were believed to be lesioned performed just as poorly as the rats that really had been lesioned.

| Table 4-6 | Median Ranks of Discrimination Learning in Four Conditions | |
|---|---|---|
| ACTUAL CONDITION | BELIEF ABOUT SUBJECT | |
|  | LESIONED | UNLESIONED |
| Lesioned | 14.0 | 14.0 |
| Unlesioned | 14.5 | 5.5 |

To summarize now what has been learned from research employing animal subjects generally, it seems that those that are expected to perform competently tend to do so while animals expected to perform incompetently tend also to perform as prophesied.

The transition from this chapter to the next comes from the results of the experiment in which rats learned their way around their Skinner boxes. At the beginning of that study experimenters assigned allegedly dull animals were of course told that they would find retarded learning on the part of their rats. They were, however, reassured that "it has been found that even the dullest rats can, in time, learn the required responses" (Rosenthal and Lawson, 1964). Animals alleged to be dull, then, were described as educable but slow. It was interesting in the light of this to learn that of the experimenters who had been assigned "dull" animals, 47 percent believed their subjects to be uneducable. Only 5 percent of the experimenters assigned "bright" rats were equally pessimistic about their animal's future $(p = .007)$. From this result one wonders about the beliefs created in schoolteachers when they are told a child is educable but slow, deserving but disadvantaged.

# PART 2

# TEACHER
# EXPECTATION ❧

# 5

# The Disadvantaged Child

It is usually in September that school opens, and thousands of near-six-year-olds from every conceivable kind of home start first grade. It is an anxious time for them, a mixture of uncertainty and excitement, confused with anticipatory feelings. "Will the teacher like me? When will I learn to read? Will she like *me*?"

Entering the first-grade classroom is a big step for a child. It can be a glowing or a devastating experience. The teacher smiles at the children, looking at them to see what the year will bring. The well-groomed white boys and girls will probably do well. The black- and brown-skinned ones are lower-class and will have learning problems unless they look exceptionally clean. All the whites who do not look tidy and need handkerchiefs will have trouble. If the teacher sees a preponderance of lower-class children, regardless of color, she knows her work will be difficult and unsatisfying. The teacher wants her children to learn, all of them, but she knows that lower-class children do not do well in school, just as she knows that middle-class children do do well. All this she knows as she smiles at her class for the first time, welcoming them to the adventure of first grade, measuring them for success or failure against the yardstick of middle-classness. The children smile back at her, unaware as yet that the first measurements have been taken. The yardstick will be used again when they speak to her, as she hears words spoken clearly or snuffled or stammered or spoken with an accent. And later they will be measured for readiness for reading or intelligence. Many times that first year the children will be examined for what they are, for what they bring with them when they come to school.

Down the hall, the second-grade teacher knows that most of *her* lower-class students are behind those of the middle class. All through the schools that first day in September the teachers look at their classes and know which children will and will not do well during the year. Sometimes the results of formal and informal measurement modify that first day's perception; a dirty child may be very bright, a brown child may learn rapidly, a black child may read like an angel, and a tidy middle-class child may be hopelessly dull. Sometimes. Usually, the teacher is right when she predicts that middle-class children generally succeed in school and lower-class children generally lag behind and eventually fail.

## THE DISADVANTAGE OF POVERTY

Currently attention has focused glaringly upon the educationally dis-advantaged children in our schools, spotlighting their scanty experience with formal language, ignorance of school culture and concomitant poor school achievement. Numerous reports indicate that the IQ scores of disadvantaged children are lower than those of middle-class children, their reading is substandard, their attitudes are negative, and their behavior is annoying to teachers (Becker, 1952; B. Clark, 1962; Davis and Dollard, 1940; Sexton, 1961). Disadvantaged children by definition come from lower socioeconomic groups where low income is married to values alien to the school culture. A larger proportion of disadvantaged children than middle-class children are failing in school.

Havighurst, who refers to the children as socially disadvantaged, predicts that American schools will spend the next ten years in a "prodigious attempt to wipe out the social disadvantage that has prevented some fifteen percent of our children from learning anything useful in school . . . and this means some thirty percent of children in the low-income sections of our big cities" (Havighurst, 1965, p. 31). The U.S. Department of Health, Education, and Welfare is encouraging this effort through making available vast sums of money for schools in low-income attendance areas. This resulted from the Elementary and Secondary Education Act of 1965, Title I, which "places the major emphasis of this new law on meeting the special needs of educationally deprived children through the largest federal grant program ever authorized for such a task" (U.S. Office of Education, 1965).

The generally low educational achievement of lower-class children has caused consternation on the federal level because of the close tie between education and the development of talent, and talent gets top place in the marketplace today. Technological innovations and international political crises demand educated manpower, which means that those disadvantaged children who have not benefited from schooling represent a waste of future national skilled manpower.

There has been in the past few years an almost overwhelming amount of literature describing the educationally disadvantaged learner, his home, family, neighborhood, and teachers, as well as the frustrations he encounters in the process of learning in the climate of a middle-class school. The sources of the disadvantages variously have been laid to economic, social, cultural, and/or linguistic factors, depending upon the orientation of the writer. Here we can only touch on some of the factors implicated.

### Income and School Success

Sexton's (1961) study on the relation between income and educational opportunity revealed that where the average family income exceeded $7000, achievement was above grade level; and where the income was below $7000, achievement was below grade level. Apparently, poor achievement is cumulative; that is, by grade eight, the lowest-income students were at least two years behind the highest-income students, a fact that confirmed Becker's (1952) widening gap, as well as being in accord with Kahl's (1961) findings that "common man" boys performed at much lower levels than high-status boys of equal intelligence by the time they were ready for grade nine, even though the boys had achieved similarly in their early school years.

Sexton found further differentiation between income groups in "Big City's" gifted-child program: out of 436 students selected for the program, not one came from an income group below $5000, whereas 148 were selected from the above $9000 group.

### Achievement Training

Research in the area of achievement motivation points out that there are class and cultural differences in family training for achievement (McClelland, 1961), differences that may cause conflict when the child attends school where middle-class values are emphasized. It is known that middle-class children, notorious for their competitiveness, have been encouraged to achieve since diaper days because the child-rearing practices of American middle-class families radiate about the concept of achievement. Children from subcultures that have a similar achievement orientation also find the school culture familiar and nurturing (Rosen, 1959; Strodtbeck, 1961). Florence Kluckhohn's (1953) value orientations show a modal profile of the dominant American who is trained at home for an activity culture with emphasis on values that lead to an achieving personality. "A child who has not acquired these particular value orientations in his home and community is not so likely to compete successfully with youngsters among whom these values are implicitly taken for granted" (Cloward and Jones, 1963, pp. 193–194).

**Impoverished Training**
Another theoretical explanation for the failure of the disadvantaged child is also based on family training, or, rather, the lack of it. Some writers postulate that the type of language spoken in lower-class families causes difficulty in children's learning at school. Working-class families use a restricted form of language whereas middle-class families use a more elaborate form. Bernstein (1960) believes that this difficulty is likely to increase as the child goes through school unless he learns the middle-class language used in the school. Loban (1964), in identifying deviations from standard English among children, found a consistent relationship between social class and communication facility.

Social-class elements other than language also appear to affect learning. Deutsch (1963) states that lower-class children have not learned to "pay attention." Their habits of seeing, hearing, and listening have not been trained in the family situation. The middle-class child, conversely, is encouraged from babyhood in discrimination of sound, sight, and judgment, all of which constitute reading readiness.

## POVERTY PROGRAMS

The findings are extensive on the disparity between middle-class and lower-class children in school performance and tested ability. In fact, the relationship of school success to social-class status has been confirmed to the extent that it may be regarded as "empirical law" (Charters, 1963, pp. 739–740). Educators, in current attempts to make this relationship historical, are establishing experimental programs to increase the educational opportunity for lower-class children—with pressure for action being levered by federal agencies. The United States Office of Education has sponsored programs for the educationally disadvantaged over the past few years. And the Elementary and Secondary Education Act signed by President Johnson in April 1965 focused an even larger spotlight on the disadvantaged children in the United States when it authorized, under Title I, over one billion dollars for them for 1966.

Faced with the chance to upgrade achievement for poverty-pocket children at federal expense, schools have been formulating programs subject to agency approval. Many of the programs are longitudinal in structure so that findings will not be conclusive for a while. Ultimate goals appear to be in accord: increase of educational opportunity through improved self-image, potential, and aspiration. The programs seem most fundamentally to be attempts to overcome learning handicaps by means of acting on the child—remedial reading, counseling and guidance, cultural experiences, parental involvement, and health and welfare services. These programs are constructed to emphasize deficiencies within the child and the home, and they are all compensatory approaches (see Wrightstone, McClelland, Krugman, Hoffman, Tieman, and Young, undated). Apparently, the varied research findings have been interpreted to mean that the disadvantaged child is somehow deficient, and that educators should be concerned about his impoverished early training and his subculturally determined differences in achievement orientation.

The premises for these expensive, special programs contain only some suggestion that the school itself may be harboring deficiencies. The premises too rarely suggest that teacher attitudes and behavior might be contributing factors to pupil failure. And yet, teacher reaction to lower-class children may well be intertwined inextricably in their lack of success.

## TEACHER VARIABLES

To say that the role of the teacher has been neglected in programs for the disadvantaged child is not to say that the teacher has been neglected by either theory or research. As will be seen from the dates of their publications, good theory was written and good research conducted even long before it was fashionable and advantageous to be concerned with the disadvantaged. Becker (1952) for example, found in his Chicago studies that teachers in slum schools use different techniques than do teachers in middle-class schools, teachers and administrators expect less from lower-class children, the gap in learning widens through the grades, teachers are offended by the attitudes and hygiene of the children, and teachers transfer to "better" schools as soon as they can. Similar findings were presented even earlier by Davis and Dollard (1940) who analyzed the operation of social-class standards in the classroom and found that the lower-class child is punished for what he is; and they found that "he is stigmatized by teachers and their favored students on grounds of the 'ignorance' of his parents, the dialect which he speaks, the appearance of his clothes, and, very likely, the darkness of his skin" (Davis and Dollard, 1940, pp. 284–285). Warner, Havighurst, and Loeb (1944) presented findings of differential attitudes in the school toward persons in different positions in the social structure.

The important work of Deutsch (1963) and Wilson (1963) lent further support to the position taken by the earlier workers. Deutsch

(1963) suggested that "It is in the school situation that the highly charged negative attitudes toward learning evolve" (p. 178), that the responsibility for disadvantagedness is the school's because the lower-class child learns his negative attitudes there. Wilson (1963) suggested after studying three socially stratified schools that the normalization of diverging standards by teachers is responsible to some degree for the divergence between aspirations and achievement among under-privileged youth; that is, that "variations in teachers' expectations and standards contribute to differences in pupil attainment and aspirations." (Passow, 1963, p. 183). Teachers in lower-class schools did not set standards as high as those in middle-class schools, nor were they as concerned with bringing their children up to grade level. Lower-strata children were overevaluated on the basis of tested performance, and higher-strata children were underevaluated.

Burton Clark's (1962) reaction to Becker's findings also holds implications for the premises upon which poverty programs are built:

> The large and continuing growth of Negro and other dark-skin minority populations in northern cities makes teacher reaction a critical aspect of the education of minorities. The northern urban situation is one in which prejudice alone is not the major factor. It is a matter of the way in which the characteristics (other than skin color and race) of the minority child affect teachers and the operation of the schools. In an important sense, doing away with prejudice would not do away with the minority problem; for as long as a sizable share of the children from culturally deprived and lower-class backgrounds are dirty, violent, and unmotivated—or appear so in the eyes of their teachers—the teachers are likely to handle them differently, teach them less, and want to escape. (p. 99)

Riessman (1965) expresses his concern through his teacher-training program "whose objective is the development of interest in and respect for low-income *culture,* as distinct from appreciating the difficulties of the low income *environment.* The theory is that this will lead to an honest 'expect more and get more' from the children and their parents." (p. 16).

Riessman's primary argument appears to be that the disadvantaged child has been underestimated and that there are positive characteristics of lower socioeconomic groups, a stand that should be adopted as a "working hypothesis, a positive myth, because by so doing we can work *with* the underprivileged rather than *upon* them" (1962, p. 106).

These writers are in agreement about at least one formulation: children defined as disadvantaged are expected by their teachers to be unable to learn. Other writers and observers agree. In his paper entitled "Not Like Other Children," Bernard Asbell (1963) reports on his visits to schools and with teachers. "Teachers everywhere I went seemed preoccupied with the idea of 'what to expect,' so seldom with what they might effect" (p. 116).

Kvaraceus (1965) who discusses the programs for the disadvantaged as "programs of promise or pretense" maintains, "We must stop projecting failure for the disadvantaged. The HARYOU studies indicate a low performance expectancy on the part of teachers which acts as a self-fulfilling prophecy. Frequently teachers use psychological tools and tests to reinforce and justify their low predictions" (p. 30).

MacKinnon (1962) observed: "If our expectation is that a child of a given intelligence will not respond creatively to a task which confronts him, and especially if we make this expectation known to the child, the probability that he will respond creatively is very much reduced" (p. 493). The same position has been stated by Kenneth Clark (1963), Hillson and Myers (1963), Katz (1964), Rivlin (undated), and Rose (1956). Kenneth Clark speaks of the deprived child becoming "the victim of an educational self-fulfilling prophecy" (1963, p. 150). Perhaps the most detailed statement of this position is that made by the authors of *Youth in the Ghetto* [Harlem Youth Opportunities Unlimited, Inc., (HARYOU), 1964]: "When teachers and principals have a low opinion of the children's learning ability, the children seldom exceed those expectations" (p. 203). Effective poverty programs, the authors continue, "will come only from a firm belief and insistence that the pupils *can* perform" (p. 244). Of their judgment of the central importance of teacher expectancy they say: "The whole weight of modern social science confirms this judgment" (p. 244). This statement means that modern social theorists often feel expectation variables to be important, but there is something more to social science than social theory, and this something more is evidence.

The evidence presented for the importance of the educational self-fulfilling prophecy was in the form of data to show that disadvantaged children fall further and further behind as they go from third to sixth grade. Data of that kind, although important to some purposes, are not enough to demonstrate the effects of teachers' expectancies. To be sure, teachers' self-fulfilling prophecies might have been responsible but so might a host of other factors.

From the theory and evidence presented so far, the most we can reasonably conclude is that disadvantaged children are not expected to do well in school. Now we need ask whether there is any good evidence that a teacher's expectations or prophecies make any difference in either her evaluation of her pupils or in their actual performance.

## PUPIL EVALUATION

When certain things are known or believed about a pupil, other things about him, true things or not, are implied. That is nothing more than the so-called halo effect, and it is well illustrated by a recent experiment by Leonard Cahen (1966), who was interested in determining whether false information about pupils' aptitudes would influence teachers' scoring of pupils' tests. Each of 256 teachers-in-training was asked to score a new test of "learning readiness." Each was told that children who scored higher on reading tests and on IQ tests also scored higher on this new test. On the front of each of the test booklets the pupil's IQ and reading level were indicated. Sometimes these fictitious scores were high, sometimes low, Cahen's results showed clearly that when the teachers-in-training scored the tests of allegedly brighter children, they gave them much greater benefit of the doubt than when they scored the tests of allegedly duller children. When one "knows" a child is bright, his behavior is evaluated as of higher intellectual quality than is the very same behavior shown by a child "known" to be dull. Such halo effects have also been shown to occur in the scoring of responses to individually administered standardized tests of intelligence for children (Sattler, Hillix, and Neher, 1967).

It has often been suggested that children from minority ethnic groups, particularly dark-skinned groups, are especially likely to suffer the disadvantages of unfavorable halo effects (HARYOU, 1964). A recent study by Jacobson (1966) serves as illustration.

Two groups of teachers were asked to rank a set of unknown children's photographs on their American or Mexican appearance. ("American" was not defined.) The teachers agreed highly on their rankings. Then these same groups of teachers were asked to rank in the same manner photographs of Mexican children who were unknown to one group but were students in the school of the other group of teachers. Here there was little agreement. The teachers at the school attended by the Mexican children saw those with higher IQs as looking more American. The significant correlation of IQ and appearance was present only where the IQ scores were available. Apparently, teachers agree in their perception of "Mexican-looking" until they know how a child tests, and then perception is changed.

This study provided further information related to disadvantaged children in the classroom. The highest achieving (in reading) Mexican children in grades one and two were seen by both teacher groups as looking significantly more Mexican. This correlation reversed itself in grades three and four, and still more so in grades five and six; that is, the highest achievers in the upper grades looked more American to both groups of teachers. The study presented the possibility that if a Mexican child looked more American (that is, Anglo-Saxon) to a teacher, academic expectations for him might be like expectations for middle-class children as compared to those for the Mexican child who looked more Mexican, or lower-class, with resultant differences in performance.

Teachers' evaluations of pupils are determined by many variables. Sometimes the teacher recognizes disadvantages and perhaps, sometimes, she creates them. An evaluation of a child, lowered or raised by halo effects, may lead to a specific expectation of performance which is communicated to the child who then may go on to fulfill the teacher's prophecy.

## PUPIL PERFORMANCE

Teacher expectations of pupil performance can derive from more than the pupil's skin color, apparent affluence, or background information. One of the most important sources of teachers' expectations about their pupils' intellectual competence comes from standardized tests of intelligence and achievement (Deutsch, Fishman, Kogan, North, and Whiteman, 1964; Gibson, 1965; Goslin, 1966; Péquignot, 1966). Even when the administration of one of these tests is more or less appropriate and valid, the results may influence the teacher's prophecy about the child's subsequent intellectual performance. In a sense, that is the purpose of aptitude and ability testing, and the advantages and disadvantages of this purpose have been as much discussed in the popular press as in the technical literature. Sometimes, however, there are special circumstances surrounding the administration of standardized tests of intelligence that throw into bolder relief the effects of test results on teachers' expectations. In such situations it may be suspected that the test results are not valid. Some examples of this type follow.

Tina was a small, mentally retarded child who spent two years in kindergarten and three in the first grade. She was tested annually because she was part of the class. Her last two scores from first grade gave her an IQ of over 140. She had memorized the preprimer and "read" it faultlessly. Her last first-grade teacher, college-fresh, until she learned of this, believed Tina to be her star pupil.

Billie, an average sixth-grade girl, in taking an achievement test for junior high school placement, used the wrong section on her IBM card and came out with a second-percentile score. The year before she had been absent for the achievement test. She was scheduled for classes for nonlearners in the new school and could not be changed until testing time at the end of the year. She spent the year, stone-faced, in her classes, and has since become a nonproductive truant.

Generally, one test will be considered along with others when children are to be placed in learning tracks or ability groups. Exceptions primarily arise during the first grade or when children transfer to a new school without former records. In kindergarten where children are first tested for IQ and first-grade placement, the cycle of expectancy may begin. High-spirited children often distract the teacher, causing a disturbance and their subsequent removal from class; frequently, the background required for taking placement tests (practicing making marks with a crayon, listening to directions, learning to turn the page, and so on) is not received. One such young man was Pedro—aggressive, bossy, boisterous, and unpredictable. Experimentally, the principal confided to his kindergarten teacher that Pedro showed all indications of being a leader. "Wasn't it marvelous to see a child today so unrestricted, a free spirit, uninhibited by middle-class artificialities?" "What would happen to this boy when he was assigned to a teacher who would seek to drain the joyousness away?" The teacher began to see Pedro in a new light, and Pedro, recognizing her approval, turned to her and became her best pupil that year. His self-pride was evident. Further, his test scores and her recommendations placed him in a top-level first grade where he continued enthusiastically through school, charming all of his teachers, the first in his large family to be an academic success.

One family came to an American school from Mexico, and the administrator, on a hunch, placed all four of the children in top-level, fast-moving classes, telling each teacher that each youngster was bright, and she need not worry that year about anything excepting encouragement in learning English. At the end of the year, the teachers asked the administrator to excuse the children from testing because their English, although fast-developing, was not sufficient for fair testing. All four children were recommended for continuance in top groups. At the end of the second year, the children scored in both intelligence and achievement where their classmates did, above average.

The stories support the proposition that intelligence test scores affect the teachers' expectations about their pupils' performance, and that the expectations may become prophecies self-fulfilled. But in all the literature on the subject, only one experiment was found which was designed specifically to test the proposition, one by Clifford Pitt (1956).

## Experimental Evidence

Pitt's (1956) sample of pupils was comprised of 165 fifth-grade boys with IQ 94 or higher, to whom a standard test of intelligence had been administered. For about one third of the boys, IQs were reported accurately to their teachers. For another third of the youngsters, the IQs were also reported to their teachers, but ten IQ points were arbitrarily added. For the final third of the sample, IQs were reported, but ten points were arbitrarily deducted from each score. All this was done in the beginning of the school year. At the end of that school year the children of the three groups were compared on school grades, achievement tests, teacher ratings, and pupil self-ratings.

Pitt's results were damaging to the hypothesis of the effects of teachers' self-fulfilling prophecies. He found essentially no effects on the objective tests of achievement of the arbitrarily raised or lowered IQs. A number of explanations are possible and are listed below.

> 1. Teacher's knowledge of a pupil's IQ really does not affect pupil performance.
> 2. There is an effect on pupil performance, but, because Pitt's teachers knew their children for seven or eight weeks before being given the IQ scores, the effect was washed out by teachers' expectations based on more personal knowledge of each boy's performance.
> 3. There is such an effect, but only when teachers are females.
> 4. There is such an effect, but only when pupils are girls.
> 5. There is such an effect, but only when teachers hold a bachelor's degree. (Very few of Pitt's teachers, 14 percent, had that much education.)
> 6. There is such an effect, but only when the children are younger than fifth graders (or older, though that seems unlikely).
> 7. There is such an effect, but only when a child's IQ is below 94.

In subsequent chapters we shall have occasion to consider some of these explanations once again. For now, however, there is no way to decide which of the alternatives listed are correct, if any, or, at least, more correct than the others.

Pitt did find some interesting effects of children's having their IQs arbitrarily increased or decreased. These effects emerged in the pupils' self-ratings. Those boys whose IQs had been fictitiously lowered came to feel that (1) they worked less hard at their school work than did other boys, (2) school was more difficult for them than for other boys,

(3) their teachers were harder on them in grading than they were on other children, and (4) school was less enjoyable. So, though teachers' beliefs about pupils' IQs did not affect pupils' academic performance, it did affect the pupils' views of themselves, of their teachers, and of the school. These findings are reminiscent of those reported by Wartenberg-Ekren (1962). She had found that examiners' expectancy was not a significant factor in the IQ scores earned by college students. Yet, in her study the subjects felt differentially treated by their examiners depending on whether the examiner expected a high or low performance level. In both of these studies, then, performance was unaffected by the expectancy of teacher or examiner yet the students could tell in some subtle way that they were being treated differently.

Many schools, perhaps most, employ the method of ability grouping or tracking in which children of similar ability are grouped together and, in tracked schools, kept together, as long as the relative homogeneity of ability is sustained. Children may move to a higher or lower group or track as changes in their performance seem to make such moves advisable. But most children do not change groups. Once placed on a fast, average, or slow track, children tend to stay there. Membership in a given group or track, like membership in a disadvantaged group, or like a particular IQ score, is a source of teacher expectation about a pupil's intellectual ability. It was this source of teacher expectancy which Charles Flowers (1966) employed in his study.

In what, to our knowledge, was the only other experimental study of the effects of teacher expectancy, Flowers employed different methods but the same logic that Pitt employed. Where Pitt employed fictitious IQ scores, Flowers employed fictitious ability grouping to learn about the effects on pupil performance of teacher expectancy.

Flowers' study was conducted in two different junior high schools located in two different cities. The two schools had in common their location in depressed areas of the city, their students were educationally disadvantaged, and grouping procedures were routine. In each of the two schools two seventh-grade classes were selected such that their "actual" abilities defined by IQ and achievement test scores were only average and comparable to each other. In each of the two schools, one of these matched pairs of classes was arbitrarily labeled as one of the top groups in the school. Teachers, of course, were not told of the arbitrary nature of the grouping of one of the classes.

At the end of the school year in which the experiment was conducted, all children were retested for ability in reading and arithmetic and for IQ, the variables on which the children had been pretested. In one of the schools, the fictitiously upgraded group (twenty-four children) performed better than its control group (nineteen children) in reading and arithmetic though the effect was a weak one statistically. There were no differences in IQ between the upgraded and the control class.

In the other school the situation was reversed. The arbitrarily upgraded group (nineteen children) showed a gain of five IQ points in excess of the gain in IQ of the control group (nineteen children), and this excess of gain was significant statistically ($p < .03$). There were no differences in arithmetic or reading achievement between the upgraded and the control class.

At the conclusion of the study Flowers asked each of the teachers of the various courses in which the children were enrolled to answer a number of questions about the children. Comparison of the replies of teachers of the upgraded and control groups suggested a number of possible differences. Compared to teachers of the control groups, teachers of allegedly superior groups (1) referred more often to what the children could do rather than to what they could not do, (2) found virtually no discipline problems in class (although discipline problems were reported by almost all teachers of control group children), (3) referred more often to efforts to motivate their pupils and less often to the inadequacy of teaching materials, and (4) preferred teaching the "higher" ability group.

More than was the case in Pitt's research, Flowers did obtain some evidence favorable to the hypothesis of educational self-fulfilling prophecies. Why he should have found achievement to be benefited by favorable expectations more in one school and IQ more in another remains a moot point. In any case the gains demonstrated were not dramatic, and there are several possible explanations.

> 1. Even when self-fulfilling prophecies occur in fact, they are not dramatic in magnitude.
> 2. Self-fulfilling prophecies may be dramatic but not when the children are already in seventh grade.
> 3. Self-fulfilling prophecies may be dramatic, but in the described study so many teachers were involved with each student that the effects were diluted from what they would have been had each group had only a single teacher.
> 4. Even the nondramatic gains demonstrated in Flowers' study may have been too high and, in fact, educational self-fulfilling prophecies do not occur.

This last possibility comes about as a result of a difference in design between the studies of Pitt and Flowers. In Pitt's design each of the teachers had an opportunity to interact with the children of his three experimental groups. Because each teacher had an equal opportunity to influence the children whose IQs had been accurately reported, fictitiously elevated, and fictitiously lowered, the effects of individual differences among teachers could not have accounted for any differences—if he had found any. That was not the case in Flowers' study. There, the experimental and control groups had different teachers for the most part so that his results might have been due to individual differences among teachers. Perhaps the teachers of the allegedly superior group were better teachers, and the group's advantage, therefore, was due more to superior teaching than to teacher expectancy. There is no way to be sure of the matter as yet, but the other side of the coin should be shown. That side suggests that individual differences among teachers were such that the control groups were the ones advantaged by teacher superiority and that otherwise the experimental groups would have shown more dramatic effects of teacher expectancy. The answer to the question with which we are left depends on additional evidence.

# 6

# The
# Oak
# School
# Experiment

In this chapter we shall describe the plan of an experiment that was designed specifically to test the proposition that within a given classroom those children from whom the teacher expected greater intellectual growth would show such greater growth. The general design (and some of the results of this experiment) have been briefly stated in preliminary reports, but here we shall be able to give the details of the procedure and subsequently the results, most of which have become available only since the preparation of our earlier reports (Rosenthal and Jacobson, 1966; in press).

## OAK SCHOOL

The experiment was conducted in a public elementary school which we shall call Oak School. It is essential for us to present some descriptions of the community from which Oak School draws its children, of the children themselves, of the educational organization of Oak School, and of its teachers.

### The Community
The community is an old part of the larger town and is fairly well divided into three parts: (1) an area of attractive middle-class homes on the hills that house few children; (2) winding streets toward the industrial section of town with tidy small cottages and new duplex units that also have few children; and (3) streets and alleys of ill-kempt deteriorated houses that are fairly bursting with children.

This old section of the city was settled several generations ago by Italian immigrants who have long since exchanged their truck-farming for real-estate enterprises, city politics, and large and small thriving businesses. Their names, though not their faces, are the heritage of many of the students at Oak School, for clearly over the years an ethnic mixture has occurred.

### The Children

Most of the children of Oak School, however, come from a preponderantly lower-class community. Their fathers, when they are part of the family unit, are mostly unskilled and semiskilled workers. Many of the children are from broken homes where their mothers work and/or the family receives welfare funds.

Still, Oak School has few desperately poor children. To a middle-class observer, some look less cared-for than others, but they are neither undernourished nor shabbily dressed; rather, they appear in need of bathing, brushing, and perhaps dental work. Few of the children need to be recommended by the teachers for free lunches in the school cafeteria. When a child's clothes are truly ragged, for example, a home visit more often reveals "poor handling" of money rather than no money. The child's lower-class status is indicated, also, by cultural impoverishment of language and experience.

Visitors to the school find the children in general to be noisy and attractive. A feeling of sociability rather than of earnest endeavor is in the atmosphere, which might be a contributing factor to the school's generally low level of achievement. There is little awe of the school office; in fact, the office seems to be a combination of a loan office and a tender-loving-care station. Children visit constantly to borrow or return lunch money as well as to have aches clucked over and treated.

About one sixth of the school's population of 650 consists of Mexican children, the only minority group enrolled. Children of the one Negro family in the attendance district appear to be quite absorbed into the majority group. The Mexican children seem to group together, which may be due to their language commonality but probably is due to their familial and social organization outside the school. Their facility in the Spanish language varies from knowledge of just a few words in English to understanding a visiting aunt from Mexico only if she speaks slowly.

Enrollment at the school is never stable. Transfers in and out seem continual to the office personnel but in reality they number approximately under 200, or about 30 percent during a single year. These transfers are frequent due to the job-seeking problems of the fathers, moves to a "better" neighborhood, and transfers to and from a nearby Catholic school. Many of the transfers out come back again within a few months.

## Ability Grouping

Oak School follows the district policy of sorting children into ability classes or tracks, with the sorting based on reading performance primarily. There are three classes each for grades one through six, termed high, middle, and low groups or fast, medium, and slow tracks. The ins and outs seldom belong to the high or top-achieving third of the school. A disproportionate number of Mexican children are found in the low groups as are children from other low-income families. The school's Mexican children constitute 17 percent of the total population, but less than 6 percent of the school's fast-track children are Mexican and nearly 29 percent of the slow-track children are Mexican, a difference in distributions that could occur by chance only very rarely.[1]

Among the Mexican children the boys and girls are equitably distributed among the three tracks. Among the non-Mexican children, however, the boys are over-represented in the slow track and the girls are over-represented in the fast track. About 53 percent of the school's non-Mexican children are boys but less than 38 percent of the fast-track children are boys, and nearly 69 percent of the slow-track children are boys, a difference in distributions that is very significant statistically.[2]

Children at Oak School are not assigned to tracks on the basis of IQ scores but rather on the basis of achievement in reading as defined by the teacher's judgment, primarily, and also by achievement test scores. Nevertheless, there are substantial differences in the average IQs of the three tracks. For a subsample of 370 children included in the experiment, nonverbal tests of intelligence had been administered before the experiment began. Table 6-1 shows the resulting mean IQs in each of the three tracks and the total school for the Mexican and non-Mexican boys and girls. In each of the four subgroups shown, the faster the track, the higher the mean IQ (the exact $p$ of such an ordering equals .0046). Table 6-1 also shows that IQs of Mexican children are substantially lower than IQs of non-Mexicans and that there is relatively little difference (9.8 points, $t = 1.53$) between the IQs of the fast and slow groups of Mexican girls compared to the great deal of difference (26.7 points, $t = 8.59$) between the fast and slow track non-Mexican girls.

Teachers' recommendations for group placement are made at promotion time for the following year. During the school year a teacher may transfer a child to a higher or lower group despite the former teacher's recommendation, but only a few such transfers occur; most of the ups and downs are proposed for the following year.

This district mandate regarding ability grouping is based on the philosophy that a narrower range of ability within a classroom results in less frustration and higher production for the children, whether high or low achievers. The achievement of Oak School is among the lowest of the twelve elementary schools in town. It should be noted that the other three lowest-achieving schools also draw enrollment from primarily lower-class and/or culturally different families. At the time of this study, the administrators of these low-achieving schools were questioning the advisability of ability grouping.

**Table 6-1**    Nonverbal IQ Scores in Three Tracks for Mexican and Non-Mexican Boys and Girls

| TRACK | BOYS | | | | GIRLS | | | |
|---|---|---|---|---|---|---|---|---|
| | MEXICAN | | NON-MEXICAN | | MEXICAN | | NON-MEXICAN | |
| | N . | IQ | N | IQ | N | IQ | N | IQ |
| Fast | 5 | 100.6 | 52 | 112.0 | 3 | 93.3 | 85 | 109.0 |
| Medium | 10 | 89.4 | 57 | 99.5 | 12 | 91.8 | 34 | 97.5 |
| Slow | 15 | 82.6 | 55 | 89.9 | 17 | 83.5 | 25 | 82.3 |
| TOTAL | 30 | 87.6 | 164 | 100.2 | 32 | 87.6 | 144 | 101.7 |

**The Teachers**

Oak School has twenty teachers of whom only two are males. Two of the teachers teach a total of four half-day kindergarten classes, and the remaining teachers are assigned to one of the three tracks at each of the remaining six grade levels. From year to year teachers tend to teach at the same grade level but there is fairly regular rotation of track assignment within grade level.

The average age of the teachers is 35.1 ($\sigma = 10.4$) with a range from 23 to over 50. In line with what we would expect from the age range, teaching experience ranges from one year to well over thirty years with a mean of 7.7 ($\sigma = 8.4$). All the teachers hold bachelor's degrees, one third earned these at universities and most of the others earned them at state and teachers' colleges.

A visitor to the school finds the teachers, like the children, attractive and sociable for the most part. There are only a few for whom teaching is just a job; most are eager to discuss their philosophy of education, the details of their teaching techniques, the assets and limitations of their pupils. Many of the teachers, then, must. be called dedicated.

## THE RESEARCH PROCEDURE

Now let us consider the research plan used at Oak School, which was patterned basically on the animal studies described in Chapter 4. There it was observed that animals alleged to be genetically inferior performed in an inferior manner for their experimenters. Animals believed by their experimenters to be genetically superior, on the other hand, performed in superior fashion. If animals become "brighter" when expected to by their experimenters, then it seemed reasonable to think that children might become brighter when expected to by their teachers.

When the subjects were animals it could be alleged of perfectly ordinary rats that they had been specially bred for brightness or dullness. That technique could hardly be employed at Oak School. It was necessary to create expectancies in some other way. Further, because animals alleged to be dull seemed to show poor learning, it would be an ethical requirement to create expectancies in only the more socially useful direction—up—rather than have any children be expected to show worsened performance.

Another requirement of the experiment was to have some measure of intellectual competence of all children in the school before the experiment began. Such a measure was necessary as a yardstick against which to measure the intellectual gains of the children of both the experimental and control groups. It is a common and methodologically defensible procedure simply to assign at random some subjects to the experimental group and some to the control group without the use of a pretest, hoping that chance will have operated to make the two groups equivalent in the first place. But, as E. G. Boring (in press) has pointed out, we can never be quite sure that the two groups formed in that way really were equivalent to begin with.

In the present experiment it was possible to combine the schoolwide administration of the pretest of intelligence with the creation of a plausible basis for creating favorable expectations for the intellectual growth of some of Oak School's children.

### The Harvard Test
### of Inflected Acquisition

In the Spring of 1964, the "Harvard Test of Inflected Acquisition" was administered to all of the children of Oak School who might return the following Fall. That meant that kindergarten children and all grades except grade six were tested. The sixth graders were headed for junior high school and would not be back. The test was purported to be a predictor of academic "blooming" or "spurting." Each teacher was given a dittoed copy of the explanation of the research several months before the first testing took place. That explanation now follows.

### ◆§STUDY OF INFLECTED ACQUISITION
(Harvard-National Science Foundation)

All children show hills, plateaus, and valleys in their scholastic progress. The study being conducted at Harvard with the support of the National Science Foundation is interested in those children who show an unusual forward spurt of academic progress. These spurts can and do occur at any level of academic and intellectual functioning. When these spurts occur in children who have not been functioning too well academically, the result is familiarly referred to as "late blooming."

As a part of our study we are further validating a test which predicts the likelihood that a child will show an inflection point or "spurt" within the near future. This test which will be administered in your school will allow us to predict which youngsters are most likely to show an academic spurt. The top 20 percent (approximately) of the scorers on this test will probably be found at various levels of academic functioning.

The development of the test for predicting inflections or "spurts" is not yet such that every one of the top 20 percent will show the spurt or "blooming" effect. But the top 20 percent of the children will show a more significant inflection or spurt in their learning within the next year or less than will the remaining 80 percent of the children.

Because of the experimental nature of the tests, basic principles of test construction do not permit us to discuss the test or test scores either with the parents or the children themselves.

Upon completion of this study, participating districts will be advised of the results.

The explanation also gave the dates of testing as May 1964; January 1965; and May 1965. No mention was made, however, of the follow-up testing scheduled for May 1966.

The ostensible reason for the testing in Oak School was to perform a final check on the validity of the test, a validity which was presented as already well established. Actually, the "Harvard Test of Inflected Acquisition" was a standardized, relatively nonverbal test of intelligence, Flanagan's (1960) Tests of General Ability (TOGA).

There were a number of reasons for using Flanagan's TOGA. First, it did not look like any intelligence test that had been routinely used at Oak School, and teachers were unlikely to have seen it elsewhere or heard of it. Second, like most such tests, it is group-administered, an essential requirement in view of the more than 2000 testings planned.[3] Third, it is a fairly homogeneous type test in the sense that for all ages at the elementary school level the type of task set for the children is similar. Finally, and perhaps most important for employment in a primarily lower-class school with a large bilingual population, TOGA was "designed to provide measures of basic learning ability" (Flanagan, 1960, p. 6) not so explicitly dependent on such school-acquired skills as reading, writing, and arithmetic.

For the elementary school grades, TOGA comes in three forms, each designed for one of the following levels: K-2, 2-4, and 4-6. For the pretest, the K-2 level was administered by the classroom teachers to all kindergarten and first-grade classes; 2-4 was administered to the second and third grades; and 4-6 was administered to the fourth and fifth grades. Retests during the following school year employed the same test level for all children so that we would expect some practice effect. Practice effect should not, however, affect the experimental and control-group children differently. It should also be recalled that in successive years a child must perform a good deal better simply to maintain his IQ score since as he ages chronologically he must develop in his performance in order only to hold his own.

Two years after the pretest the children were retested again. This time those who at the time of pretest had been in kindergarten, second grade, and fourth grade again had the same form of TOGA, while those who had been in the first and third grades were tested with the next-higher-level form. Pretest fifth graders were not retested on the two-year follow-up as they had become seventh graders and were no longer at Oak School.

At all levels, TOGA is composed of two relatively independent subtests, one measuring verbal ability, and the other, reasoning. Verbal subtest items are designed to measure level of information, vocabulary, and concepts. An example of a verbal item on the K-2 level shows pictures of a suit jacket, a flower, an envelope, an apple, and a glass of water. Children are asked to mark with a crayon "the thing that you can eat." Though performance at such items depends on the child's being able to understand English, it is not necessary for him to speak, read, or write English as it is in many other tests of intelligence.

Reasoning subtest items are designed to test the ability to understand relationships and form concepts. In each item there are five abstract line drawings, one of which differs from the other four in some respect and must be indicated. An example of such an item on the K-2 level shows four squares and a circle. The circle must be crossed out with a crayon. The correlation between scores on the reasoning and verbal subtests for our sample was +.42; the median correlation obtained by Flanagan (1960) in ten studies was +.43.

There is an important difference in the administration of the two subtests. The verbal items are all read aloud to the children, and the teacher is required to make frequent trips up and down the aisles to see that children are all on the correct page of the test booklet. The reasoning items are self-administered by the children except that two examples are solved by the teacher in front of the class as an illustration before pupils begin to work on their own. The reasoning subtest is also timed. In short, there is considerably more teacher-pupil interaction during the administration of the verbal subtest than there is during the administration of the reasoning subtest. We shall have occasion later to refer back to that fact.

## The Assessment
## of Intellectual Growth

Intellectual growth was defined as the difference between a child's pretest IQ and his IQ on a post-test. The basic experiment was intended to show whether those children of whom the teachers held especially favorable expectations would show greater intellectual growth than the remaining or control-group children. The basic post-test was administered eight months after the experimental treatment (described below) was administered, and one year after the pretest.

Two other retests were also administered. One of these was a follow-up testing two years after the pretest. The purpose of this testing was to learn, in case there were some effects of teachers' favorable expectations, whether these effects would last at least another year. That would be important to know because in any change experiment, one wants to know if changes appear quickly only to disappear quickly. In addition, since in this experiment the teacher was the agent of change, it was important to know whether any expectancy-derived gains would be maintained even after the children left their change agent for another teacher who had not been given special expectations about any of the children.

The other retest was administered before, rather than after, the basic post-test. It came at the end of the first semester, midway between the administration of the experimental change program and the basic post-test. The purpose of this preliminary retest was to learn, in case there were some effects of the change program, whether these effects occurred early or late during the year. That would be useful information since it might suggest whether the advantage of favorable expectations, if any, grew gradually over the year, developed quickly without further change over the year, or showed an incubation effect with no change early in the year followed by a true "late blooming" of the advantages of favorable expectations.

This preliminary retest and the basic post-test were administered by the classroom teachers who had been given the favorable expectations. The follow-up test was also administered by the classroom teachers, but these were new teachers to whom the children had since been promoted; and these teachers did not know which of their children had, the year before, been in the experimental or control groups. In principle they could have known this if the teachers of the year before had told them, but, in fact, they did not know. While, as teachers do, "last year's" teachers told "next year's" teachers about their prospective class, none of "last year's" teachers told their heirs which of the class had been experimental-group and which had been control-group children. Indeed, the evidence suggested that "last year's" teachers could not have told because they did not know. A memory test administered to the teachers showed that they could not recall accurately, nor even choose accurately from a larger list of names, the names of their own pupils designated as experimental-group children.

Of the more than 500 children pretested, there were less than 400 remaining for the first year's retests, partly because of transfers out of school and partly because of illness during the periods of retesting. For the two-year follow-up testing there were less than 300 children remaining, partly for the same reasons but also because the entire pretest fifth grade had by then left Oak School for junior high school. Only those children can be said to have been in the experiment for whom a pretest IQ was available and at least one retest IQ.

Retests were not explained to teachers as retests but were designed to appear as further efforts to predict intellectual growth.

Although teachers administered the tests, they did not score them. All tests, pretests, preliminary retests, post-tests, and follow-up tests were scored twice, and independently, by research assistants who did not know which children were part of the control group and which were part of the experimental program of intellectual change defined below.

## The Program
## for Intellectual Change

At the end of the Summer of 1964, the classes already having been pretested, 20 percent of the children of Oak School were designated as academic "spurters" just before the teachers met their new classes. The background of plausibility for this designation had been established in the Spring of the preceding school year. It remained now actually to institute the program of intellectual change.

The program was instituted by the distribution of eighteen sheets of paper, one each to the teachers of the new grades one through six, one class per grade in each of the three tracks, fast, medium, and slow. On each teacher's sheet were listed the names of from one to nine children, those children in her class who were allegedly in Oak School's top 20 percent scorers on the "Harvard Test of Inflected Acquisition." The lists of names contained a total of 20 percent of the school's children, but it was felt to be more plausible if each teacher did not have exactly the same number or percentage of her class listed.[4] As a reason for their being given the lists of names, teachers were told only that they might find it of interest to know which of their children were about to bloom. They were also cautioned not to discuss the test findings with their pupils or the children's parents.

The names of the 20 percent subsample of "special" children had been selected by means of a table of random numbers. The difference between the children earmarked for intellectual growth and the undesignated control children was in the mind of the teacher.

✎§

[1] For a subsample of 370 children included in our experiment, the Mexican and non-Mexican children differed in their distribution among the three tracks at $p$ much less than .001 ($\chi^2 = 24.9$, $df = 2$).

[2] For a subsample of 308 non-Mexican children included in our experiment, the boys and girls differed in their distribution among the three tracks at $p$ much less than .001 ($\chi^2 = 23.8$, $df = 2$).

[3] The logistics of the situation required a group test, and there is a general feeling that group tests are justified only on logistic grounds. There may be some more positive reasons, however, for preferring a group test that have to do with the lessened degree of personal interaction between examiner and examinee. When it becomes important to control for the unintended effects of the examiner's expectancy, for example, the evidence presented in Chapter 4 suggests that group testing may provide a better safeguard than individual

testing. It is difficult for the examiner to behave in very different ways to different examinees during his reading of the instructions to a group. It is even more difficult, perhaps, for the examiner *not* to treat his individually instructed examinees quite differently.

4 For the same reason the proportion of either boys or girls on each teacher's list was allowed to vary from a minimum of 40 percent of the designated children to a maximum of 60 percent of the designated children.

# 7

# The
# Magic
# Children
# of
# Galatea

The basic question to be answered in this chapter is
whether in a period of one year or less the children
of whom greater intellectual growth is expected will show greater
intellectual growth than the undesignated control-group children.
There are also four important subsidiary questions. If there were some
advantages to a child whose teacher had favorable expectations for his
intellectual development, would these expectancy advantages be greater
for:

1. Children in the lower grades or higher grades?
2. Children in the fast track, or medium track, or slow track?
3. Children of one sex rather than the other?
4. Children of minority group or nonminority group status?

## THE MAJOR VARIABLES

### Age
The folk knowledge of our culture, current theories of human development, especially psychoanalytic theory, and the work of the develop-
mental and experimental psychologists and of the ethologists are in
agreement on the importance of age as a factor in determining the
degree to which an organism can be shaped, molded, or influenced
(Scott, 1962). In general, the younger the organism, the greater is
thought to be the degree of susceptibility to social influence. In his
classic monograph, Coffin (1941) concluded that influenceability increased from infancy to ages seven to nine but decreased after that.
More recently in a summary of the evidence bearing on overt social

influence on children, Stevenson (1965) reported the greater influenceability of five-year-olds than twelve-year-olds, a finding consistent with
Coffin's summary. Both Coffin and Stevenson were writing about more
overt social influence than the subtle, unintended influence of teachers'
prophecies. Still, it would be interesting to know whether influence
processes of a more subtle, unintended form would also show younger
children to be the more susceptible.

## Ability
We are also interested in learning whether the children of the three
tracks differ in the degree to which they profit from the teachers'
favorable expectations. In the case of ability, however, the literature
is not so helpful in telling us what we might find. Stevenson (1965)
suggested that susceptibility to social influence may not be too contingent on the child's intellectual status, and we know that the three
tracks differ considerably in average IQ. One of the most recent dis-
cussions of intellectual gains is by Thorndike (1966) who reports that
there are only modest correlations between initial intellectual status
and changes in intellectual status. In the present research, in any case,
we are not so much interested in gains *per se* but rather in the excess
of gain that might be shown by the "special" children over the
"ordinary" undesignated children. In short, we are interested in differences among the tracks in the degree of expectancy advantage that
may be found, but we hardly know what to expect. The matter is
further complicated by the fact that the other two variables in which
we are interested, sex and minority group status, are not independent
of track placement. In the last chapter we saw that boys tend to overpopulate the slow track relative to girls who tend to overpopulate the
fast track. Mexican children, Oak School's minority group, tend to
overpopulate the slow track and underpopulate the fast track.

## Sex
Whether boys or girls are the more susceptible to social influence
processes depends on whether the influencer is male or female (Stevenson, 1965). Since the overwhelming majority of Oak School's teachers
are females, the findings from research with lady influencers interest
us most. Those findings, summarized by Stevenson (1965), suggest
that boys should be the more suspectible to social influence. As in the
case of the children's age, however, the social influence processes
employed were neither unintended nor very subtle. Effects of teachers'
expectations are likely to be both.

## Minority Group Status

The reasons for our interest in the variable of minority-group status need little justification. So much of the literature on the disadvantaged child focuses on the minority-group child that "disadvantaged" almost means "minority group." One of the best known publications dealing with the disadvantaged is called *Youth in the Ghetto*. We shall be especially interested, then, if expectancy advantages occur at all, in whether they benefit minority-group children more or less than non-minority-group children.

At Oak School the minority-group child is Mexican. The definition of a minority-group child in this research, however, was more stringent than simply whether the name was Mexican. To qualify as a "minority-group child," either the child himself or his parents had to come from Mexico, Spanish had to be spoken at home, and the child had to be present for the administration of certain procedures. These procedures, in connection with another study (Jacobson, 1966), included administration of an IQ test in Spanish, a test of reading ability, and the taking of photographs of the child himself. Within this sample of Mexican minority-group children there were variations in how "Mexican" each child looked. A group of ten teachers with no connection to Oak School or its children rated each photograph on "how Mexican the child looked." The definition of how clearly Mexican a child "really" looked was the average rating of all ten teachers. These ratings were highly reliable. The average rating of the same children by the teachers of Oak School was correlated .97 with the ratings of the judges who were not associated with Oak School.

## INTELLECTUAL GROWTH

### Expectancy Advantage
### by Grades

The bottom row of Table 7-1 gives the over-all results for Oak School. In the year of the experiment, the undesignated control-group children gained over eight IQ points while the experimental-group children, the special children, gained over twelve. The difference in gains could be ascribed to chance about 2 in 100 times ($F = 6.35$).[1]

The rest of Table 7-1 and Figure 7-1 show the gains by children of the two groups separately for each grade. We find increasing expectancy advantage as we go from the sixth to the first grade; the correlation between grade level and magnitude of expectancy advantage ($r = -.86$) was significant at the .03 level. The interaction

**Figure 7-1**   Gains in total IQ in six grades.

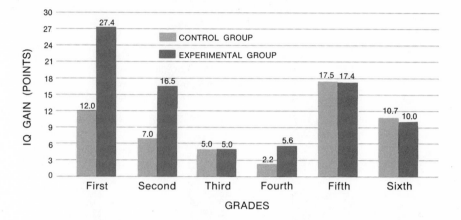

effect, or likelihood that at different grades there were significantly greater expectancy advantages, was significant at the .07 level ($F = 2.13$). (Interactions, however, are not sensitive to the ordering of differences unless one makes them so with further statistical efforts; that is, the $p$ of .07 is conservative.)

**Table 7-1**   Mean Gain in Total IQ after One Year by Experimental- and Control-Group Children in Each of Six Grades

| GRADE | CONTROL | | EXPERIMENTAL | | EXPECTANCY ADVANTAGE | |
|---|---|---|---|---|---|---|
| | $N$ | GAIN | $N$ | GAIN | IQ POINTS | ONE-TAIL $p < .05$[a] |
| 1 | 48 | +12.0 | 7 | +27.4 | +15.4 | .002 |
| 2 | 47 | + 7.0 | 12 | +16.5 | + 9.5 | .02 |
| 3 | 40 | + 5.0 | 14 | + 5.0 | − 0.0 | |
| 4 | 49 | + 2.2 | 12 | + 5.6 | + 3.4 | |
| 5 | 26 | +17.5 (−) | 9 | +17.4 (+) | − 0.0 | |
| 6 | 45 | +10.7 | 11 | +10.0 | − 0.7 | |
| TOTAL | 255 | + 8.42 | 65 | +12.22 | + 3.80 | .02 |

[a] Mean square within treatments within classrooms = 164.24

In the first and second grades the effects of teachers' prophecies were dramatic. Table 7-1 shows that, and so does Table 7-2 and Figure 7-2. There we find the percentage of experimental- and control-group children of the first two grades who achieved various amounts

**Figure 7-2**          Percentages of first and second graders
                        gaining ten, twenty, or thirty
                        total IQ points.

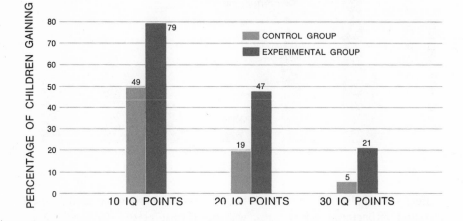

of gain. In these grades about every fifth control-group child gained
twenty IQ points or more, but of the special children, nearly every
second child gained that much.

---

**Table 7-2**          Percentages of First and Second
                       Graders Gaining at Least Ten,
                       Twenty, or Thirty Total IQ Points

| IQ GAIN AT LEAST | CONTROL $N = 95$ | EXPERIMENTAL $N = 19$ | ONE-TAIL $p$ OF DIFFERENCE |
|---|---|---|---|
| 10 points[a] | 49% | 79% | .02 |
| 20 points[b] | 19% | 47% | .01 |
| 30 points | 5% | 21% | .04 |

[a] Includes children gaining twenty and thirty points or more.
[b] Includes children gaining thirty points or more.

---

So far we have told only of the effects of favorable expectancies on
total IQ, but Flanagan's TOGA yields separate IQs for the verbal and
reasoning spheres of intellectual functioning. These are sufficiently
different from each other so it will not be redundant to give the results of each. In the case of verbal IQ the control-group children of
the entire school gained just less than eight points, and the special
children gained just less than ten, a difference that could easily have

arisen by chance. The interaction term was not very significant ($p < .15$) so that we can not conclude greater expectancy advantage at some grade levels than at others. But we do have a special interest now in the first and second graders, and it will do no harm to see what happened there in particular. In those combined grades, the control-group children gained 4.5 verbal IQ points, and the special children gained exactly 10 points more, or 14.5. If we may have the $t$ test (even though the interaction effect was not significant) we would find $t = 2.24$, $p < .02$, one-tail.

Table 7-3    Mean Gain in Verbal IQ after One Year by Experimental- and Control-Group Children in Grades One–Two and Three–Six

| GRADES | CONTROL | | EXPERIMENTAL | | EXPECTANCY ADVANTAGE | |
|---|---|---|---|---|---|---|
| | N | GAIN | N | GAIN | IQ POINTS | ONE-TAIL $p < .05$[a] |
| 1–2 | 95 | +4.5 | 19 | +14.5 | +10.0 | .02 |
| 3–6 | 174 | +9.6 | 49 | + 8.0 | − 1.6 | |
| TOTAL | 269 | +7.79 | 68 | + 9.85 | + 2.06 | |

[a] Mean square within = 316.40.

For grades three through six the control gained 1.6 points more than the experimental group, a difference not nearly significant. Table 7-3 summarizes these results.[2]

Table 7-4    Mean Gain in Reasoning IQ after One Year by Experimental- and Control-Group Children in Grades One–Two and Three–Six

| GRADES | CONTROL | | EXPERIMENTAL | | EXPECTANCY ADVANTAGE | |
|---|---|---|---|---|---|---|
| | N | GAIN | N | GAIN | IQ POINTS | ONE-TAIL $p < .05$[a] |
| 1–2 | 95 | +27.0 (−) | 19 | +39.6 (+) | +12.7 | .03 |
| 3–6 | 160 | + 9.1 (−) | 46 | +15.9 (+) | + 6.9 | .06 |
| TOTAL | 255 | +15.73 | 65 | +22.86 | + 7.13 | .005 |

[a] Mean square within = 666.58.

The advantage of favorable expectations showed itself more clearly in reasoning IQ as shown in Table 7-4. For the school as a whole, the advantage of favorable expectations was a seven point net gain in reasoning IQ ($F = 6.98$), and there were no significant differences in the six grades in degree of expectancy advantage.[3] Once again, the younger children benefited most. While we are not especially interested in the magnitude of IQ gain of the control group, it does seem remarkable that the younger children of even the control group should gain so heavily in reasoning IQ. Table 7-1 shows that control-group children gained substantially in total IQ and not only at the younger ages where we might expect practice effects to be most dramatic. There is no way to be sure about the matter (we shall return to it in a later chapter), but it may be that experiments are good for children even when the children are in the untreated control group.

## Expectancy Advantage
## by Tracks and Sex

None of the statistical tests showed any differences among the three tracks in the extent to which they benefited from teachers' favorable prophecies. That was the case for total IQ, verbal IQ, and reasoning IQ. When the entire school benefited as in total IQ and reasoning IQ, all three tracks benefited; and when the school as a whole did not benefit much, as in verbal IQ, none of the tracks showed much benefit. For all three IQ measures, the tendency was for the middle track, the more average children, to benefit most from being expected to grow intellectually, but the difference could easily have occurred by chance.

In total IQ, girls showed a slightly greater advantage than boys of having been expected to show an intellectual spurt; but to see what really happened we must look at boys' and girls' expectancy advantages for the two subtypes of IQ. Table 7-5 shows the gains in all three types of IQ by boys and girls of the experimental and control groups. In verbal IQ it was the boys who showed the expectancy advantage (interaction $F = 2.13$, $p = .16$); in reasoning IQ it was the girls who showed the advantage, and it was dramatic in size (interaction $F = 9.27$, $p = .003$). Just why that should be is not at all clear. On the pretest, boys had shown a higher verbal IQ than girls (4.4 points), and girls had shown a higher reasoning IQ than boys (8.5 points). Apparently each group profited more from teachers' prophecies in the area of intellectual functioning in which they were already a little advantaged.[4]

It was mentioned earlier that expectancy advantage was not dependent on placement in any one of the three tracks. That conclusion is modified when we examine expectancy advantages in the three tracks separately for boys and girls. Only for reasoning IQ is there a statistically significant effect (triple interaction $F = 3.47$, $p < .04$). Table 7-6 shows the excess of gain in reasoning IQ by the experimental over the control boys and girls in each of the three tracks. We already knew that girls showed the greater expectancy advantage in reasoning IQ, and from Table 7-6 we see that this was significantly more true in the medium track, the track with the more average children.

| Table 7-5 | | | | | Mean Gain in Three IQ Scores after One Year by Experimental and Control Boys and Girls | | |
|---|---|---|---|---|---|---|---|
| | CONTROL | | EXPERIMENTAL | | EXPECTANCY ADVANTAGE | | |
| | $N$ | GAIN | $N$ | GAIN | IQ POINTS | ONE-TAIL $p < .06$ | |
| *Total IQ* | | | | | | | |
| Boys | 127 | + 9.6 | 32 | +12.5 | + 2.9 | | |
| Girls | 128 | + 7.3 | 33 | +12.0 | + 4.7 | .04 | |
| *Verbal IQ* | | | | | | | |
| Boys | 136 | + 8.4 (−) | 34 | +13.9 (+) | + 5.6 | .06 | |
| Girls | 133 | + 7.2 | 34 | + 5.8 | − 1.4 | | |
| *Reasoning IQ* | | | | | | | |
| Boys | 127 | +19.2 | 32 | +15.3 | − 3.9 | | |
| Girls | 128 | +12.3 | 33 | +30.2 | +17.9 | .0002 | |

We knew also that girls are over-represented in the fast track. These are the brighter girls from whom a lot is already expected. The slow track girls tend to be relatively very slow at Oak School, and we know that girls only rarely are placed there, and that they represent a real challenge to Oak School's teachers. Of the middle-track girls there is little to say—teachers tend to find them uninteresting; pre-existing expectations about their intellectual ability are neither favorable as in the fast track nor very unfavorable and challenging as in the slow track. Perhaps when teachers are given favorable expectations about these children a greater increment of interest results than when expectations are given of girls in the outer tracks. That is a possible explanation of the greater effect in the average track of teachers' favorable expectations for girls' intellectual growth. Why the growth should be in reasoning IQ in particular is not at all clear, but we do know that for the girls in this experiment when there are advantages of teacher prophecies they tend to occur in the reasoning sphere of intellectual functioning.

| Table 7-6 | Excess of Gain in Reasoning IQ by Experimental over Control Boys and Girls in Three Tracks after One Year | |
|---|---|---|
| TRACK | BOYS | GIRLS |
| Fast | − 2.6 | + 9.1 |
| Medium | −12.0 | +42.0[a] |
| Slow | − 0.3 | +12.5 |
| TOTAL | − 3.9 | +17.9 |

[a] $p = .00003$, one-tail.

A pupil's sex turned out to be a factor complicating the amount of expectancy advantage found in the three tracks. Sex also complicated the magnitude of expectancy advantage found in the younger children of the first two grades compared to the older children of the upper four grades. Table 7-7 shows the number of IQ points by which the gains of the experimental-group children exceeded the gains of the control-group children. These expectancy advantage scores are shown separately for each of the three IQ measures for boys and girls in the lower and upper grades. For total IQ, although the "special" boys of the lower grades did profit from being expected to grow intellectually, the girls of the lower grades gained nearly three times as many IQ points as a function of favorable expectations (triple interaction $F = 2.96$, $p = .09$). For verbal IQ there was no difference between boys and girls at either grade level in the amount of profit from favorable expectations (triple interaction $F < 1$), although, as we learned earlier, boys and girls of the lower grades were helped more than children of upper grades three through six. For reasoning IQ, boys and girls at different grade levels did show very different magnitudes of expectancy advantage. Boys in higher grades performed better in contrast to girls in lower grades who performed better when they were expected to do better (triple interaction $F = 8.14$, $p < .005$). Most of that effect was due to the extraordinary performance of the first- and second-grade girls of the experimental group who gained over forty IQ points more than did the control-group girls of the first and second grade.

| Table 7-7 | Excess of Gain in Three IQ Scores by Experimental over Control Boys and Girls in Two Grade Levels after One Year | |
|---|---|---|
| | BOYS | GIRLS |
| *Total IQ* | | |
| Grades 1–2 | + 6.1 | +17.1[b] |
| Grades 3–6 | + 2.3 | − 0.1 |
| *Verbal IQ* | | |
| Grades 1–2 | +10.8[a] | + 9.5 |
| Grades 3–6 | + 2.8 | − 5.8 |
| *Reasoning IQ* | | |
| Grades 1–2 | −10.7 | +40.2[c] |
| Grades 3–6 | + 3.6 | +10.0[a] |

[a] $p < .05$, one-tail (or .10 two-tail).
[b] $p < .0002$, one-tail.
[c] $p < .00002$, one-tail.

To summarize our somewhat complex findings involving pupil's sex as a factor, we may say most simply that girls bloomed more in the reasoning sphere of intellectual functioning, and boys bloomed more in the verbal sphere of intellectual functioning when some kind of unspecified blooming was expected of them. Furthermore, these gains were more likely to occur to a dramatic degree in the lower grades. That susceptibility to the unintended influence of the prophesying teacher should be greater in the lower grades comes as no special surprise. All lines of evidence tend to suggest that it is younger children who are the more susceptible to various forms of influence processes. The influence of a teacher holding favorable expectations may not be so very different. Why the boys gained more in verbal IQ when expected to gain intellectually, and why the girls gained more in reasoning IQ is not so easily explained. Earlier we did mention the possibility that children profit more from vague teacher expectations in those spheres of intellectual functioning in which they tend to be slightly advantaged to begin with. In Oak School, the pretest verbal

IQs were higher for boys than for girls by over four points; the pretest reasoning IQs were higher for girls than for boys by over eight points.

**Expectancy Advantage
by Minority-Group Status**
In total IQ, verbal IQ, and especially reasoning IQ, children of the minority group were more advantaged by favorable expectations than were the other children though the differences were not statistically significant.

For each of the Mexican children, the magnitude of expectancy advantage was computed by subtracting from his or her IQ gain the IQ gain made by the children of the control group in his or her class-room.[5] The resulting magnitudes of expectancy advantage were then correlated with the "Mexican-ness" of the children's faces. Table 7-8 shows the correlations obtained among Mexican boys and girls when expectancy advantage was defined by total, verbal, and reasoning IQs. For total IQ and reasoning IQ, those Mexican boys who looked more Mexican benefited more from teachers' favorable expectations than did the Mexican boys who looked less Mexican. There is no clear explanation for these findings, but we can speculate that the teachers' pre-experimental expectancies of the more Mexican-looking boys' intellectual performance was probably lowest of all. These children may have had the most to gain by the introduction of a more favorable expectation into the minds of their teachers.

| Table 7-8 | | Correlations between Mexican Facial Characteristics and Advantages of Favorable Expectations after One Year | | | |
|---|---|---|---|---|---|
| | BOYS | | GIRLS | | TOTAL |
| | $N$ | $r$ | $N$ | $r$ | $N$ | $r$ |
| Total IQ | 7 | +.70[a] | 9 | −.14 | 16 | +.27 |
| Verbal IQ | 7 | +.54 | 10 | −.11 | 17 | +.21 |
| Reasoning IQ | 7 | +.75[b] | 9 | −.01 | 16 | +.14 |

[a] $p = .08$, two-tail.
[b] $p = .05$, two-tail.

**SOME DISCUSSION**

The results of the experiment we have described in some detail provide further evidence that one person's expectations of another's be-havior may come to serve as a self-fulfilling prophecy. When teachers

expected that certain children would show greater intellectual development, those children did show greater intellectual development. For
the basic year of the experiment, the self-fulfilling prophecy was in
evidence primarily at the lower grade levels; it is difficult to be certain
why that was the case. A number of interpretations suggest themselves,
and these are not mutually exclusive.

First, younger children are generally regarded as more malleable,
less fixed, more capable of change, more subject to the effects of
critical periods (Scott, 1962). It may be, then, that the experimental
conditions of our experiment were more effective with younger children simply because younger children are easier to change than older
ones. (It should be recalled that when we speak here of change we
mean it as change relative to control-group change. Table 7-1 showed
that even fifth graders can change dramatically in IQ, but there the
change of the experimental-group children was not greater than the
change of the control-group children.)

A second interpretation is that younger children within a given
school have less well-established reputations within the school. It then
becomes more credible to a teacher to be told that a younger child will
show intellectual growth. A teacher may "know" an older child much
better by reputation and be less inclined to believe him capable of
intellectual growth simply on someone else's say-so.

A third interpretation is a combination, in a sense, of the first two.
It suggests that younger children show greater gains associated with
teachers' expectancies not because they necessarily *are* more malleable
but rather because they are believed by teachers to be more malleable.

A fourth interpretation suggests that younger children are more
sensitive to and more affected by the particular processes whereby
teachers communicate their expectations to children. Under this interpretation, it is possible that teachers react to children of all grade
levels in the same way if they believe them to be capable of intellectual
gain. But perhaps it is only the younger children whose performance is
affected by the special things the teacher says to them, the special ways
in which she says them, the way she looks, postures, and touches the
children from whom she expects greater intellectual growth.

A fifth interpretation suggests that the effects of teachers' expectations were more effective in the lower grade levels not because of any
difference associated with the children's age but rather with some
correlated sampling "errors." Thus it is possible that the children of
the lower grades are the children of families that differ systematically
from the families of the children of the higher grade levels.

A sixth interpretation also suggests that the greater IQ gain in younger children attributable to teacher expectation is a result of sampling "error," not in the sampling of children this time but in the sampling of teachers. It may be that in a variety of demographic, intellectual, and personality variables, the teachers of the younger children differed from the teachers of the older children such that they may have (1) believed the communications about their "special" children more or (2) been more effective communicators to their children of their expectations for the children's performance.

There is some evidence to suggest that teachers of the lower grades do in fact differ from the teachers of the upper grades of Oak School. Two administrators who were well acquainted with all the teachers rated them on over-all effectiveness as teachers. The two administrators agreed well in their ratings ($r = +.88$) and, although there were many exceptions, teachers of the lower grades were judged to be more effective teachers by both administrators (average $r$ between effectiveness and teaching grade $= -.57$, $p < .02$).

The finding that only the younger children profited after one year from their teachers' favorable expectations helps us to understand better the results of two other experimenters, Clifford Pitt (1956) and Charles Flowers (1966) (see Chapter 5). Pitt, it will be recalled, divided his sample of fifth-grade boys into three groups. For one group he reported the boys' IQ scores to the teachers after having arbitrarily added ten points. For another group he reported the boys' IQ scores after having deducted ten points. For the third group he reported the boys' actual IQ scores. Pitt found that there were no effects on school achievement at the end of the year of teachers having been given false information about their pupils' IQ.

The results of our own study suggest that after one year, fifth graders may not show the effects of teacher expectations though first and second graders do. Pitt's study differed in too many ways from our own to make direct comparisons possible, however. Pitt did not, for example, retest the children on IQ *per se* but only on school achievement. More important perhaps, is the fact that Pitt's teachers knew their pupils for nearly two months before being given pupils' IQ scores. That was long enough for teachers to have developed realistic expectations of pupils' performance more powerful than the expectations that could have been induced by adding or deducting IQ points.

The equivocal results of Flowers' experiment are also not directly comparable to our own data. Flowers' pupils were also older children (seventh graders) and each child had many different teachers rather than just one. Perhaps the effects of teachers' expectations were diluted by being distributed over many teachers. In the case of Flowers' study, we must bear in mind, too, that the classes arbitrarily labeled as brighter had been assigned different teachers than had been assigned to the control-group classes. Therefore, any differences between the experimental- and control-group classes could have been due to differences in the quality of teachers assigned to each.

## A MAGIC DOZEN

An often-paid price of experimental, quantitative, behavioral research is a loss of any immediate awareness of the human beings whose behavior is being studied. In order that we identify and describe the human element, as well as the quantitative units of measurement of the Oak School Experiment let us present, in a little detail, the school behavior of a number of Oak School's children. Of the children whose teachers had been led to have favorable expectations for their intellectual ability, twelve have been selected for personal descriptions, six boys and six girls.

Because the effects of favorable teacher expectations were dramatic only in the first and second grades, the youngsters to be described were drawn from these grades. For each sex, two children were included who showed the greatest gains in total IQ after one year, those two children who showed the midmost amount of gain, and those two children who showed the least amount of gain. For each child, the pretest IQ, the post-test IQ, and the gain score is indicated as well as whether he or she was in the first or second grade during the year of the experiment. The descriptions themselves are based on personal acquaintance with each child and on school records, but the names, of course, are fictitious and some details have been altered to ensure anonymity.

### Highest Gains

*Mario*   Pretest IQ:   133   Mario is a tall, good-looking blue-
          Post-test IQ:  202   eyed blond of Italian and Nordic descent.
          IQ gain:      +69   He is the older of two boys. His father
          Grade:          2   is a semiskilled factory worker and his
                              mother works as a typist. Mario and his
brother are cared for during the day by their grandmother who speaks only Italian. The family has lived in the same house since Mario entered Oak School as a kindergartner.

In the first grade Mario had no academic problems; but in the beginning of his second year he had difficulty in word mastery and oral reading, and his printing showed many reversals of letters. By the end of his second year, the year in which he was designated as a "bloomer," he had improved in his reading skills. His third-grade teacher found that he expressed his ideas well in written composition. He also began speech therapy for a defect that had not been noticed before. At the time of his promotion to grade four, comment was made that he was a conscientious, precise worker who shouldn't be pressured to work faster. Some restlessness was noticed during the third grade. In the third grade his teacher did not know that he was a "special" child, and it is tempting to speculate that he was, therefore, relatively less challenged and, therefore, became more bored. Such speculation is possible because we know a good deal about each of the children in an historical sense, but at the same time such speculation serves to illustrate the hazards of historical reconstructions. We will never know whether there is merit to the speculation.

Parent-conference notes showed that when his parents were told of his reading problems at the beginning of the second grade they tried to help him evenings. The parents show interest and concern in his school progress. When his class enacted a brief one-act play that he had written and directed, his mother took time off from work to see it performed.

Mario is a serious boy who smiles only rarely. He is friendly with class members, and has never been sent to the office for disciplinary action. He appears poised and mature.

Mario has been in a high ability (fast-track) group since the first grade and apparently will continue in one.

*José*  Pretest IQ:      61      José is a good-looking Mexican boy with
        Post-test IQ:  106      a slight Spanish accent. His father is a
        IQ gain:      +45       skilled worker in a foundry, and his mother
        Grade:          1       is a meat packer. Both parents were born in
                                Mexico. The fact that José's mother is employed is unusual in Mexican families in the community, as is the fact that José has but one sibling, a younger brother. A Spanish-speaking aunt is their baby-sitter. The family has lived in two houses since José entered kindergarten at Oak School.

José had been recommended to a low-ability first-grade group by his kindergarten teacher, was in a low group also in grade two, and will go to a middle group for his third-grade year.

José's first-grade teacher found him anxious to learn. That was the year in which he was designated as a "spurter." He made good progress but had started behind and so had farther to go. His second-grade teacher stated that he was attentive, courteous, and kind. He tried to do his best in the second grade.

Parent-conference notes show no conferences were held in first grade, and in grade two José's mother hoped he could move up to a middle group. Comments made at the time of his promotion to grade three indicated that he showed great interest in reading. His mother listens to him read in the evenings. He started a second-grade reader three months before completion of the second grade and will continue the book in the middle third-grade class.

José is a little aloof, but appears to have no social problems. He seems quiet and secure. He has never received office discipline.

*Maria*  Pretest IQ:    88     Maria is a sparkly little blue-eyed
         Post-test IQ:   128    blonde girl whose light complexion is
         IQ gain:        +40    unusual for a child of Mexican ancestry.
         Grade:          1      She speaks no Spanish but understands
                                simple family phrases. She walks as
though she's dancing, and when she moves her tiny golden earrings flash. She is one of five children, the next to the youngest, and is the most attractive of all. Her father is a storekeeper and her mother a housewife. The family has lived in the same house since she entered Oak School for kindergarten.

Maria had been recommended for a middle first grade by her kindergarten teacher. At the beginning of the first grade, the grade in which she was designated a potential bloomer, the teacher found her to be a precise and conscientious worker. A remarkable artistic talent was evident, and the teacher recommended to the mother that special art classes would be appropriate. The teacher's notes at the end of the first grade showed that the child was doing well in all subjects except arithmetic. Exceptional artistic talent was noted. She was recommended for a top second grade at promotion time.

Second grade progress was fair in the beginning. Reading comprehension seemed a bit weak. The end of the second grade found Maria's reading much improved. She did well in arithmetic and showed much over-all academic improvement.

Parent-conference notations show that the parents were very interested in Maria's progress and were pleased that she was advanced to a top group for the second grade. The mother agreed to help her at home in reading when she had trouble in the second grade.

Maria is not aggressive, but cannot be considered shy. She receives much adult praise for her artwork which is unusually good for so

young a child. During recess she plays primarily with her sister who
is one year older. Family ties seem close.

*Violet*  Pretest IQ:        60        Violet is a small wiry tomboy with
          Post-test IQ:      97    little black eyes and a shorn head
          IQ gain:          +37    cropped like a boy's because her hair is
          Grade:              1    too curly to comb. Her ancestry is French
                                            and Portuguese, but only English is
spoken in the home. Violet is the next to youngest of six children,
most of whom attend Oak School. The family has lived in the same
house since Violet was in kindergarten. Her father is a butcher, her
mother, a housewife. The father occasionally leaves home due to
marital conflicts. When in the midst of such a family fracas, the father
comes to school, tells of his problems and checks daily on the children's
attendance. When he is part of the family unit, he is a frequent visitor
to his children's classrooms. His interest in his children causes problems for school personnel at times. Violet, for example, has been
vigorously encouraged to be aggressive, and she is a small tiger on the
playground. Also, her language is inappropriate at times for a little
girl. She has been sent to the office frequently for fighting or for de-
fiant behavior toward classroom and playground teachers.

Violet was started in the low first-grade class, was in the low second-
grade class and will continue in the low group in grade three. Her
first-grade teacher noted that the child was inattentive, noisy, and diso-
bedient, but that her responses were good when she paid attention. It
was in the first grade that she was designated as a potential spurter.
The second-grade teacher commented on her sulky attitude when she
didn't get her own way. At the beginning of grade two the teacher
noted that she showed no interest in reading but could do better work
when she tried. At the end of the second grade, comments showed that
she was trying to do her best in reading and that she was a capable,
creative child in art.

Violet has emotional and behavioral problems, both in the classroom and on the playground. She does not relate well to other children.
Her relations to one sister at school, who is a year older, swing from
close protection to fairly wild demonstrations of antagonism, such as
biting, scratching, and kicking. Her attitude toward school personnel
is somewhat influenced by her father's who has stated often in the
classrooms and office that Oak School teachers are responsible for his
children's poor school work. The mother seldom enters the school
picture. She seems quiet, amenable, and somewhat shy. Violet's father
claims that his wife can neither read nor write and that his children

must have inherited these conditions. To the school's personnel he is a very colorful but very exasperating character. Violet seems to be following in her father's footsteps rather than her mother's.

## Midmost Gains

*Constantine*  Pretest IQ:  116  Constantine is a sweet-faced boy, slight and gentle, whom each of his teachers has dearly loved. He is of Greek ancestry and understands that language. He has lived in the same house since starting at Oak School, and lives with his father, who is a semiskilled worker, and his mother, who is a skilled technician. He is an only child.

| | | |
|---|---|---|
| Pretest IQ: | 116 |
| Post-test IQ: | 137 |
| IQ gain: | +21 |
| Grade: | 1 |

Notes from the teacher made during the first few months of grade one show that Constantine was doing very well in skills. He preferred being alone. After Christmas of the year in which he was designated a potential bloomer, he was advanced from the middle level to the top first grade. His new teacher commented that he was working well in all areas and had adjusted well to the transfer. He still was a "loner" and preferred talking to the teacher to playing at recess.

His second-grade teacher found Constantine to be very musically inclined. His reading was progressing well.

Parent-conference notes showed that the parents did not come to the first-grade conferences. Second-grade conference notes indicated that the mother agreed to take Constantine to the library. She in turn asked the teacher to encourage him to participate more in sports.

Constantine prefers adult company. He shows little inclination to rough-house or play aggressively with the other children. He is somewhat timid but talks freely when he feels confident of acceptance.

*Kathy*  Pretest IQ:  105  Kathy is a very shy, thin girl who is growing fast. She is freckled and blue-eyed and has long light hair. Kathy has not yet grown into her teeth. She is the oldest of three girls. The father is a fireman and the mother, a housewife. The family has lived in two houses since she entered Oak School in the middle of grade one when she was placed in the top group.

| | | |
|---|---|---|
| Pretest IQ: | 105 |
| Post-test IQ: | 125 |
| IQ gain: | +20 |
| Grade: | 2 |

Teacher comments indicate that Kathy is somewhat babied at home. She is reportedly allergic to various kinds of foods. Her first-grade teacher found her to be inattentive and immature. In the second grade, the grade in which she was designated as a potential spurter, her shyness was noted but so was a very gradual development in confidence. Kathy showed a lack of arithmetic understanding in the beginning of the second grade. By the end of the year, she had improved in arithmetic. Kathy had a poor understanding of what she read. The grade-three teacher noted that she continued to have some problem with arithmetic, handwriting, and comprehension.

Parent-conference notes indicated that Kathy's father always attended the meetings. He apparently was most anxious for her to succeed in school because he had not. He admitted he was impatient with her so that it was the mother who helped her with her homework. The father had been asked to praise Kathy for completion of her work rather than to criticize her for her "pokiness."

Kathy is very shy. She blushes brightly when addressed and stares at her shoes when smiled at. She does not have social problems with her peers, however. The shyness seems to be related only to contacts with adults. She is known in the office because of her father's visit to the principal regarding Kathy's apparent fear of a cafeteria teacher. Because the child is obviously distressed by adult attention, it is difficult to get to know her.

*Betsy*   Pretest IQ:       95      Betsy is an imp-faced, fastidious little
       Post-test IQ:   113   girl with dark crinkled eyes and long
       IQ gain:     +18   brown hair. She has two older sisters and
       Grade:        1   some younger half-siblings. Just recently
she and her older sisters were adopted by their stepfather. They had been using his name because they didn't want a different name than their mother and the babies had. Betsy has lived in the same house since she entered Oak School in kindergarten. Her stepfather has a managerial job and her mother is a housewife.

Betsy had been recommended by the kindergarten teacher for the top-level first-grade class. Her first-grade teacher noted at the beginning of the year, the year in which she was designated as a potential bloomer, that she was a conscientious, eager learner and was making satisfactory progress. Her second-grade teacher found that she worked too rapidly. Betsy showed keen interest in science. Comments at the end of grade two stated that she was very capable but that she needed to be encouraged or else she tended to become lax.

Parent-teacher conference notes indicated that Betsy's mother was highly interested in her progress. She has worked with the child in an effort to improve study habits, and was quite pleased when improvement occurred. Betsy is a merry child, careless about school, loving, and friendly. She presented no discipline problems. Her concerns seemed primarily social.

*Tony*  Pretest IQ:      109       Tony is a black-eyed, fat little boy
         Post-test IQ:    123    with enormous front teeth, very rosy
         IQ gain:         +14    cheeks, and a wide smile. He is the
         Grade:             2    youngest of two children. Tony's parents
                                  and his older sister would be described
by most as "beautiful" people, and Tony is indeed a very handsome youngster. He has lived in the same house since entering Oak School in kindergarten. His father is in the produce business and his mother is a housewife. An Italian-speaking grandmother lives with the family.

Tony was recommended for the top first grade and has remained in a top group ever since. His first-grade teacher found him to be an extremely observant child who had an unusually large vocabulary. He cried frequently that year. In the second grade, the year in which he was designated as a potential spurter, his self-control improved, although he continued to seek the teacher's praise and direction. Teacher's notes at the end of the second grade indicated that Tony showed a lack of responsibility at home and at school. In the third grade, his study habits seemed poor. He had difficulty completing assignments.

Parent-conference notes showed that his father did not want Tony helping around the house with "women's chores."

This young man is charming and irresponsible. His grades have been average to poor, and he is apparently underachieving. He seems to feel secure at school and shows more maturity there than at home.

## Lowest Gains

*Louise*  Pretest IQ:      101       Louise is a tall, blonde, blue-eyed,
          Post-test IQ:    114    serious child who shows an unusual
          IQ gain:         +13    maturity. She is unchildlike in her atti-
          Grade:             2    tudes and feelings of responsibility. She
                                   is highly dependable. Louise and her
younger brother lived in an apartment with their parents from the time she entered kindergarten at Oak School until the family moved out of town at the end of her second-grade year. The father is an aerospace technologist and the mother is a housewife.

The kindergarten teacher recommended her for a top-level first-grade classroom, and she was also in a top class for grade two, the year in which she was designated as a potential bloomer.

Some of Louise's school records were sent to the new school, so teacher comments were not available. The child, however, was well known in the office where she was often employed as a messenger. Office personnel found her reliable, diligent, and delightful in her serious aspect. She seldom smiled, but was, rather, busy with the business of life. Her grades, of course, were excellent. Louise would have considered nothing less acceptable.

*Patricia* Pretest IQ:  89  Patricia is a scrub-faced, tall, heavy
     Post-test IQ: 90  child who has a quick smile and a very
     IQ gain:   +1  pleasant disposition, and she is inclined
     Grade:    2  to giggle. She is the youngest of four
               girls. The family has lived in the same
house since she entered kindergarten at Oak School. Her father is a salesman and her mother a cashier-waitress.

There are almost no teacher comments in Patricia's school records. She was in a middle-level group for grades one and two and apparently performed at an above-average level during grade two because she was advanced to the top group for grade three. It was in the second grade that she was designated as a potential spurter.

Parent-conference notes are scanty, also, perhaps because Patricia's mother works and was unable to attend conferences, or perhaps because she did not care to, until the girl was in third grade at which time telephone conferences were held. At that time, the mother was informed that Patricia worked somewhat carelessly although her overall progress was satisfactory.

Patricia presented no particular problems—academic, personal, or social. She gave the impression of being happy and well adjusted.

*Douglas* Pretest IQ:  111  Douglas is a dark, tall, thin boy
     Post-test IQ: 107 who always looks polished and well
     IQ gain:   −4 groomed. He has four older sisters
     Grade:    2 and one younger brother. The family
              has lived in the same house since he
entered kindergarten at Oak School. His father is self-employed at home in an unknown capacity and the mother is a secretary.

Doug appeared highly nervous to his first- and second-grade teachers. In the middle of his first year he was moved from a low to a middle group because of his good performance in the first grade. He remained in a middle group throughout his second- and third-grade year. While in the second grade, he was designated as a potential bloomer. Teachers have commented that he worked carelessly and rushed through his assignments.

Parent-teacher conference notes showed that Doug's mother always attended the meetings. She was worried when he was in the second grade that perhaps he did not belong in a middle group. She appears content with his progress and is not pressuring him.

Doug is a withdrawn, serious child. He is friendly with his peers but does not participate in aggressive play. The mother is better known to the office personnel than is Doug.

*Juan*   Pretest IQ:    123      Juan, a slight, dark boy with green
       Post-test IQ:   117   eyes, has a speech defect that is becoming
       IQ gain:       &minus;6   less noticeable. He has lived in the same
       Grade:        2   apartment with his mother, father, and
younger sister and brother since he entered kindergarten at Oak School. Juan's father is a skilled worker and his mother is a housewife. The boy is of Portuguese and Mexican descent, but only English is spoken in the home.

According to teacher comments, Juan has been a model child since entering school. In the first grade, he appeared somewhat timid, but overcame this. Teachers of grades two and three found his academic work strong and his behavior outstanding. It was in the second grade that he was designated as a potential spurter. He is unusually neat and careful for a little boy. He does resent correction of his speech, but otherwise conforms remarkably well to the demands of the school world.

Parent-teacher conference notes showed that Juan's mother was pleased with his excellent progress. She showed concern that he was continuing to attend speech classes which may be responsible for his impatience.

Juan is a little perfectionist. His teachers have found him to be a good boy but not particularly an endearing one. He does not seem to show much "personality" at school, which is noticeable because his younger brother is widely loved by the teachers for his charm and appeal. Juan has always been in a top group and will probably continue in the fast track.

**Some Impressions**
These children are probably typical of Oak School's children. Some of the dozen were very bright to begin with, some were not. A third have some knowledge of another language. Several are non-Anglo-Saxon. They come from large and small families. Two of the dozen could clearly be described as educationally disadvantaged, and these two were among the highest gainers in intellectual ability. Though the descriptions given were brief and restricted, some impressions emerge.

Case histories, biographies, and anecdotes are not usually employed

most usefully to test scientific hypotheses. They can, however, be especially useful in generating such hypotheses. In the descriptions given,
for example, we are struck by two threads running through the stories
of those children who benefited most from favorable teacher expectations. Their parents seemed especially interested in their academic
progress,[6] and they were often described as children unusually attractive in physical appearance. Not to test these hypotheses but rather
to formulate them more clearly, each of the twelve children was ranked
on the degree of interest his or her parents showed in their school
work and also on their physical attractiveness. These rankings were
made by one of the authors who knew the children quite well. The
rankings might have been contaminated by the ranker's approximate
knowledge of the magnitude of IQ gain shown by each child. Such
warnings seem less critical considerations, however, in the generating
of hypotheses for future test than in the actual testing of hypotheses.

The correlation between IQ gain and parental interest among the
twelve children was +.40, that between IQ gain and physical attractiveness was +.48, and the correlation between these variables was
+.43. None of these correlations was significant statistically at even
the .10 level. When the ranks of parental interest and attractiveness
were added together and reranked, the correlation between this new
combined variable and IQ gain was found to be +.62 ($p < .04$,
two-tail). The six children ranked highest on this combined variable
gained an average of over twenty IQ points more than did the six
children ranked lowest on the combined variable. These six low-
ranked children, however, still gained over seven IQ points more than
did the average control group child of the first and second grades.

It would be interesting to learn whether all children, and not just
those of whom special growth is expected, gain more in intellectual
ability when their parents are more interested in their school work
and they are more physically attractive. Presumably, it would be in the
early grades that such a combination would be both most helpful and
also most likely to occur. A child's attractive appearance and his
parents' interest are unlikely to change dramatically from year to year.
If present at all, they are likely to be present from the first day of
school.

✑§

[1] The reader interested in the more technical aspects of the design and analysis
of experiments will recognize our presentation as following the plan of a
multifactorial analysis of variance with interest focused on the main effect

of treatments, the two-way interactions of treatments by grades, treatments by tracks, treatments by sex, and treatments by minority-group status. Three-way interactions were also computed for treatments by sex by tracks, treatments by sex by grade levels, and treatments by minority-group status by sex. All other possible three-way and higher-order interactions yielded one or more empty cells or a number of cells with $N$s so small as to weaken any confidence in the results even though the analyses were possible in principle.

All two-way and three-way analyses had unequal and nonproportional $N$s per cell, and Walker and Lev's (1953) approximate solution was employed. Since all double interactions were computed directly and also were estimated in one or more of the three-factor analyses of variance, it should be pointed out that whenever the discussion is of a simple interaction, the $F$ test was based on the two-way analysis rather than on the three-way analysis because the greater $N$ per cell of the two-way analysis provided a more stable estimate. When a given double interaction, however, also entered into a significant triple interaction, that fact is indicated in the text, and the interpretation of the two-way interaction is modified accordingly. The main effect of treatments was of course obtained in each of the analyses of variance, and $p$ values associated with the $F$s ranged from .05 to .002.

When we consider classrooms as the sampling unit $(N = 17)$, we find that in eleven of the seventeen classes in which the comparison was possible (one class was inadvertently not post-tested for reasoning IQ) children of the experimental group gained more in total IQ than did children of the control group. The one-tail $p$s associated with the sign test, the Wilcoxon matched-pairs signed-ranks test, and the $t$ test for correlated means were .17, .06, and .03, respectively. Table A-7 of the Appendix gives the required data. Tables A-1 to A-6 give the means, $N$s, and standard deviations of the pretest and post-test total, verbal, and reasoning IQs in both experimental conditions within all classrooms.

[2] Considering classrooms as the sampling unit $(N = 18)$, we find children of the experimental group gained more in verbal IQ than did children of the control group in twelve of the eighteen classes. The one-tail $p$s associated with the sign test, Wilcoxon test, and $t$ test were .12, .23, and .25, respectively. Table A-8 of the Appendix gives the required data and shows that in one of the classrooms there was a significant reversal with the children of the control group gaining more than the children of the experimental group. In giving the results of the Oak School Experiment, one-tail tests have been employed when the direction of difference was predicted. Following strictly the logic of one-sided tests would not permit us to consider such unpredicted results as the one shown in Table A-8. Nevertheless, we have given two-tail $p$ values for unexpected results as an aid to those who would prefer the use of two-tail tests throughout and who will have to double all $p$s given as one-tail.

[3] Considering classrooms as the sampling unit $(N = 17)$, we find the advantage of favorable expectations to occur in fifteen of the seventeen classrooms. The one-tail $p$s associated with the sign, Wilcoxon, and $t$ tests were

.001, .003, and .003, respectively. Table A-9 of the Appendix gives the required data. Comparison of the expectancy advantages shown in verbal and reasoning IQs (Tables A-8 and A-9) shows the advantage to be greater in reasoning IQ than in verbal IQ in fourteen of the seventeen classes. The two-tail $p$s associated with the sign, Wilcoxon, and $t$ tests were $< .02$, $< .05$, and $< .20$, respectively.

[4] This footnote will serve to illustrate the complexity of nature and the need for noncomplacency in the behavioral researcher. Preliminary results of a study conducted with Judy Evans give just the opposite results and with an equally significant probability level. The same basic experiment conducted at Oak School was repeated in two elementary schools located in a small Midwestern town. Unlike Oak School, which drew its pupils from a lower-class community, these schools drew their pupils from a substantial middle-class community. Oak School's student body included a large proportion of minority-group members; the two Midwestern schools did not. The mean pretest total IQ at Oak School was 98, compared to the pretest total IQ of 105 found in these Midwestern schools. Eight months after the teachers had been given the names of their "special" children, retests were administered. The results of the studies at the two schools were sufficiently similar that the results could reasonably be combined. No expectancy advantage was found for either boys or girls as measured by total IQ or verbal IQ. For reasoning IQ, however, the results were opposite to those found at Oak School. Now it was the boys who showed the benefits of favorable teacher expectations. Those who had been expected to bloom gained over sixteen IQ points compared to the less than nine gained by control-group boys. Among the girls it was the control-group children who gained about fifteen IQ points while those of the experimental group gained just over five IQ points. (The interaction $F$ was 9.10, $p < .003$) In these schools, just as in Oak School, boys had shown higher pretest verbal IQs than girls while girls had shown higher pretest reasoning IQs than boys. Therefore, in these middle-class schools it was not true that each sex benefited most from favorable teacher expectations in those areas in which they were already somewhat advantaged. At the time of this writing there appears to be no ready explanation for this dramatic and very highly statistically significant reversal ($p = .00004$) in the two studies. But now we know for sure that Oak School's results, like the results of all behavioral experiments, are not universal.

[5] All of the control-group children in each classroom were employed as the basis of comparison rather than just the Mexican children. This was done to provide a more stable estimate of control-group gains, there being too few Mexican children in some classrooms. Among the children of the control group there was a high rank correlation between the IQ gains of the Mexican and non-Mexican children; $+.74$ for the fifteen classrooms in which the comparison could be made ($p < .003$). The corresponding correlation between IQ gains of all children and just the Mexican children was $+.90$ ($p < .001$).

⁶ A recent study by Brookover, Erickson, Hamachek, Joiner, LePere, Patterson, and Thomas (1966) suggests that increasing parents' interest in their children's scholastic work and ability may significantly improve the children's scholastic achievement.

# 8

# Teachers' Assessments

It appears now that teachers' favorable expectations can be responsible for gains in their pupils' IQs and, for the lower grades, that these gains can be quite dramatic. But a raised IQ, even a dramatically raised IQ, does not guarantee that its possessor will show his profits in situations more "real life" than the situation of taking an IQ test. To the child in school there is no situation more "real life" than the situation of the classroom itself. We want to know, therefore, whether the gain in IQ attributable to teachers' favorable expectations was reflected also in the more directly observable classroom behavior of the special children. Ideally, independent observers would have been employed to record the pupils' classroom behavior but that method was not possible in the Oak School Experiment.

For the observation of the children's classroom behavior we must, therefore, depend on the teacher's own assessment of the children's academic performance and of their general schoolroom behavior. There are advantages and disadvantages to the use of teachers' assessments as sources of information about children. On the one hand, there is a rich tradition of educational research to show that teachers are often inaccurate in their assessment of pupils' intelligence and personal adjustment. On the other hand, in the development of even the most sophisticated tests of intelligence and personal adjustment, one frequently employed definition of a pupil's "true" ability and adjustment is the teacher's assessment of these attributes. That is not hard to understand since no adult knows a child's classroom behavior as well as his teacher knows it.

—In the present study there is the special problem that teachers' observations of pupils' behavior in the classroom may have been affected by the experimentally created expectations. It was possible that teachers would ascribe more desirable behavior to the special children even if the actual classroom behavior of the special children did not differ from the behavior of the control-group children. That is the nature of the halo effect, and we know from Cahen's (1966) study, described earlier, that teachers' expectations can color their assessments of pupils' performance. There is no way to be sure from the present study whether teachers' assessments were subject to halo effects; but even if they were, the ecological validity or "real-lifeness" of teachers' assessments is not impaired. Halo effects occur in real life, too, and a teacher's evaluation of her pupil, haloed or not, has very real consequences for that pupil's future, both academic and non-academic. Before proceeding to the teachers' assessments we should recall that although we know that the children expected to gain more intellectually actually did gain more than the control-group children, the teachers did not know that fact. If the teachers were observing with a halo in their eye, at least they did not have that halo reinforced by the knowledge that the alleged bloomers really did bloom.

## ACADEMIC PERFORMANCE

All teachers routinely assess the academic performance of their pupils, and usually they code their assessments in terms of letter grades and record them on report cards. Oak School uses grades "A," "B," "C," and "D," for passing grades and "U" for a failing grade. All children are graded each report-card period in the following subjects: reading, arithmetic, language, handwriting, social studies, science, health, physical education, arts and crafts, and music. In addition, grades three through six are graded in spelling, but grades one and two are not.

In the comparison of the academic classroom performance of the children expected to grow intellectually with the children of the control group, the same method of analysis was employed as when the comparison was of the gains in IQ. For each child in Oak School, on both occasions, the final report-card grades of the Spring 1964 term served as the "pretest," and the final report-card grades of the Spring 1965 term served as the "post-test." Letter grades were converted to numbers ranging in integers from four points for an "A" grade to zero points for a "U" grade. Pretest scores were subtracted from post-test scores to yield gain scores and, just as in the case of IQ, the gains of the special children were compared statistically with the gains of the control-group children.

When the entire school was considered, there was only one of the eleven school subjects in which there was a significant difference between the grade-point gains shown by the special children and the control-group children. That subject was reading, and the children of whom greater intellectual gains were expected showed the greater gain.

### Expectancy Advantage
### by Grades
The results for the school as a whole are shown in the bottom row of Table 8-1.[1] It will be seen that the effects were small only when the

**Figure 8-1**            Gains in reading grades in six grades.

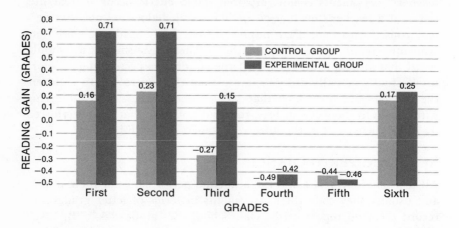

school was considered as a whole. The rest of Table 8-1 (and Figure 8-1) shows the gains in reading grade points by the children of the two groups for all six grade levels. Just as in the case of IQ we find increasing expectancy advantage as we go from the sixth to the first grade; the correlation between grade level and magnitude of expectancy advantage $(r = -.91)$ was significant at the .02 level.[2] That correlation was very close to the one found when it was expectancy advantage in IQ that was correlated with grade level $(r = -.86)$. The more a given grade level benefited in IQ gain from favorable expectations, the more that same grade level benefited in reading gains $(r = +.74, p < .05,$ one-tail). It seems especially interesting that the expectancy advantage in terms of reading scores is so parallel to the expectancy advantage in terms of IQ scores in view of the fact that the IQ test was especially selected so that no reading ability would be required to take the test. Of the remaining ten school subjects there was one more that showed the same pattern of expectancy advantage for the different grade levels. That subject was arithmetic, which for the school as a whole showed no significant advantage associated with teachers' favorable expectations. Nevertheless, in the lower grades the special children showed greater gains in arithmetic than did the control children, though the latter showed greater gains in higher grades. The correlation between grade level and expectancy advantage in arithmetic was $-.87$ $(p < .03,$ two-tail). The more a given grade level benefited in arithmetic gains the more that grade level had benefited in IQ gains $(r = +.90, p < .01,$ one-tail) and also in reading gains $(r = +.89, p < .01,$ one-tail). It seems fairly clear that in at least two school subjects—and two of the most important ones—younger children benefit more from having been expected to grow intellectually.

Table 8-1       Mean Gain in Reading Grades after One Year by Experimental- and Control-Group Children in Each of Six Grades

| GRADE | CONTROL | | EXPERIMENTAL | | EXPECTANCY ADVANTAGE | |
|---|---|---|---|---|---|---|
| | | | | | | ONE-TAIL |
| | N | GAIN | N | GAIN | GRADE POINTS | $p < .05^a$ |
| 1 | 49 | +0.16 | 7 | +0.71 | +0.55 | .03 |
| 2 | 39 | +0.23 | 7 | +0.71 | +0.48 | .05 |
| 3 | 26 | −0.27 | 13 | +0.15 | +0.42 | .04 |
| 4 | 47 | −0.49 | 12 | −0.42 | +0.07 | |
| 5 | 41 | −0.44 | 11 | −0.46 | −0.02 | |
| 6 | 47 | +0.17 | 12 | +0.25 | +0.08 | |
| TOTAL | 249 | −0.09 | 62 | +0.08 | +0.17 | .05 |

[a] Mean square within treatments within classrooms = .484.

When expectancy advantage was reckoned in terms of total IQ the lowest two grade levels were the ones showing the greatest benefit. When expectancy advantage was reckoned in terms of reading scores the lowest two grade levels were again benefited most but grade three turned out to have profited just about as much.

## Expectancy Advantage by Tracks and Sex

Relative to the reading gains made by the control-group children, the reading gains made by the children earmarked for growth varied in the three tracks of Oak School (interaction $F = 2.49$, $p = .09$). Table 8-2 shows that the children of the fast track were not benefited in reading scores by virtue of their teachers' favorable expectations. The children of the medium track, however, and to a lesser degree, the children of the slow track, were substantially benefited when their teachers expected intellectual growth. We recall that when the discussion dealt with expectancy advantage in terms of IQ gain, it was also the special children of the middle track who benefited most though their advantage was not significantly greater statistically than the expectancy advantages shown by the special children of the other two tracks.

Table 8-2                    Mean Gain in Reading Grades after One
                             Year by Experimental- and Control-Group
                             Children in Each of Three Tracks

| TRACK | CONTROL | | EXPERIMENTAL | | EXPECTANCY ADVANTAGE | |
|---|---|---|---|---|---|---|
| | | | | | | ONE-TAIL |
| | $N$ | GAIN | $N$ | GAIN | GRADE POINTS | $p < .05$ |
| Fast | 99 | −.09 | 27 | −.15 | −.06 | |
| Medium | 68 | −.31 | 17 | +.18 | +.49 | .007 |
| Slow | 82 | +.09 | 18 | +.33 | +.24 | |

The bottom row of Table 8-3 shows that for the school as a whole, boys and girls showed the same degree of expectancy advantage. The rest of Table 8-3 shows that boys and girls differed in expectancy advantage depending upon their track placement ($F$ for triple interaction $= 4.63$, $p = .02$). For the girls there were advantages to favorable expectations only in the top two tracks; for the boys only in the bottom two tracks. Column 3 of Table 8-3 shows in which of the three tracks girls were more benefited than boys, while Column 4 shows the analogous data based on gains in reasoning IQ, the only measure of IQ to show significant differences between boys and girls of different tracks in amount of expectancy advantage. It is interesting that in the track where girls profited most in reasoning IQ relative to boys, they profited least in reading grades relative to boys. Where girls profited least in reasoning IQ they profited most in reading gains. Actually, girls in the fast track did not really benefit any more than girls of the medium track from the favorable expectations of their teachers; but the boys of the fast track were somewhat disadvantaged in reading scores if intellectual gains were expected of them ($p = .06$). It seems unlikely that these boys actually read less well when expected to bloom. More likely, teachers graded them more strictly when more was expected of these already above-average readers. The evidence that these boys were probably not actually affected negatively by their teachers' favorable expectations comes from the fact that fast-track boys showed greater gains in total IQ and verbal IQ than did the boys of the other two tracks. It seems intuitively unlikely that actual reading losses would occur where gains in IQ are greatest, especially gains in verbal IQ.

When expectancy advantage had been defined in terms of gains in IQ, pupil's sex had complicated the magnitude of expectancy advantage found in the younger children of the first two grades compared to the older children of the upper four grades. When expectancy advantage was defined in terms of reading gains, no such complication was found (triple interaction $F < 1$). In the upper grades, boys and girls showed only slight and nearly equal amounts of expectancy advantage ($+.13$ and $+.16$, respectively). In the lower grades, boys and girls both showed a much larger expectancy advantage and that shown by boys was about twice that shown by girls though the difference was not significant statistically ($+.69$ and $+.35$, respectively).

| Table 8-3 | | Excess of Gain in Reading Grades by Experimental over Control Boys and Girls in Three Tracks after One Year | | |
|---|---|---|---|---|
| TRACK | BOYS | GIRLS | DIFFERENCE FAVORING GIRLS | |
| | | | READING | REASONING IQ |
| Fast | −.50 | +.27 | +.77[a] | +11.7 |
| Medium | +.83[b] | +.23 | −.60 | +54.0[c] |
| Slow | +.42 | −.04 | −.46 | +12.8 |
| TOTAL | +.17 | +.18 | +.01 | +21.8[b] |

[a] $p < .05$, two-tail.
[b] $p < .01$, two-tail.
[c] $p < .0005$, two-tail.

In total IQ and reasoning IQ, the younger girls had benefited much more than the younger boys from their teachers' favorable expectations. In verbal IQ, however, the younger boys benefited a bit more than the younger girls which is what we might expect in view of these boys' greater gains in reading scores.

In the last chapter, when we summarized the effects on IQ gains of teachers' favorable expectations, we concluded that girls bloomed more in the reasoning sphere of intellectual functioning while boys bloomed more in the verbal sphere, especially in the lower grades. We wondered, then, whether blooming was more likely to occur in those spheres in which children tended to be slightly advantaged to begin with. Girls at Oak School had started out with a higher reasoning IQ than boys, and boys had started out with a higher verbal IQ than girls. It would have been very consistent with our interpretation to have found that boys started out with better grades in reading than girls, but that was not the case. The point biserial correlation between being a boy and pretest reading grades was −.25 ($p < .001$). Girls in Oak School earned the higher reading grades and, in fact, earned higher pretest grades in all other subjects as well ($p < .001$, mean $r_{pb} = -.22$).

Partial support for the interpretation that between the sexes "that which has more profits more" comes from looking at the correlation between sex and pretest reading score separately for the lower and upper grades. In the upper four grades that correlation was —.33, in the lower two grades that correlation was —.02 with the difference between these correlations significant at $p < .01$. Relatively speaking, boys in the lower grades did better in reading to begin with than boys in the higher grades, and it was in the lower grades that the boys tended to gain more in reading scores.

## Expectancy Advantage
## by Minority-Group Status

There were no significant differences between the Mexican and non-Mexican children in the magnitude of expectancy advantage shown either in reading scores or in the sums of all report-card grades. When the Mexican and non-Mexican boys and girls were considered separately, there were still no differences in degree of expectancy advantage in reading scores. But, for the sum of all scores, and for most of the individual school subjects, the Mexican boys showed the greatest advantage of having been expected to grow intellectually. Table 8-4 shows the magnitude of expectancy advantage separately for Mexican and non-Mexican boys and girls for all eleven school subjects. There were only five Mexican boys for whom pretest and post-test grades were available and of whom special growth was expected. All five of these boys, one each in grades one, two, four, five, and six, gained more in total grade points than did their average Mexican control-group counterparts (sign test $p = .03$, $t$ test $p < .005$). None of the other subgroups showed any significant effects on over-all grade averages of having been expected to grow intellectually.

On the whole, the effects on school grades of teachers' favorable expectations were less dramatic than the effects of such expectations on IQ. The one exception to this seemed to occur in the case of reading scores, which seemed to profit about as much as did IQ scores. We can not say to what extent the expectancy advantage in reading scores was due to real improvement in reading ability or only to halo effects. It does seem though, that halo effects would have operated more in such subjects as health, physical education, arts and crafts, and music, but in those subjects there were no effects on school marks of having been expected to bloom.

Rather than teachers' expectations for superior performance leading to higher marks for the special children, these expectations could also have led to lower marks. That seemed likely for the special boys of the fast track who were graded lower than their more ordinary counterparts. The same thing may have operated in other subgroups as well, such that the now brighter children were required to perform better than formerly in order to be given the same evaluation by their teacher. The performance that once may have satisfied the teacher just may no longer do so.

| Table 8-4 | Excess of Gain in School Subjects by Experimental over Control Children after One Year | | | |
|---|---|---|---|---|
| SUBJECT | MEXICAN | | NON-MEXICAN | |
| | BOYS | GIRLS | BOYS | GIRLS |
| Reading | +.24 | −.05 | +.15 | +.28 |
| Arithmetic | +.24 | −.17 | −.41 | −.05 |
| Language | +.49 | +.39 | −.23 | −.01 |
| Spelling | +.53 | +.47 | −.07 | −.10 |
| Handwriting | −.05 | +.38 | −.07 | −.11 |
| Social studies | +.39 | +.10 | +.17 | −.06 |
| Science | −.12 | +.04 | −.06 | −.01 |
| Health | +.23 | −.41 | −.14 | −.08 |
| Physical education | +.19 | +.16 | −.14 | −.03 |
| Arts and crafts | −.02 | −.21 | −.03 | −.02 |
| Music | +.40 | −.06 | −.01 | +.06 |
| MEAN | +.23 | +.06 | −.08 | −.01 |
| N EXPERIMENTAL | 5 | 9 | 25 | 23 |
| N CONTROL | 19 | 18 | 109 | 103 |

## Objective Assessments

As a check on whether teachers' assessments of academic achievement were biased by their expectations, it would have been desirable to have available some more objective measures of achievement for all the children of Oak School. That was not entirely possible but, fortunately, it was partly possible. In the Spring of 1964 the Iowa Tests of Basic Skills were administered to all the children then in grades four and five. The following November, these tests were readministered to the same children, now in grades five and six, as well as to the new fourth graders who had not been tested the preceding Spring. One year later, in October of 1965, the same tests were administered once again to the children who had just begun grades five and six. The achievement testing schedule then, did not coincide with the report-card grading schedule. The closest fit between the interval of one year between pre- and postreport-card grading was the one-year interval between the second and third administration of the achievement tests. The interval was identical, but the November 1964 achievement tests were administered after the teachers had already been given the names of the special children. The effect of using that testing as a "pretest" would be to diminish any gains the special children might have actually made. The earlier the effects of teachers' expectations began to operate, the more serious would the problem be. In principle, all the effects of self-fulfilling prophecies might have come about within those first few weeks so that our achievement "pretest" was really more of a post-test. That possibility could be checked.

There are five main subtests to the Iowa Tests of Basic Skills: reading comprehension, language usage, arithmetic, vocabulary, and a work-study Skills subtest that assesses such things as the ability to use maps, graphs, and references. The first three subtests listed were also categories in which the children were assessed by their teachers. For these three subject areas the gains in percentile units from the Spring of 1964 to November of 1964 were calculated for the experimental- and control-group children.[3] Perhaps because of the intervening summer vacation, all the children lost a few percentile points. The children of the control group lost an average of 4.6 percentile units, and the children of the experimental group lost 4.4 percentile units. Obviously there was no effect in the first few weeks of the experiment of teachers' expectations on these three achievement subtests.

For comparison purposes the gains in report-card grades from the end of the Spring, 1964, semester to the end of the Fall, 1964, semester were also calculated for the same three subject areas. The control-group children lost an average of .10 of a grade point and the experimental-group children lost .09 of a grade point. In both the teachers' assessments and objective achievement tests there were no advantages to favorable expectations after one month in the three subject areas compared. The teachers' and the tests' verdicts were so similar that we gain some confidence that, at least after one month, teachers' assessments are unlikely to have been affected by their expectations.

The details of the comparison are found in Table A-10 of the Appendix. The units of gain, percentile points in one case, grade points in the other, are not directly comparable so that we do best to compare the $t$ tests themselves because $t$s are not so fussy about the units of measurement involved. The median of the three $t$s based on the achievement tests was $+.37$, a value identical to the median $t$ based on teachers' assessments. The mean $t$s were $+0.01$ and $+0.15$, respectively.

The results just presented were based on the children who in the

Fall of 1965 were in grades five and six. The following Fall (1966) the sixth graders had left the school for junior high school, the fifth graders had become sixth graders and the fourth graders who took their first achievement tests in the Fall of 1965 were fifth graders. For these last two grade levels, then, it was possible to compare the gains in achievement of the experimental- and control-group children both in test scores (November 1964–October 1965) and in teachers' grades (June 1964–June 1965). We feel better about this comparison (based, in the case of the achievement test, on a "pretest" which came a month after the experimental program had been initiated) knowing that the three school subjects in question had not been affected by the teachers' expectations by the time of the "pretest."

The details of the comparison are given in Table A-11 of the Appendix, but they are easily summarized. The results show that when achievement is defined by the more objective test, the effects of teacher expectations are larger for all three subject areas. In the area of language both measures of achievement showed the special children gaining more than the control children though the magnitude of advantage was not dramatic. That should not be surprising because we had learned earlier that in the upper grades (three to six) very little IQ gain had resulted from teachers' favorable expectations, and during the basic year of the experiment, the 1964–1965 school year, these children had been in the fourth and fifth grades, grades which showed little expectancy advantage.

In both reading and arithmetic achievement the objective test showed a small and not very significant expectancy advantage, but in both cases the teachers' assessments of achievement showed an expectancy disadvantage. The median of the three $t$s based on the achievement tests was $+1.41$ (mean $= +1.28$) while the median $t$ based on teachers' evaluations was $-0.69$ (mean $= -0.05$), not quite as large numerically but in the opposite direction.

These findings lend support to the hypothesis advanced earlier that when children are expected to gain intellectually they are more likely to be evaluated by their teachers against a higher standard. Wilson (1963) found that teachers hold up lower standards for children from the "poor part of town" than for children from the "better part of town." This lowering of standards, or grading too high for a given performance level, may actually result in the lessened profit from education found among disadvantaged children. It seems important, then, that additional research be directed to the hypothesis presented on the basis of our own analysis. Changes in the teacher's expectations about a pupil's intellectual performance may result in her setting different standards for his assessment. Teachers may not only get more when they expect more, they may also come to expect more when they get more. Not all cycles are "vicious"; some are benign.

## CLASSROOM BEHAVIOR

Teachers' assessments of their pupils' academic performance are routinely available in the form of report-card grades. Teachers' assessments of pupils' classroom behavior that is less directly related to academic achievement are not so routinely available. Therefore, toward the end of the school year of the basic study, all teachers were asked to make a number of judgments about the general classroom behavior of all their pupils. For each child, the teacher was asked to say how successful he would be in the future, the degree to which the child's behavior reflected intellectual curiosity, and the extent to which the child could be described as interesting, happy, appealing, well adjusted, affectionate, hostile, and motivated by a need for approval. Each child was rated by the teacher on each of these nine variables on a scale that went from 1 ("not at all happy") to 9 ("extremely happy").

This part of the research involved a so-called after-only design. That is, we had no pretest scores available for the children so that we shall be comparing only the postexperimental ratings of the children of the experimental and control groups. Because the children of the experimental program had been selected at random, this lack of pretest should not be too serious a problem, but we must recognize that the post-test-only measures are less precise than the change or gain scores employed in other phases of our research.

For each of the nine classroom behaviors, the mean rating assigned the children of the experimental group was compared to the mean rating assigned the children of the control group. Table 8-5 shows the nine comparisons. The children from whom intellectual growth was expected were described as significantly more likely to succeed in the future, as more interesting, as showing greater intellectual curiosity, and as happier. Children who were expected to grow intellectually seem to have benefited in other ways as well.

Earlier, when we considered expectancy advantages in terms of IQ gains and academic achievement, we wanted to know whether age, initial ability, sex, and minority-group status affected the magnitude of expectancy advantage. We want to have the same information for expectancy advantage as defined by classroom behavior. However, the complex analyses required, if applied to nine different measures, might be difficult to interpret since it was likely that some of the nine behaviors were even more strongly related to one another than were verbal IQ and reasoning IQ ($r = +.42$). It was decided, therefore, to reduce the nine variables to a smaller number of sets of variables each of which would not be too highly related to variables of the other sets.

| Table 8-5 | Classroom Behavior after One Year of Children in Experimental and Control Groups | | | |
|---|---|---|---|---|
| BEHAVIOR | CONTROL | EXPERIMENTAL | DIFFERENCE | $p \leqq .20$, TWO-TAIL |
| Curious | 5.50 | 6.25 | .75 | .01 |
| Interesting | 5.46 | 6.43 | .97 | .0008 |
| Future success | 5.53 | 6.48 | .95 | .0006 |
| Adjusted | 5.67 | 6.04 | .37 | |
| Appealing | 5.78 | 6.23 | .45 | .14 |
| Happy | 5.77 | 6.33 | .56 | .05 |
| Affectionate | 5.72 | 6.01 | .30 | |
| Hostile | 3.84 | 3.97 | .13 | |
| Needs approval | 5.35 | 4.97 | —.38 | .20 |
| $N \geqq$ | 279 | 68 | | |

When all nine variables were correlated with one another, three satisfactory sets of behaviors emerged, each showing higher relationships with the other variables in the same set than with the variables not in the set.[4]

The first set or cluster of variables was composed of ratings of intellectual curiosity, likelihood of a successful future, and being interesting. This seemed to be something of an intellectual curiosity cluster; and if that were an apt label, we might expect that children scoring higher on these three variables would have scored somewhat higher on the pretest and post-test IQs. That did turn out to be the case; the average correlation between the variables of this cluster with pretest IQ scores was $+.34$, and with post-test IQ scores it was $+.33$ ($p < .0001$).

The second cluster of variables was comprised of ratings on the dimensions adjusted, happy, appealing, affectionate, and nonhostile.[5] This seemed to be an adjustment-friendliness cluster and if it were, its variables should not correlate as highly with IQ scores as the variables of the intellectual curiosity cluster. The average correlation of the "adjustment" cluster variables with both pretest and post-test IQ turned out to be only $+.11$ which, while greater than zero ($p < .05$),

was much less than either of the correlations of .33 and .34 found
between IQ and the intellectual curiosity cluster ($p < .0001$).[6]

The third "cluster" stood quite alone both in terms of being made
up of only a single variable, need for approval, and in terms of showing
relatively little relationship to any other variables. The highest degree
of association between need for approval was with the variable of adjustment. The correlation was —.29 ($p < .0001$), very similar in magnitude to the correlation of —.25 between need for approval and
manifest anxiety reported by Crowne and Marlowe (1964) but un-
expectedly in the opposite direction, since presumably adjustment and
anxiety are in part opposite sides of the same coin. It was the important
work of Crowne and Marlowe on the psychological importance of the
need for approval that led to its inclusion in the present study.
Crowne and Marlowe had found no relationship between intelligence and their measure of need for approval. Similarly, we also
found no relationship between IQ and our measure of need for approval ($r = $ —.06 with pretest IQ, $r = $ —.08 with post-test IQ).[7]

For each of the three clusters of variables the children of the experimental group were compared with the children of the control group
to determine whether there was any expectancy advantage for the
three clusters of behaviors as there had been for some of the behaviors taken individually. In addition, for each cluster, magnitudes
of expectancy advantage were examined to learn whether they were
affected by pupils' age, initial ability, sex, and minority-group status.
The formal statistical analyses were carried out on cluster scores just
as they had been for IQ and for academic achievement.

## Expectancy Advantage
## by Grades
### INTELLECTUAL CURIOSITY

The results for the school as a whole are shown in the bottom row
of Table 8-6. Children expected to show intellectual growth were
judged by their teachers to show appreciably greater intellectual curiosity in their classroom behavior. The rest of Table 8-6 (and Figure
8-2) shows the assessments of intellectual curiosity of the experimental-
and control-group children for each of the six grades.[8] Just as we have
by now come to expect, the two lowest grades show large differences
between the groups. But there is also a surprise for us here, and that
is the finding that the special children of the sixth grade also showed
an expectancy advantage in classroom intellectual behavior as seen by
their teachers. What made that surprising, of course, was the fact that
these sixth-grade special children had shown no expectancy advantage

**Figure 8-2**  Ratings of intellectual curiosity in six grades.

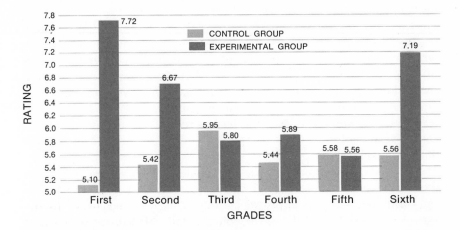

in terms of IQ gains. Still, when expectancy advantages of the first two grades were compared to those of the last four grades, the younger children showed the significantly greater advantage (interaction $F = 4.65$, $p = .04$).

**Table 8-6**  Intellectual Curiosity of Experimental- and Control-Group Children in Each of Six Grades after One Year

| GRADE | CONTROL | | EXPERIMENTAL | | EXPECTANCY ADVANTAGE | |
|---|---|---|---|---|---|---|
| | N | MEAN | N | MEAN | DIFFERENCE | ONE-TAIL $p < .05$[a] |
| 1 | 50 | 5.10 | 7 | 7.72 | +2.62 | .001 |
| 2 | 46 | 5.42 | 14 | 6.67 | +1.25 | .03 |
| 3 | 43 | 5.95 | 12 | 5.80 | −0.15 | |
| 4 | 50 | 5.44 | 12 | 5.89 | +0.45 | |
| 5 | 44 | 5.58 | 12 | 5.56 | −0.02 | |
| 6 | 46 | 5.56 | 11 | 7.19 | +1.63 | .02 |
| TOTAL | 279 | 5.50 | 68 | 6.38 | +0.88 | .002 |

[a] Mean square within treatments within classrooms = 4.3037.

Because of the unexpected expectancy advantage in the sixth grade, the correlation between grade level and expectancy advantage was not large or significant ($r = -.41$). However, despite the sixth-grade surprise, the more a given grade level benefited in IQ gains from favorable expectations, the more that same grade level also tended to benefit in ratings on the intellectual curiosity cluster ($r = +.75$, $p < .05$, one-tail).

ADJUSTMENT

For the school as a whole and for all the six grades taken individually, teachers' expectations showed no relationship to the cluster of variables labeled "adjustment." For the school as a whole the children expected to gain intellectually were regarded as happier, after one year, than the children of the control group. Happiness, however, was only one of the five variables in the adjustment cluster, and the lack of difference in the other four was sufficient to reduce the advantage for the cluster as a whole.

NEED FOR APPROVAL

Table 8-7 shows that only in the first grade and, to a lesser extent in the second grade, were there any effects of teacher expectations on the children's need for approval as judged by their teachers.[9] In the eyes of their teachers, at least, the younger children who were expected to gain intellectually were seen as more autonomous and less dependent upon the approval of others. The lower the grade the more this was the case ($r = +.79$, $p = .07$, two-tail); and the more a particular grade had benefited in IQ gains from favorable expectations, the more it benefited in increased autonomy ($r = -.87$, $p = .03$).

| Table 8-7 | | | Need for Approval of Experimental and Control Group Children in Each of Six Grades after One Year | | | |
|---|---|---|---|---|---|---|
| GRADE | CONTROL | | EXPERIMENTAL | | EXPECTANCY ADVANTAGE | |
| | N | MEAN | N | MEAN | DIFFERENCE | TWO-TAIL $p < .05$[a] |
| 1 | 49 | 5.59 | 7 | 3.43 | −2.16 | .02 |
| 2 | 47 | 5.24 | 14 | 4.22 | −1.02 | |
| 3 | 44 | 5.46 | 13 | 5.38 | −0.08 | |
| 4 | 51 | 5.10 | 12 | 5.66 | +0.56 | |
| 5 | 44 | 5.44 | 12 | 5.00 | −0.44 | |
| 6 | 48 | 5.29 | 12 | 5.59 | +0.30 | |
| TOTAL | 283 | 5.35 | 70 | 4.97 | −0.38 | |

[a] Mean square within treatments within classrooms = 4.724.

In general, then, when there were expectancy advantages to be had in the observed behavior of the children as was the case for increased intellectual curiosity and decreased need for social approval, the advantages accrued to the same grade levels that had benefited most in terms of IQ gain. These grade levels, with one exception, tended to be the lower grades.

## Expectancy Advantage
## by Tracks and Sex

### INTELLECTUAL CURIOSITY

Though there was a tendency for the special children to be judged highest on intellectual curiosity relative to the control group children in the medium-track, the expectancy advantage in that track was not significantly greater than that in the other two tracks. Disregarding treatment conditions, however, the fast-track children were rated higher on intellectual curiosity (6.34) than were the children of either the medium (5.28) or slow (5.20) tracks.[10] Ordinarily, we would not be so interested in a finding that is unrelated to the effects of our treatment program. In this case, however, the differences in tracks give additional evidence for the validity of the teachers' ratings of intellectual curiosity. We might expect that children in the fast track would show greater intellectual curiosity, and it is well to know that teachers' ratings reflect that reasonable state of affairs.

Boys and girls did not differ significantly in the extent to which they were seen as intellectually curious, neither for the school as a whole, nor when considering boys and girls of the two treatment conditions, the three tracks, or the lower two and upper four grades separately or in combination. Girls had shown greater expectancy advantages in reasoning IQ than boys, and especially so in the medium track and in the lower grades. Actually, girls did show a greater expectancy advantage in intellectual curiosity and especially so in the medium track and in the lower two grades, but the differences from the boys' expectancy advantages were not significant statistically. Table 8-8 gives the relevant data.

### ADJUSTMENT

For the adjustment-friendliness variables taken together there were no advantages to be had for the children of the experimental group over the children of the control group. That was equally true for all three tracks and each of the sexes. Disregarding treatment conditions, for the school as a whole, girls were seen as higher on adjustment-friendliness (6.14) than boys (5.62), a finding ($p < .03$, two-tail) that interests us primarily because it helps to establish the reasonableness of the cluster. By most other criteria girls are also regarded as better adjusted, friendlier, or at least less troublesome than boys.

| Table 8-8 | Excess of Ratings of Intellectual Curiosity of Experimental over Control Boys and Girls in Three Tracks and Upper and Lower Grades | | |
|---|---|---|---|
| | BOYS | GIRLS | DIFFERENCE |
| *Track* | | | |
| Fast track | +0.21 | +0.90[a] | +0.69 |
| Medium track | +1.16[a] | +2.22[b] | +1.06 |
| Slow track | +0.17 | +0.66 | +0.49 |
| *Grade* | | | |
| Lower two grades | +1.27[a] | +2.34[c] | +1.07 |
| Upper four grades | +0.26 | +0.64[a] | +0.38 |
| TOTAL | +0.65[a] | +1.14[b] | +0.49 |

[a] $p < .10$, one-tail.
[b] $p < .0025$, one-tail.
[c] $p < .001$, one-tail.

NEED FOR APPROVAL

Earlier we saw that it was the younger children who showed less need for approval when they were in the experimental group. Now we find that when tracks are considered, it is the children of the middle track who show the greatest difference in need for approval depending on whether they were in the experimental or control group (Table 8-9).[11] It was these children of the middle track who had tended to gain the most in IQ and especially in reading grades when they were expected to gain intellectually.

| Table 8-9 | | | | Need for Approval of Experimental- and Control-Group Children in Each of Three Tracks after One Year | | |
|---|---|---|---|---|---|---|
| TRACK | CONTROL | | EXPERIMENTAL | | EXPECTANCY ADVANTAGE | |
| | N | MEAN | N | MEAN | DIFFERENCE | TWO-TAIL $p < .05$ |
| Fast | 107 | 5.05 | 30 | 5.20 | +0.15 | |
| Medium | 89 | 5.71 | 18 | 4.33 | −1.38 | .02 |
| Slow | 87 | 5.35 | 22 | 5.18 | −0.17 | |

There was no effect on teachers' ratings of need for approval that was attributable to the sex of the children considering separately or in combination the experimental or control groups, the higher or lower grades, or the different tracks.

## Expectancy Advantage
## by Minority-Group Status

It was only for the intellectual curiosity cluster that there were differences in magnitude of expectancy advantage between the Mexican and non-Mexican children. Table 8-10 shows that while there was ample advantage to the non-Mexican children, boys and girls alike, of having been expected to bloom intellectually, there was no such advantage to the Mexican children.[12] That was surprising because, in general, the Mexican children had benefited somewhat more than the non-Mexican children from favorable expectations in terms of gains in both IQ and reading grades. Because of the small number of Mexican boys and girls in the experimental group, the difference between them in expectancy advantage was not significant statistically. Still, it is worth noting that the Mexican boys showed the least benefit of any group of having been expected to bloom. That was especially surprising because it was the Mexican boys who had gained the most in IQ and in total report-card grades when they were expected to spurt intellectually.

| Table 8-10 | | Intellectual Curiosity of Mexican and Non-Mexican Experimental- and Control-Group Children after One Year | | | | |
|---|---|---|---|---|---|---|
| | CONTROL | | EXPERIMENTAL | | EXPECTANCY ADVANTAGE | |
| | N | MEAN | N | MEAN | DIFFERENCE | ONE-TAIL $p < .05$ |
| *All Children* | | | | | | |
| Mexican | 42 | 5.91 | 18 | 5.61 | −0.30 | |
| Non-Mexican | 237 | 5.42 | 51 | 6.66 | +1.24 | .0001 |
| *Boys* | | | | | | |
| Mexican | 22 | 6.22 | 8 | 5.17 | −1.05 | |
| Non-Mexican | 121 | 5.57 | 26 | 6.68 | +1.11 | .008 |
| *Girls* | | | | | | |
| Mexican | 20 | 5.56 | 10 | 5.97 | +0.41 | |
| Non-Mexican | 116 | 5.27 | 25 | 6.64 | +1.37 | .002 |

One would not think that favorable expectations would benefit these boys more in the more objectively measured IQ and in the possibly more objectively measured report-card grades than in the probably less objectively measured view of the boys' intellectual curiosity in the classroom. For these puzzlements there is no simple explanation clamoring to be heard, but one wonders whether among

these minority-group children who over-represent the slow track and
the disadvantaged of Oak School their gains in intellectual competence
may not be easier for teachers to bring about than to believe.

## CLASSROOM BEHAVIOR
## AND INTELLECTUAL GROWTH

Considering Oak School as a whole, the behavior of the children who
had been expected to gain more intellectually was described in more
favorable terms by Oak School's teachers than was the behavior of the
other children. Teachers made their judgments of the children's classroom behavior toward the end of the school year, by which time there
was more than an expectancy in the teachers' minds to distinguish
the special children from the children of the control group. The
special children had by then gained significantly more in IQ than the
control-group children. It was entirely possible, therefore, that the
perceived behavioral differences between special- and control-group
children were due to the greater IQ gains of the former children. That
possibility could be examined more closely.

Although greater gains in IQ occurred among the children of the
experimental group, there were many children in the control group
who also gained a good deal in IQ during the year of the experiment.
If it were the case that gains in IQ led to more favorable assessments
of classroom behavior, then those control-group children who gained
more in IQ should be evaluated more favorably by their teachers.
To test this suggestion one has only to compute the correlations between gains in IQ (total, verbal, and reasoning) and teachers' assessments of classroom behavior. These correlations were computed separately for the children of the experimental and control groups in
each of the three tracks. The correlations found in the fast and middle
tracks were so similar that they could be combined.

The surprising details of the analysis are found in Tables A-13,
A-14, and A-15 of the Appendix where the arrays of correlations are
presented for total IQ, verbal IQ, and reasoning IQ. Table 8-11 summarizes the detailed analyses by listing all those behaviors associated
with greater gains in IQ (at $p < .10$, two-tail) separately for the
experimental- and control-group children of the upper two tracks
and the experimental- and control-group children of the slow track.

Looking first at the upper tracks we find that the greater the IQ
gain of one of the special children, the more favorably he was evaluated in every respect by his teacher. Not so, however, for the upper-
track children of the control group. There, the more a child gained in

IQ, the less favorably he was evaluated as to adjustment, happiness, and affectionateness. Hostility, though, was judged to be less among the children who gained more in IQ. The results for these control-group children of the upper track, then, are equivocal; the big IQ gainers win a little but lose a little more in their teacher's eye. In any case, since there were at least 165 children in this group, it took only a small degree of relationship to reach the required level of statistical significance, and most of the correlations were trivial in size. We conclude safely, however, that among children of the upper tracks, those who gain more in IQ are seen more favorably only when they have been expected to gain more intellectually.

| Table 8-11 | Classroom Behavior Associated with Greater IQ Gain after One Year among Experimental- and Control-Group Children of Slow and Upper Tracks | | | |
|---|---|---|---|---|
| | CONTROL ($df \geq 165$) | | EXPERIMENTAL ($df \geq 37$) | |
| *Upper Tracks* | less adjusted | (V) | more interesting | (T)[a] (V)[b] (R)[c] |
| | less happy | (V) | more successful | |
| | less affectionate | (V) | future | (T) (V) |
| | less hostile | (R) | more adjusted | (T) (R) |
| | | | more appealing | (T) |
| | | | more affectionate | (T) (R) |
| | ($df \geq 74$) | | ($df \geq 17$) | |
| *Slow Track* | less need for approval | (V) | less need for approval | (T) (R) |
| | less interesting | (T) (R) | less affectionate | (T) (V) |
| | less curious | (R) | | |
| | less adjusted | (R) | | |
| | less appealing | (R) | | |
| | less happy | (R) | | |
| | less affectionate | (R) | | |

[a] Total IQ.
[b] Verbal IQ.
[c] Reasoning IQ.

Among those children of the slow track who were expected to gain intellectually, those who gained more in IQ are seen as more autonomous but less affectionate. We cannot, therefore, say that they were clearly affected either positively or negatively by having shown greater

IQ gains. In any case, they were not as favorably seen as the high-gaining special children of the upper tracks, even though objectively they had gained as much intellectually as the special children of the fast track.

We need have little hesitation about interpreting the situation for those children of the slow track who were not expected to gain intellectually. The more such a child gained in IQ, the more unfavorably he was evaluated by his teacher in almost every respect.

How are these counterintuitive results to be understood? The upper-track children of the experimental group had two things in their favor: their upper-track status and the special expectations about their intellectual growth given to their teachers. These were the children who, as seen by their teachers, benefited most from having gained more in IQ. The upper-track children of the control group and the lower-track children of the experimental group each had only one thing in their favor; track status in one case, special expectations in the other. These two groups of children did not benefit much as seen by their teachers when they gained more in IQ. The lower-track children of the control group had nothing in their favor, neither their track status nor the specially created expectancies.[13] When they showed greater gains in IQ, they were seen much more unfavorably than when they showed those more modest gains that were expected of them.

From this we suggest the proposition for further research: If a child is to show intellectual gains, it may be better for his intellectual vitality and for his mental health as seen by his teacher, if his teacher has been expecting him to gain intellectually. It appears that there may be psychological hazards to unexpected intellectual growth.

◆§

[1] The statistical analysis proceeded in the same fashion as described in the last chapter, that is, by means of two-way and three-way analyses of variance. The $p$ value for the over-all difference in reading gains shown in Table 8-1 was based on the over-all $t$. However, $F$s for the main effect of treatments were obtained in all the analyses of variance, and the $p$ values associated with the various $F$s ranged from .23 to .005 with a median two-tail $p$ of .04.

Considering classrooms as the sampling unit ($N = 17$; report cards from one class were not available), we find that children of the experimental group gained more in reading scores than did children of the control group in fourteen of the seventeen classes. The one-tail $p$s associated with the sign, Wilcoxon, and $t$ tests were .006, .002, and .002, respectively. Even allowing for the fact that reading was the only school subject to reach a $p < .10$ of a total of eleven school subjects, these obtained $p$s for reading seem too low to justify our ascribing them to chance. If the eleven subjects were independent, which they were not (mean intercorrelation among post-test grades $= +.47$) we might expect on the average to find by chance one $p < .09$, and that expected $p$ is about ten times larger than those obtained when classrooms served as sampling units.

[2] The interaction between the two treatments and six grade levels was not significant $(F < 1)$.

[3] Often when percentages are used in statistical analyses they are first transformed to a corresponding angle. This procedure was not employed since the percentages involved were all close to 50 percent. The mean total test percentile level of all children tested in the Spring of 1964 was 49.6 percent, based on the national sample.

[4] For each of the sets or clusters, the ratio of the square of the mean of the intercorrelations among variables within a cluster to the square of the mean of the correlations of variables in a cluster with variables not in the cluster was 3.00 or greater. Table A-12 of the Appendix shows all the intercorrelations between and within cluster members.

[5] The variable "nonhostile" was coded for each child by subtracting from 10 the rating on hostility.

[6] Clusters I and II were not, of course, completely independent of each other. The mean correlation between the variables of Cluster (I) with the variables of Cluster II was $+.36$. That was a lower correlation than the one between the verbal IQ and reasoning IQ tests.

[7] The mean correlation of Cluster (III) with the variables of Cluster (I) was $-.07$; with the variables of Cluster (II) it was $-.13$.

[8] The interaction between treatments and grade levels was significant at $p < .05$ $(F = 2.33)$. Depending upon the particular analysis of variance, the $p$ values associated with the main effect of treatments ranged from .20 to .0003 with a median two-tail $p$ of .002. Considering classrooms as the sampling unit, we find children of the experimental group judged higher than the children of the control group on intellectual curiosity in fourteen of the eighteen classrooms. The one-tail $p$s associated with the sign, Wilcoxon, and $t$ tests were identical $(p = .02)$.

[9] The interaction $F = 1.89$, $p < .10$. For main effects of treatments $p$ values associated with $F$s ranged from .28 to .04 with a median $p$ of .10. Considering classrooms as the sampling unit, the children of the experimental group showed a lower need for approval in twelve of the eighteen classrooms. The two-tail $p$s associated with the sign, Wilcoxon, and $t$ tests were .24, .12, and .09, respectively. When the first two grades were compared to the last four grades on magnitude of expectancy effect, the lower grades showed the

greater difference between the children of the experimental and control groups, interaction $F = 6.22$, $p < .02$.

[10] Main effects of tracks was significant at the .004 level, $F = 6.07$.

[11] The interaction $F = 2.48$, $p = .09$.

[12] The two-way interaction $F = 5.34$, $p < .03$; the triple interaction adding pupil sex as a factor yielded an $F < 1$.

[13] For another group of subjects who "had little in their favor," Katz and Cohen (1962) found evidence to suggest that increases in Negroes' perceived ability were reacted to with hostility by their white coworkers.

# 9

# The
# Process
# of
# Blooming

The evidence presented in the last two chapters suggests rather strongly that children who are expected by their teachers to gain intellectually in fact do show greater intellectual gains after one year than do children of whom such gains are not expected. But important questions regarding the acquisition and maintenance of expectancy advantage have not been discussed. Some of these questions can be partially answered, and that is the purpose of this chapter.

Under ideal conditions we would learn most about the process of acquisition and maintenance of any expectancy advantage by beginning our measurements immediately after the initiation of the experimental program and by recording responses continuously for as long as we could maintain contact with the children. Under these ideal conditions of measurement we might be able to state (1) exactly when the process of expectancy blooming began, (2) the rates and rates of changes in the acquisition process at various points in time, and finally, (3) the point at which the effects of favorable expectations disappear. But schools, teachers, and pupils have other things to do than provide behavioral researchers with data. The realities of the situation were such that we could make measurements of the effects of teachers' expectancies at only two other points in time. The first of these measurements was made halfway through the academic year of the experiment. The second of these was made at the end of the academic year following the year of the basic experiment. This latter measurement was designed to show whether the effects of favorable teacher expectancies could last as long as two academic years. The former measurement was designed to tell something of how soon the effects of favorable expectations showed themselves. If the effects found at the end of our basic academic-year study were present in full strength after only one

semester, we would at least know that one semester was all the time
the effect required, though we would not know in how much less time
the effect reached its full magnitude. If the effects found at the end
of the school year were nowhere in evidence after only one semester,
that might suggest an incubation or delayed-action hypothesis. If the
effects found at the end of the first semester were larger than they were
at the end of that academic year, there might be a good argument
made for the ephemeral nature of expectancy advantages—dramatic
at first, but quick to disappear. That same pattern of results might
also suggest that the communication of teachers' favorable expectations
occurred not so much on a daily basis but only during her administration of the tests themselves. Later evidence will be presented to show
that teachers soon "forgot" which of their pupils were "magic" children. Considering what we know of curves of forgetting, teachers
should have recalled the names of the special children better after one
semester than after two. If the effects of the teacher's expectations were
greater after one semester than after two, it might be due to her having
treated the special children more preferentially during the one-semester
retest than during the two-semester retest. At this latter time, chances
would be greater that she could not remember which of her pupils
were on the list of special children.

Perhaps the most likely outcome to anticipate, however, was that
in which children would show after one semester some of, but not all
of, the expectancy advantage found after two semesters. That would
suggest a somewhat linear curve of acquisition during the basic year
of the experiment.

## THE ONSET
## OF EXPECTANCY ADVANTAGES

The comparison of the gains in intellectual performance after one
semester by children of the experimental and control groups proceeded
just as had the analysis of gains after one year. We shall examine in
turn the effects of favorable expectancies as a function of pupils' grades,
tracks, sex, and minority-group status.

### Expectancy Advantage
### by Grades
IQ
The bottom row of Table 9-1 gives the over-all results for Oak School.
After one semester, the undesignated control-group children had
gained about three IQ points while the special children had gained

**Figure 9-1**                Gains in total IQ in six grades
                             after one semester.

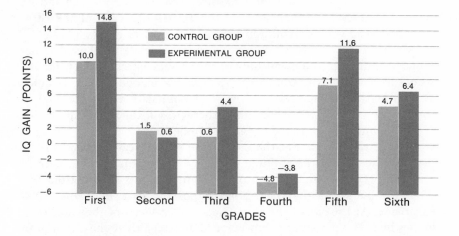

over five IQ points. Though the difference in IQ gains was neither large nor very significant statistically, it appeared that, over-all, expectancy advantages were beginning to show themselves after one semester.[1]

**Table 9-1**                Mean Gain in Total IQ after One Semester
                            by Experimental- and Control-Group
                            Children in Each of Six Grades

| GRADE | CONTROL | | EXPERIMENTAL | | EXPECTANCY ADVANTAGE | |
| --- | --- | --- | --- | --- | --- | --- |
| | $N$ | GAIN | $N$ | GAIN | IQ POINTS | ONE-TAIL $p < .05$[a] |
| 1 | 51 | +10.0 | 9 | +14.8 | +4.8 | |
| 2 | 48 | + 1.5 | 14 | + 0.6 | −0.9 | |
| 3 | 47 | + 0.6 | 14 | + 4.4 | +3.8 | |
| 4 | 55 | − 4.8 | 12 | − 3.8 | +1.0 | |
| 5 | 44 | + 7.1 | 14 | +11.6 | +4.5 | |
| 6 | 49 | + 4.7 | 13 | + 6.4 | +1.7 | |
| TOTAL | 294 | + 3.01 | 76 | + 5.30 | +2.29 | (.08) |

[a] Mean square within treatments within classrooms = 155.92.

The rest of Table 9-1 (and Figure 9-1) shows that magnitudes of expectancy advantage did not vary with grade levels after one semester as they had after two semesters (interaction $F < 1$). The children of grades one, three, and five gained somewhat more than the children of grades two, four, and six. We should make little of this fact because it could easily have occurred by chance. We should recall, however, that children of grades one and two, three and four, and of five and six each had taken a different form of the IQ test. In each of the three test forms, the younger children showed the greater gains.

When verbal IQ is considered separately, grade level is still not found to influence the magnitude of expectancy effect. In fact, for the school as a whole, the control-group children gained almost as much (3.0 points) as the special children (3.5 points). Even at the end of the school year, it will be recalled, there was little benefit to verbal IQ of having been expected to bloom intellectually.

Just as was the case at the end of the school year, the end of the first semester found the children of the special group gaining more in reasoning IQ than the children of the control group. The bottom row of Table 9-2 shows that fact. The rest of the data in Table 9-2 is surprising. At the end of the school year the children of the two lowest grades had shown a greater expectancy advantage than the children of grades four to six. That had been shown earlier in Table 7-4. Now we find that after one semester the younger children had not shown any expectancy advantage whatever. The older special children had gained all they were going to gain in reasoning IQ after one semester but the younger special children had yet to begin their gaining of any advantage. Why there should be this delayed-action effect for the younger children, and only as measured by reasoning IQ gains, is hardly obvious intuitively.

Table 9-2          Mean Gain in Reasoning IQ after One Semester by Experimental- and Control-Group Children in Grades One to Two and Three to Six

| GRADES | CONTROL | | EXPERIMENTAL | | EXPECTANCY ADVANTAGE | |
|--------|---------|------|--------------|------|-----------|------------------|
|        | N | GAIN | N | GAIN | IQ POINTS | ONE-TAIL $p < .05$[a] |
| 1–2 | 99 | +18.8 | 23 | +14.5 | −4.3 | |
| 3–6 | 195 | + 0.8 | 53 | + 8.7 | +7.9 | .008 |
| TOTAL | 294 | + 6.86 | 76 | +10.43 | +3.57 | (.09) |

[a] Mean square within = 427.42.

REPORT CARDS

At the end of the first semester of the experiment, each of Oak School's children was graded on the eleven school subjects described in the last chapter. Just as before, children of the experimental and control groups were compared on the basis of their gains in report-card grades from the end of the preceding school year. It may be recalled that at the end of two semesters the special children had benefited significantly only in reading grades. The second largest expectancy advantage for Oak School as a whole had been in gains in social studies, but that advantage had not been significant statistically. Now, after only one semester, these two school subjects both showed a significant effect of teachers' favorable expectations, and they were the only school subjects to do so. The control-group children lost .17 of a grade point in social studies after one semester and the experimental-group children gained .02 of a grade point ($p < .03$, one-tail). In reading, the control group lost .21 of a grade point while the experimental group gained .03 of a grade point ($p = .004$, one-tail). Because the results for reading scores after two semesters had been analyzed in detail, the same analyses were also carried out for reading gains after one semester. Only minority-group status turned out to be a factor affecting the magnitude of expectancy advantage in reading grades so that further discussion is best postponed until the variable of minority-group status is discussed.[2]

ACHIEVEMENT TESTS

For just grades five and six the Iowa Tests of Basic skills (ITBS) were available in November of the first semester as were pretest scores obtained the preceding Spring. In the last chapter when we compared ITBS gains with report-card gains we reported that there were no expectancy advantages to be found after just the first few weeks of the experiment in the ITBS scores in reading, language, or arithmetic. These were subtests for which the report-card grades contained analogues. The ITBS, however, has two other subtests for which there are no report-card analogues. One of these subtests is vocabulary, the other is work-study skills. The latter is designed to assess such things as the ability to use maps, graphs, and references.

After just these few weeks of the "treatment program" the special children had gained nearly five percentile units more than the control-group children in vocabulary scores ($p = .08$) and over ten percentile units more in work-study skills ($p < .003$). These expectancy advantages among the fifth and sixth graders suggested that we had erred in waiting to do the first retest until the end of the first semester. It appears likely that some of the effects of favorable teacher expectations begin to manifest themselves within just the first few weeks of the changing of the expectations. (Tables A-22 and A-23 of the Appendix show for each classroom the gain in percentile-unit scores of the experimental- and control-group children in vocabulary and work-study skills.)

While reporting these results for vocabulary and work-study skills after just a few weeks of the experiment had elapsed, we can also report the results of retesting almost a full year later in October of 1965. Only the fifth graders, now in sixth grade, were left, the sixth graders having gone on to junior high school. In vocabulary, the special children lost some but not all of their expectancy advantage. In work-study skills, the special children gained a little more expectancy advantage but neither of these "one-year-later" changes in expectancy advantage was significant statistically. The gains that had been made by pupils of the teacher who held favorable expectations were maintained after promotion to a new teacher who had been given no special expectations about the children's performance.

## Expectancy Advantage
## by Tracks and Sex

Quite unlike the situation at the end of the school year, at the end of the first semester, expectancy advantages were quite unrelated to pupils' sex and track status. That was the case for total, verbal, and reasoning IQs when sex and track were considered either independently or jointly.

| Table 9-3 | | | Mean Gain in Reasoning IQ by Mexican and Non-Mexican Experimental- and Control-Group Children after One Semester | | | |
|---|---|---|---|---|---|---|
| | CONTROL | | EXPERIMENTAL | | EXPECTANCY ADVANTAGE | |
| | *N* | GAIN | *N* | GAIN | IQ POINTS | ONE-TAIL $p < .05$ |
| *Boys* | | | | | | |
| Mexican | 22 | +10.5 | 8 | +26.4 | +15.9 | .04 |
| Non-Mexican | 133 | +11.0 | 31 | + 7.4 | − 3.6 | |
| *Girls* | | | | | | |
| Mexican | 22 | + 9.0 | 10 | + 6.4 | − 2.6 | |
| Non-Mexican | 117 | + 1.1 | 27 | +10.7 | + 9.6 | .02 |

## Expectancy Advantage
## by Minority-Group Status

It was only when the measure was of reasoning IQ that the minority-group status of the pupil was a factor related to magnitude of expectancy effects; and then it was complicated by the sex of the pupil (triple interaction $F = 5.84$, $p < .02$). Table 9-3 shows that it was the

Mexican boys and the non-Mexican girls who showed this early expectancy advantage and showed it to a dramatic degree while the Mexican girls and non-Mexican boys showed a very slight expectancy disadvantage. By the end of the school year the Mexican girls had more than caught up with the Mexican boys in expectancy advantage though the Mexican boys' expectancy advantage held up well. The non-Mexican boys, however, never did catch up with the Mexican boys in terms of expectancy advantage.

For each of the Mexican children, the magnitude of expectancy advantage was computed by subtracting from his or her IQ gain the IQ gain made by children of the control group in his or her classroom. These individual magnitudes of expectancy advantage were then correlated with the "Mexican-ness" of the children's faces. Table 9-4 shows the correlations obtained among Mexican boys and girls when expectancy advantage was defined by total, verbal, and reasoning IQs. In general, and especially when expectancy advantage was reckoned in reasoning IQ, those Mexican boys who looked more Mexican showed the greater expectancy advantage. Two chapters ago we saw the same relationship to apply after two semesters as well. At that time we suggested the possibility that teachers' pre-experimental expectancies of the more Mexican-looking boys' intellectual performance might have been lowest of all. These children might, therefore, have stood to gain the most by the introduction of a more favorable expectation into their teachers' minds. That seems not too far-fetched, but what is there to be said about finding the same relationship among Mexican girls? Those correlations, we learned earlier, tended to become negative at the end of the school year. Perhaps we can evade responsibility for interpreting this strange finding by noting that, in any case, after one semester there had been no expectancy advantage for the Mexican girls as a group, though there had been for the Mexican boys.

| Table 9-4 | Correlations between Mexican Facial Characteristics and Advantages of Favorable Expectations after One Semester | | | | | |
|---|---|---|---|---|---|---|
| | BOYS | | GIRLS | | TOTAL | |
| | N | r | N | r | N | r |
| Total IQ | 8 | +.47 | 10 | +.69[b] | 18 | +.51[b] |
| Verbal IQ | 8 | +.15 | 10 | +.51 | 18 | +.25 |
| Reasoning IQ | 8 | +.69[a] | 10 | +.14 | 18 | +.38 |

[a] $p = .06$, two-tail.
[b] $p \le .04$, two-tail.

| Table 9-5 | Excess of Gain in School Subjects by Experimental- over Control-Group Children after One Semester | | | |
|-----------|-------------------|-------|-------------|-------|
| SUBJECT | MEXICAN | | NON-MEXICAN | |
|  | BOYS | GIRLS | BOYS | GIRLS |
| Reading | −.40 | +.28 | +.41 | +.25 |
| Arithmetic | −.50 | +.28 | −.08 | +.11 |
| Language | +.36 | +.13 | −.28 | −.02 |
| Spelling | +.55 | +.44 | −.12 | −.10 |
| Handwriting | −.19 | +.28 | +.09 | +.07 |
| Social Studies | +.11 | +.28 | +.21 | +.16 |
| Science | −.16 | −.09 | +.03 | −.02 |
| Health | +.54 | −.46 | −.06 | +.15 |
| Physical Education | +.30 | +.27 | −.02 | +.04 |
| Arts and Crafts | +.14 | −.10 | +.11 | +.05 |
| Music | +.51 | −.14 | −.02 | +.16 |
| MEAN | +.11 | +.11 | +.02 | +.08 |
| N EXPERIMENTAL | 5 | 9 | 30 | 32 |
| N CONTROL | 19 | 18 | 130 | 120 |

REPORT CARDS

The top row of Table 9-5 shows the expectancy advantages in reading scores for Mexican and non-Mexican boys and girls. After one semester, the Mexican boys were the only group not to benefit in reading grades from having been expected to bloom intellectually (triple interaction $F = 3.40$, $p = .07$). Yet it was the Mexican boys who had shown the greatest expectancy advantage in reasoning IQ. Also, in six of the eleven school subjects they showed the greatest expectancy advantage of any group as the rest of Table 9-5 shows; but of the five remaining school subjects, they showed the lowest expectancy advantage.[3] In terms of grades assigned by their teachers, then, Mexican boys were most affected by their teachers' expectations but sometimes for better and sometimes for worse. Inspection of the school subjects in which the Mexican boys profited most compared to those in which they profited least showed no clear pattern of differentiation. By the end of the school year these differences in variability had vanished and the Mexican boys emerged as the group benefiting most clearly in report-card grades from favorable teacher expectations (see Table 8-4 for comparison purposes).

Just as was the case after two semesters, the Mexican children showed slightly greater over-all expectancy advantages after one semester though they did not profit significantly more than did the non-Mexican children.

## THE DURABILITY
## OF EXPECTANCY ADVANTAGES

At the end of the school year of 1965–1966, the children of Oak School were tested for the fourth and final time. This follow-up testing took place some twenty months after the initiation of our "program for intellectual change," and some two years after the initial pretesting. The reason for this follow-up testing, of course, was to see whether any advantages of favorable teacher expectations could last that long, especially after the additional year had been spent in a classroom whose teacher had not been told which of the children were "special."

The children who, during the year of the basic experiment, had been sixth graders, had now left Oak School for junior high school. They were unavailable for the follow-up testing. All the other children had moved up one grade, but to make comparisons with earlier reported data simpler we shall continue to refer to them as first graders, if that is what they were during the year of the basic experiment. We need only keep in mind that the children of grades one through five during the follow-up year were actually in grades two through six.

The analysis of the effects of "last year's" teachers' favorable expectations proceeded just as had the analysis earlier in this chapter. The gains in intellectual performance after two years of the children of the experimental and control groups were compared as a function of pupils' grades, tracks, sex, and minority-group status.

### Expectancy Advantage
### by Grades

The bottom row of Table 9-6 shows the over-all results for Oak School. After two years the overall magnitude of expectancy advantage had increased slightly over what it had been after only one semester but decreased slightly over what it had been after one year. When only those children were considered who had taken both the one-year post-test and the two-year follow-up test there was a significant reduction of expectancy advantage in total IQ ($p < .05$, two-tail) although a moderate degree of expectancy advantage still remained after two years.[4]

Examination of the rest of Table 9-6 (and Figure 9-2) shows us that there was only one grade level to benefit after two years from teachers' favorable expectations, and that grade was the original fifth grade (now the sixth grade). That was a surprise because on the

**Figure 9-2**    Gains in total IQ in five grades
after two years.

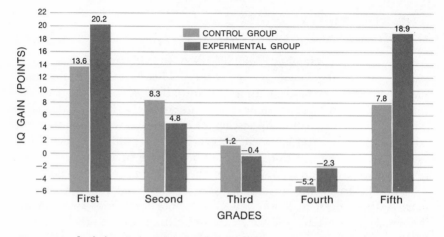

post-test administered one year earlier those children had shown no
expectancy advantage whatever. Why fifth graders, expected to bloom
in one year, should show such large expectancy advantages during
a subsequent year in a classroom taught by a teacher given no special
expectation for their intellectual performance remains a baffling question.

**Table 9-6**    Mean Gain in Total IQ after Two
Years by Experimental- and Control-Group
Children in Each of Five Grades

| GRADE | CONTROL | | EXPERIMENTAL | | EXPECTANCY ADVANTAGE | |
|---|---|---|---|---|---|---|
| | *N* | GAIN | *N* | GAIN | IQ POINTS | ONE-TAIL $p < .05$[a] |
| 1 | 36 | +13.6 | 6 | +20.2 | + 6.6 | |
| 2 | 39 | + 8.3 | 9 | + 4.8 | − 3.5 | |
| 3 | 36 | + 1.2 | 10 | − 0.4 | − 1.6 | |
| 4 | 47 | − 5.2 | 11 | − 2.3 | + 2.9 | |
| 5 | 38 | + 7.8 | 11 | +18.9 | +11.1 | .01 |
| TOTAL | 196 | + 4.63 | 47 | + 7.30 | + 2.67 | (.13) |

[a] Mean square within treatments within classrooms = 194.36.

When verbal IQ and reasoning IQ were considered separately, fifth
graders continued to show the largest expectancy advantages though
these advantages were greater in verbal than in reasoning IQ. That
was the case not only for fifth graders but for all of Oak School as well.

In reasoning IQ the average expectancy advantage for Oak School was just over one IQ point, a difference easily attributed to chance. In verbal IQ the average expectancy advantage for Oak School was just under four points ($p = .08$, one-tail).[5]

| Table 9-7 | | | | | Mean Gain in Three IQ Scores after Two Years by Experimental and Control Groups in Three Tracks | |
|---|---|---|---|---|---|---|
| TRACK | CONTROL | | EXPERIMENTAL | | EXPECTANCY ADVANTAGE | |
| | N | GAIN | N | GAIN | IQ POINTS | ONE-TAIL $p < .10$ |
| *Total IQ* | | | | | | |
| Fast | 72 | + 7.5 | 20 | + 4.7 | − 2.8 | |
| Medium | 60 | + 3.8 | 12 | +13.4 | + 9.6 | .02 |
| Slow | 64 | + 2.2 | 15 | + 5.9 | + 3.7 | |
| TOTAL | 196 | + 4.63 | 47 | + 7.30 | + 2.67[a] | (.13) |
| *Verbal IQ* | | | | | | |
| Fast | 72 | + 3.3 | 20 | + 4.2 | + 0.9 | |
| Medium | 60 | − 2.6 | 12 | + 4.5 | + 7.1 | .10 |
| Slow | 64 | − 5.9 | 15 | − 1.5 | + 4.4 | |
| TOTAL | 196 | − 1.50 | 47 | + 2.43 | + 3.93[b] | .08 |
| *Reasoning IQ* | | | | | | |
| Fast | 72 | +13.8 | 20 | + 7.4 | − 6.4 | |
| Medium | 60 | +15.3 | 12 | +32.1 | +16.8 | .04 |
| Slow | 64 | +19.3 | 15 | +18.1 | − 1.2 | |
| TOTAL | 196 | +16.04 | 47 | +17.13 | + 1.09[c] | (.39) |

[a] Mean square within = 194.36.
[b] Mean square within = 278.19.
[c] Mean square within = 606.13.

## Expectancy Advantage by Tracks and Sex

After the first year of the experiment there had been a tendency, not significant statistically, for the children of the middle track to benefit most from favorable teacher expectations. Now after the second year of the experiment this tendency became more pronounced, and it reached statistical significance for total IQ and reasoning IQ and tended toward statistical significance for verbal IQ.[6] On both theoretical and psychometric bases, we might have expected the children of the slow track to benefit most from their teachers' favorable expectations. But, as we have seen, it was the more average children who

profited most, and especially after they had been promoted to a
teacher who had been given no special expectation for their intellectual
development (Table 9-7).

One year earlier, at the conclusion of the basic experiment, the
girls had shown a somewhat greater expectancy advantage in total IQ.
Now, one year later, that was still true, as shown in Table 9-8. (The
reader may wish to compare Table 9-8 with Table 7-5.) After the first
year of the experiment the results for total IQ obscured the interesting
fact that it was in reasoning IQ that the girls benefited more from
favorable expectations while in verbal IQ, the boys benefited more.
Now, after the follow-up testing, the same results emerged. Only the
girls showed a significant expectancy advantage in reasoning IQ and
only the boys showed one in verbal IQ.[7] On the initial pretest, two
years earlier, boys had shown a higher verbal IQ than girls, while girls
had shown a higher reasoning IQ than boys. That may simply be coincidence, but it is at least possible that each sex benefits most from
favorable expectations in the area of intellectual functioning in which
they are already relatively more advantaged.

| Table 9-8 | | | | | Mean Gain in Three IQ Scores after Two Years by Experimental and Control Boys and Girls | |
|---|---|---|---|---|---|---|
| | CONTROL | | EXPERIMENTAL | | EXPECTANCY ADVANTAGE | |
| | N | GAIN | N | GAIN | IQ POINTS | ONE-TAIL $p < .10$ |
| *Total IQ* | | | | | | |
| Boys | 107 | + 7.5 | 21 | + 9.3 | + 1.8 | |
| Girls | 89 | + 1.2 | 26 | + 5.7 | + 4.5 | .08 |
| *Verbal IQ* | | | | | | |
| Boys | 107 | − 0.5 | 21 | + 6.5 | + 7.0 | .05 |
| Girls | 89 | − 2.7 | 26 | − 0.9 | + 1.8 | |
| *Reasoning IQ* | | | | | | |
| Boys | 107 | +21.5 | 21 | +14.6 | − 6.9 | |
| Girls | 89 | + 9.5 | 26 | +19.2 | + 9.7 | .05 |

From the finding that girls show greater expectancy advantages,
especially in reasoning IQ, and from the finding that middle-track
children profit most from favorable expectations, we might in part have
predicted the results shown in Table 9-9. There we see that among
girls those in the middle track benefited most and especially so in
reasoning IQ.[8] (Table 7-6 had given the analogous data for reasoning
IQ after the one-year post-test.) Among the boys, however, the results
were less predictable. Boys of the fast track tended to show something

of an expectancy disadvantage after two years in all three measures of IQ. Boys of the medium and slow tracks, however, in both verbal IQ and total IQ tended to show advantages of favorable expectations.

| Table 9-9 | Excess of Gain in Three IQ Scores by Experimental over Control Boys and Girls in Three Tracks after Two Years | |
|---|---|---|
| | BOYS | GIRLS |
| *Total IQ* | | |
| Fast | − 9.6[b] | + 1.6 |
| Medium | + 8.4 | +15.3[d] |
| Slow | + 9.2[c] | − 0.2 |
| *Verbal IQ* | | |
| Fast | − 2.8 | + 3.5 |
| Medium | +11.9[c] | + 6.3 |
| Slow | +12.6[c] | − 1.3 |
| *Reasoning IQ* | | |
| Fast | −14.4[a] | − 1.5 |
| Medium | − 2.2 | +39.5[e] |
| Slow | + 0.1 | − 3.1 |

[a] $p < .12$, two-tail.
[b] $p < .07$, two-tail.
[c] $p \leq .07$, one-tail.
[d] $p < .007$, one-tail.
[e] $p < .0002$, one-tail.

When expectancy advantages accrue to girls they tend to accrue to the average girls. In Oak School, teachers tend to find these girls uninteresting, and pre-existing expectations for their intellectual performance are neither high as in the case of fast-track girls nor low but challenging as in the case of slow-track girls. As was suggested earlier, it may be that in terms of teacher interest, medium-track girls have the most to gain from having their "potential" pointed out to their teacher. These gains then hold up very well over the course of an additional year in which they are taught by a teacher who had been given no special expectation about the girls' intellectual development.

When long-term expectancy advantages accrue to boys, they tend to accrue to the average and slow-track boys. One year earlier that had not been the case, a fact that makes any interpretation very tenuous indeed. That fact, coupled with the borderline statistical significance of the results for boys, leads us to forego any interpretation at this time.

At the end of the first year of the experiment, magnitudes of expectancy advantage had been fairly homogeneous among children of the lowest two grades and among children of the highest four grades. At the end of the second year's follow-up testing that homogeneity had been lost. Nevertheless, to provide data comparable to that shown earlier in Table 7-7, Table 9-10 was prepared.[9] For total IQ, younger girls showed greater expectancy advantages than younger boys after one year and after two years. Similarly, on both retests, older boys benefited just a bit more than did older girls. At the time of both post-tests the special boys of both grade levels gained more in verbal IQ than did the special girls (relative to the control group boys and girls). In reasoning IQ, after the first year of the experiment, girls showed the greater expectancy advantage at both grade levels but especially among the younger children. The younger boys, in fact, tended to show an expectancy disadvantage as measured by reasoning IQ. That same pattern of results was also obtained after the two year follow-up retesting.

| Table 9-10 | Excess of Gain in Three IQ Scores by Experimental over Control Boys and Girls in Two Grade Levels after Two Years | |
|---|---|---|
| | BOYS | GIRLS |
| *Total IQ* | | |
| Grades 1–2 | − 4.4 | + 6.3 |
| Grades 3–5 | + 6.5[a] | + 3.9 |
| *Verbal IQ* | | |
| Grades 1–2 | + 4.7 | + 1.3 |
| Grades 3–5 | + 8.5[b] | + 2.3 |
| *Reasoning IQ* | | |
| Grades 1–2 | −19.7[c] | +16.7[b] |
| Grades 3–5 | + 3.3 | + 7.2 |

[a] $p < .07$, one-tail.
[b] $p < .05$, one-tail.
[c] $p < .06$, two-tail.

In our earlier presentation of the results of the first year of the experiment, we summarized the complex findings involving pupils' sex as a factor complicating the operation of expectancy effects. On the basis of the two-year follow-up testing, there is only little need to modify that summary. Although this follow-up year was spent with a teacher who had been given no special expectations about pupils' performance, the patterning of expectancy advantage remained essentially the same. After one year and after two, girls bloomed more in the reasoning sphere of intellectual functioning, and boys bloomed more in the verbal sphere when some kind of unspecified blooming was expected of them. When dramatic sex differences in expectancy advantage occurred they were more likely to be found among younger children and among children of the medium track.

### Expectancy Advantage
### by Minority-Group Status
After the first year of the experiment, the Mexican children of Oak School had shown greater benefits of favorable teacher expectations than had the non-Mexican children. The difference favoring the Mexican children had not, however, been significant statistically. Now, another year later, the Mexican children maintained their advantage in total IQ, increased their advantage in verbal IQ, but lost their advantage in reasoning IQ. The differences in expectancy advantage between Mexican and non-Mexican children still did not reach statistical significance, however.

| Table 9-11 | Correlations between Mexican Facial Characteristics and Advantages of Favorable Expectations after Two Years | | | | | |
|---|---|---|---|---|---|---|
| | BOYS | | GIRLS | | TOTAL | |
| | N | r | N | r | N | r |
| Total IQ | 4 | +.79 | 8 | +.12 | 12 | +.36 |
| Verbal IQ | 4 | +.90[a] | 8 | +.54 | 12 | +.54[a] |
| Reasoning IQ | 4 | +.67 | 8 | −.35 | 12 | −.18 |

[a] $p \leq .10$, two-tail.

Just as had been done before, an expectancy advantage score was computed for each Mexican child by subtracting from his or her IQ gain, the IQ gain made by the children of the control group in his or her classroom. The resulting expectancy advantage scores were then correlated with the "Mexican-ness" of the children's faces. Table 9-11 gives the correlations obtained among Mexican boys and girls when expectancy advantage was in terms of total, verbal, and reasoning IQs. Among the Mexican boys, those who looked more Mexican tended to show the greater expectancy advantage after two years just as they had after one semester and after one year of the experiment. The same general relationship had been found among the Mexican girls after one semester, but after two semesters and now, after two years, that relationship had become equivocal. Earlier we suggested the possibility

**Figure 9-3**          Expectancy advantage after four, eight, and
twenty months among boys, girls, and all
children (asterisk indicates $p < .10$, two-tail).

that boys who looked more Mexican might have surprised the teachers
most by turning up on a list of children destined to bloom. Interest
may have followed surprise, and greater interest, in turn, may have led
to the greater expectancy advantage found among these children. If
this speculation were entertained, we might expect that other boys of
whom little is ordinarily expected would also benefit more from an
increased interest in them by their teacher. Such boys are those of
the slow track. Table 9-9 shows that at the time of the two-year
follow-up, the boys of the slow track were the ones to show the greatest
benefit from their teacher having been given a favorable expectation
about their future intellectual development.

## A LONGER VIEW

For each of the retests employed, the results have now been presented
to show the effects of teacher expectations on children's IQ gains.
The three retests, it will be recalled, were administered four months,
eight months, and twenty months after the initiation of the experimental program for intellectual change. At each succeeding retest,
fewer children were available to whom the pretest had been administered. Thus, for example, after four months, 370 children who had
been pretested were retestable, but after twenty months, there were
only 243 such children. In spite of the fact that not all children were
available for all retests, it may be useful to examine the magnitude
of expectancy advantage at the time of each retesting for those children who were available. As usual, magnitude of expectancy advantage
is defined as the gain in IQ of the control-group children subtracted
from the gain in IQ of the experimental-group children. Thus, expectancy advantage is, as usual, an excess of gain of experimental- over
control-group children.

Figure 9-3 shows expectancy advantages measured at three points
in time for total, verbal, and reasoning IQ for all children, for boys,
and for girls. All special children showed slight advantages in IQ gains
after only four months, greater advantages after eight months, and,
after twenty months, continued increase in advantage in verbal IQ
but decrease in advantage in reasoning and total IQ. The trend over
time for boys differed from that for girls. For total IQ, girls showed
their expectancy advantage earlier, maintained it at a higher level, and
lost virtually none of it even after twenty months. Boys' gains were

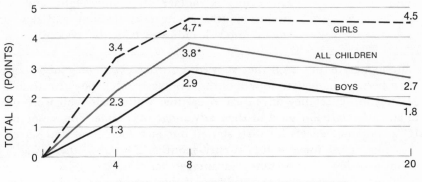

MONTHS SINCE INITIATION OF TREATMENT

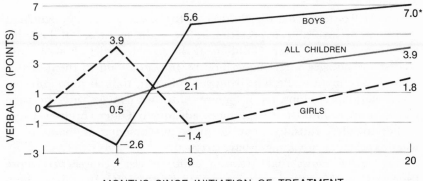

MONTHS SINCE INITIATION OF TREATMENT

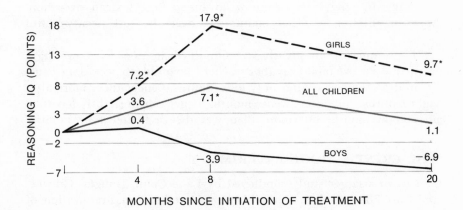

MONTHS SINCE INITIATION OF TREATMENT

**Figure 9-4**             Expectancy advantage after four, eight, and
                          twenty months among fast, medium, and slow
                          tracks (asterisk indicates $p < .10$, two-tail).

more moderate, but even they showed a greater expectancy advantage
after twenty than after four months. For verbal IQ, boys continued
gaining in expectancy advantage over time while girls who were off
to an early start lost most of their advantage over time. For reasoning
IQ, expectancy effects for girls started out at a high level and stayed
at a high level for the full twenty months. For boys, there was a
progressive loss of expectancy advantage over time.

Figure 9-4 shows that the children of the three tracks diverged over
time in their degree of expectancy advantage. Increasingly over time,
children of the medium track were most advantaged by favorable
teacher expectations, and children of the fast track were least advantaged.

Figure 9-5 shows that the children of the lower two grades benefited
greatly from favorable expectations after eight months but lost this
advantage one year later. Children of the upper grades showed more
modest advantages after eight months but maintained them better
after twenty months. Perhaps younger children, though more affected
by teacher expectations, require more continued contact with the same
teacher to maintain their expectancy advantage. Older children, while
harder to affect initially, may be more autonomous in maintaining
what expectancy advantages have accrued.

Figure 9-6 shows that Mexican children were consistently more
benefited by the experimental program in total IQ than were non-
Mexican children. For verbal IQ, this advantage of the Mexican
children increased steadily over the twenty-month retest period. For
reasoning IQ, the early excess of advantage by Mexican over non-
Mexican children was not maintained over the full twenty-month
period.

To summarize in greatly oversimplified fashion what we have
learned so far, we might say that teachers' favorable expectations benefit children somewhat after only four months, benefit them more after
eight months, and, after twenty months, benefit them slightly less than
after eight months but more than was the case after four months.


## THE CREST SCHOOL EXPERIMENT

As part of a larger study conducted by Lane Conn, Douglas Crowne,
and Carl Edwards, it was possible to undertake a quasireplication of

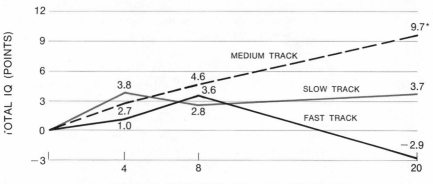

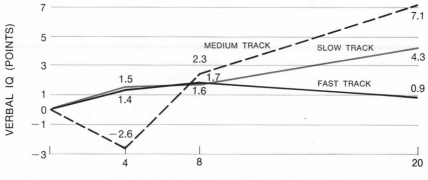

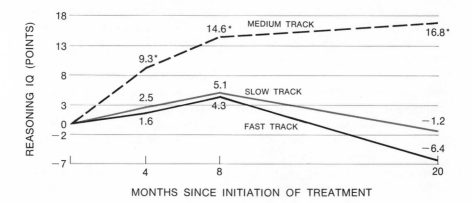

**Figure 9-5**          Expectancy advantage after four, eight and
                        twenty months among upper and lower (two)
                        grades (asterisk indicates $p < .10$, two-tail).

the Oak School experiment (Conn, Edwards, Rosenthal, and Crowne,
1967). Crest School is located some 3000 miles from Oak School and
differs considerably from it in the social-class background of its children. Oak School's children were from a lower-class community and
there was substantial minority-group representation. Crest School's
children are from a middle- or upper-middle-class community and there
is no sizeable minority group represented. There is a very substantial
difference in IQ between the children of the two schools even when
the IQ test is the one especially employed at Oak School in order
to minimize the differences attributable to disadvantagedness. The
mean pretest total IQ at Oak School was 98; at Crest School it was 109.

The general procedure was just as it was at Oak School but with
this important exception. The children were pretested (during the
academic year 1965–1966) at the beginning of the second semester.
Teachers were given the names of the "special" children very shortly
thereafter. Once again, of course, the special children's names were selected at random but the teachers were led to believe that the status of
being "special" was based on scores on the "Harvard Test of Inflected
Acquisition." That test, Flanagan's IQ test as before, actually served
only as a pretest.

We were aware that giving teachers their special expectations for
intellectual development after a full semester of contact with their
pupils would probably weaken the effect of teacher expectations. After
that much contact teachers have considerable basis for forming expectations about their pupils and they would probably be less influenced by our predictions for individual children than if they had
no basis for deciding whether our predictions were plausible or not.
That there was so little likelihood of any effect of teacher expectations
under these circumstances made it all the more interesting to see what
would happen.

At the end of the school year of 1965–1966, about four months
after the teachers had been given their expectations for the blooming
of an average of 23 percent of their pupils, the post-test was administered. For purposes of comparison with all of Oak School, the reader
may wish to refer to some of the tables and figures of this chapter,
especially, perhaps Figures 9-3 and 9-4. The Crest School results after
one semester are shown together with the one semester results from just
the fast track of Oak School. The average pretest total IQ of the fast

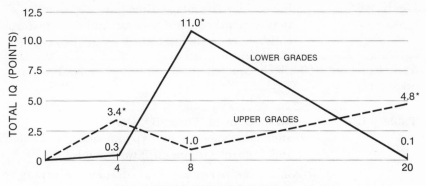

MONTHS SINCE INITIATION OF TREATMENT

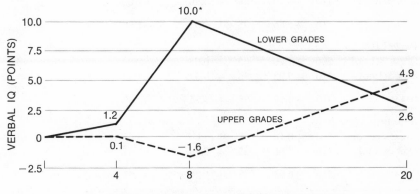

MONTHS SINCE INITIATION OF TREATMENT

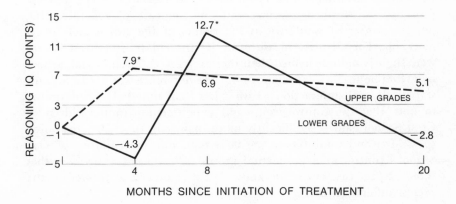

MONTHS SINCE INITIATION OF TREATMENT

**Figure 9-6**         Expectancy advantage after four, eight, and
twenty months among Mexican and non-Mexican
children (asterisk indicates $p < .10$, two-tail).

track had been 109 which equated nicely the Crest School average
pretest IQ.

**Table 9-12**         Mean Gain in Three IQ Scores
after One Semester by Experimental
and Control Groups in Two Schools

|  | CONTROL | | EXPERIMENTAL | | EXPECTANCY ADVANTAGE | |
|---|---|---|---|---|---|---|
|  | N | GAIN | N | GAIN | IQ POINTS | TWO-TAIL $p < .20$ |
| *Total IQ* | | | | | | |
| Crest School | 206 | +7.22 | 63 | + 8.98 | +1.76 | |
| Oak School | 110 | +3.38 | 35 | + 4.40 | +1.02 | |
| TOTAL | 316 | +5.88 | 98 | + 7.34 | +1.46 | |
| *Verbal IQ* | | | | | | |
| Crest School | 206 | +7.79 | 63 | +10.63 | +2.84 | |
| Oak School | 110 | +3.93 | 35 | + 5.37 | +1.44 | |
| TOTAL | 316 | +6.45 | 98 | + 8.75 | +2.30 | |
| *Reasoning IQ* | | | | | | |
| Crest School | 206 | +8.18 | 63 | +14.06 | +5.88 | .10 |
| Oak School | 110 | +4.66 | 35 | + 6.23 | +1.57 | |
| TOTAL | 316 | +6.95 | 98 | +11.26 | +4.31 | .10 |

Table 9-12 shows that after four months the children of Crest
School, like the fast-track children of Oak School, showed a slight
expectancy advantage. The magnitude of the effect is small and approaches statistical significance only in the case of reasoning IQ,
but the degree of similarity in the results of the two schools is remarkable. For all three measures of IQ the children of Crest School
were slightly more benefited than the fast-track children of Oak School
by favorable teacher expectations but the difference was not significant
statistically (all interaction $F$s were less than unity). It is interesting
to note that the control-group and experimental-group children of
Crest School gained significantly more in verbal ($p < .05$) reasoning
($p < .04$) and total IQ ($p < .008$) than did the children of Oak
School's control or experimental groups. We do not know why that
should be the case but we do know that it cannot be attributed to any
pretest differences in IQ.

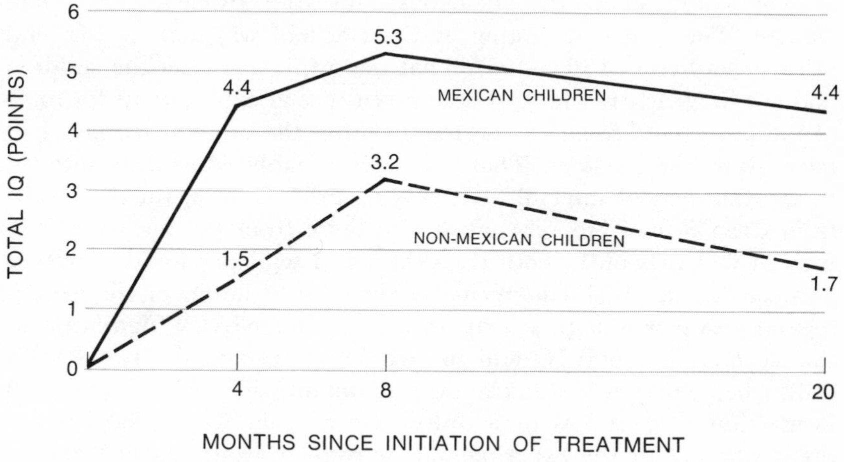
TOTAL IQ (POINTS)
6
5
4
3
2
1
0
5.3
4.4
MEXICAN CHILDREN
4.4
3.2
NON-MEXICAN CHILDREN
1.5
1.7
4
8
20
MONTHS SINCE INITIATION OF TREATMENT

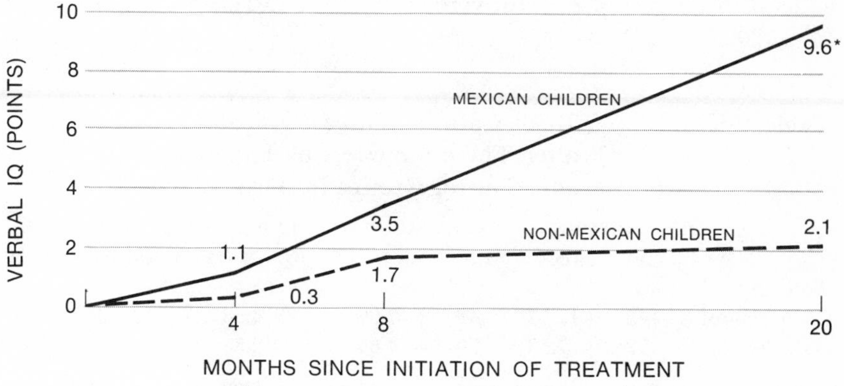
VERBAL IQ (POINTS)
10
8
6
4
2
0
9.6*
MEXICAN CHILDREN
3.5
NON-MEXICAN CHILDREN
2.1
1.1
1.7
0.3
4
8
20
MONTHS SINCE INITIATION OF TREATMENT

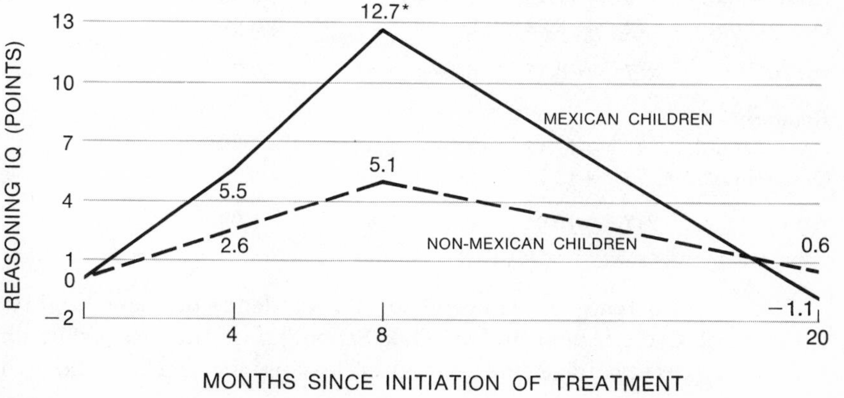
REASONING IQ (POINTS)
13
10
7
4
1
0
−2
12.7*
MEXICAN CHILDREN
5.1
5.5
2.6
NON-MEXICAN CHILDREN
0.6
−1.1
4
8
20
MONTHS SINCE INITIATION OF TREATMENT

Table 9-13 shows the analogous data after three semesters had elapsed. The follow-up testing at Crest School was done at the end of the school year of 1966–1967. That was a full year after the children had left the teachers who had been given special expectations for some of the pupils and some sixteen months after the original teachers had been given their names. That was a reasonably equivalent interval to the Oak School interval of twenty months. Once again the results from Crest School are very much like those from the fast-track children of Oak School. In both cases there is a tendency for the control-group children to gain more in IQ than the children of the experimental group. For both schools combined, this effect is significant at the .06 level for total IQ and for reasoning IQ and the two schools show the expectancy disadvantage to about the same degree (all interaction $F$s were less than unity). Once again Crest School's children, whether in the experimental or control group showed greater gains in total IQ ($p = .06$), verbal IQ ($p < .01$), and reasoning IQ ($p > .20$).

| Table 9-13 | | Mean Gain in Three IQ Scores after Three Semesters by Experimental and Control Groups in Two Schools | | | |
|---|---|---|---|---|---|
| | CONTROL | | EXPERIMENTAL | | EXPECTANCY ADVANTAGE |
| | N | GAIN | N | GAIN | IQ POINTS    TWO-TAIL $p < .20$ |
| *Total IQ* | | | | | |
| Crest School | 145 | +12.57 | 43 | + 7.99 | −4.58 | .08 |
| Oak School | 72 | + 7.53 | 20 | + 4.65 | −2.88 | |
| TOTAL | 217 | +10.90 | 63 | + 6.93 | −3.97 | .06 |
| *Verbal IQ* | | | | | |
| Crest School | 145 | +11.19 | 43 | +10.60 | −0.59 | |
| Oak School | 72 | + 3.28 | 20 | + 4.15 | +0.87 | |
| TOTAL | 217 | + 8.57 | 63 | + 8.55 | −0.02 | |
| *Reasoning IQ* | | | | | |
| Crest School | 145 | +17.18 | 43 | + 9.82 | −7.36 | .11 |
| Oak School | 72 | +13.75 | 20 | + 7.40 | −6.35 | |
| TOTAL | 217 | +16.04 | 63 | + 9.05 | −6.99 | .06 |

There is no ready explanation for the tendency of these brighter children of Crest School and of Oak School's fast track to suffer an expectancy disadvantage one year after leaving the teacher who had been given favorable expectations about their intellectual development. Perhaps they suffered a relative deprivation in moving into a classroom in which the teacher had no special expectation for their intellectual growth and this disappointment may have been reflected in their intellectual performance. Why that should happen only in the case of these brighter children and not in those of more nearly average IQ we cannot say. Figure 9-4 shows us that the more average children of Oak School's medium track, during the year spent with a new teacher who had been given no special expectation for intellectual development, showed a continued growth of the advantage of having been expected to bloom.

In any case, before we feel too sorry for these brighter children of Crest School and Oak School's fast track we should remind ourselves that their already high pretest total IQs were augmented by an average of seven more IQ points.

᪣᪣

[1] The main effect of treatments was obtained in each of the analyses of variance and the $p$ values associated with these $F$s ranged from .03 to .28 with a median two-tail $p$ of .14.

When we consider classrooms as the sampling unit ($N = 18$) we find that in twelve of the eighteen classes children of the experimental group gained more in total IQ than did children of the control group. The one-tail $p$s associated with the sign, the Wilcoxon, and $t$ tests were .12, .08, and .10, respectively. The analogous $p$ values based on differences in gains in verbal IQ were .59, .56, and .36; those based on reasoning IQ were .02, .01, and .03. Tables A-16, A-17, and A-18 show the means and standard deviations of total, verbal, and reasoning IQs after one semester in both experimental conditions within all classrooms. Tables A-19, A-20, and A-21, give the analogous data for gains in IQ from the pretest to the one-semester retest.

Preliminary results of an experiment conducted with Don Anderson suggest that teacher expectations can significantly affect students' intellectual performance in a period as short as two months. In this small experiment, the twenty-five children were mentally retarded boys with an average pretest IQ of 46. Expectancy effects were significant only for reasoning IQ and only in interaction with membership in a group receiving special remedial reading instruction in addition to participating in the school's summer day-camp program ($p \leq .03$, two-tail). Among these specially tutored boys those who were expected to bloom showed an expectancy disadvantage of nearly twelve IQ points; among the untutored boys who were participating only in the school's summer day-camp program, those who were expected to bloom showed an expectancy advantage of just over three IQ points. (For verbal

IQ, in contrast, the expectancy disadvantage of the tutored boys was less than one IQ point, while the expectancy advantage for the untutored boys was over two points.)

2 The main effect of treatments on reading scores after one semester was obtained in each of the analyses of variance, and the $p$ values associated with these $F$s ranged from .003 to .26 with a median two-tail $p$ of .008. When classrooms were considered as the sampling units, the one-tail $p$ values associated with the sign, Wilcoxon, and $t$ tests were .11, .005, and .005, respectively.

3 $F$ max was 13.99, $p < .01$. In the different school subjects, mean expectancy advantages were most variable among Mexican boys ($S^2 = .1433$) and least variable among non-Mexican girls ($S^2 = .0102$). Mexican children showed a greater variability of expectancy advantage than non-Mexican children ($F = 4.98$, $p < .05$).

4 For total IQ, the main effect of treatments was obtained in each of the analyses of variance and the associated $p$ values ranged from .09 to .26 with a median two-tail $p$ of .17.

When classrooms were considered as the sampling unit ($N = 15$) we find that in ten of the fifteen classes children of the experimental group gained more in total IQ than did children of the control group. One-tail $p$s associated with the sign, Wilcoxon, and $t$ tests were .15, .20, and .23, respectively. The analogous $p$ values based on differences in gains after two years in verbal IQ were .06, .14, and .19; those based on reasoning IQ were .50, .52, and .47. Tables A-24, A-25, and A-26 show the means and standard deviations of total, verbal, and reasoning IQs after two years in both experimental conditions within all classrooms. Tables A-27, A-28, and A-29 give the analogous data for gains in IQ from the pretesting to the two-year follow-up testing.

5 For verbal IQ, $p$s associated with the main effects of treatments ranged from .05 to .18 for the various analyses of variance and the median two-tail $p$ was .10.

6 Interaction $p$s were $< .10$ for the treatment by track analyses of variance only for total and reasoning IQs.

7 In the treatment by sex analyses of variance the interaction approached significance only for reasoning IQ ($p < .05$).

8 The treatment by tracks by sex interaction reached a $p < .10$ only for reasoning IQ but the pattern of expectancy advantages is nevertheless given for total IQ (interaction $p < .18$) and for verbal IQ ($p > .20$).

9 The treatment by grade levels by sex interaction reached a $p < .10$ only for reasoning IQ, but the pattern of expectancy advantages is given also for total IQ (interaction $p < .20$) and for verbal IQ ($p > .20$).

PART 3

# IMPLICATIONS

# 10

# Pygmalion's Medium

The purpose of this chapter will be to consider how we may best account for the results of the experiment described. Using the term "theory" in a rather loose sense, there are a number of theories that can be advanced to account for the results of the research reported.

## ACCIDENT THEORIES

The "accident" theories maintain that there really is nothing to explain. In one way or another the results of the experiment are seen simply as artifacts, and teachers' expectations are felt not to be significant determinants of pupils' intellectual growth.[1]

### Test Reliability
One interpretation of the results of the experiment suggests that because group-administered tests of intelligence are less reliable than individually administered IQ tests, therefore, the results are attributable to the unreliability of the instrument. The argument is statistically unsound, but because it is common it will be discussed.

The term "reliability" has several meanings, but the one in which we are most interested means simply that on successive occasions of testing, people's scores will maintain their relative position in the group of scores. A test would be maximally reliable if, on successive retests, each person obtained the same score with or without a constant added to each person's score. An important point here is that a test can be completely reliable even though no member of a group has obtained the same score on a retest that he obtained on the pretest. The crucial requirement for perfect reliability is that the change from pretest to retest be constant for all members of the group.

On an intuitive basis, it is difficult to see how the unreliability of a test could contribute to the statistically significantly greater gain in IQ of an experimental group of children relative to the gain in IQ of a control group of children. In fact, on a more rigorous basis, it can be shown that the less reliable a test, the more difficult it is to obtain systematic, significant differences between groups when such differences do, in fact, exist. In summary, there seems to be no way in which the "unreliability" of our group measure of intelligence could account for our results although it could, in principle, account for the results' not having been still more dramatic.[2]

**Pretest IQ Differences**
In spite of random allocation of pupils to the experimental condition, the children of the experimental group scored slightly higher in pretest IQ than did the children of the control group. This fact suggested the possibility that those children who were brighter to begin with might have been the ones who would in any case have shown the greater gains in intellectual performance. As one check on this hypothesis, the correlations were computed between children's initial pretest IQ scores and the magnitude of their gains in IQ after one year. If those who were brighter to begin with showed greater gains in IQ, the correlations would be positive. In general, the over-all correlations were negative; for total IQ $r = -.23$ ($p < .001$); for verbal IQ, $r = -.04$ (not significant); and for reasoning IQ, $r = -.48$ ($p < .001$). (A detailed presentation of these correlations is found in Table A-31 of the Appendix.) Although for the school as a whole the correlations between initial IQ and gain in IQ were somewhat less negative among the children of the experimental group than among the children of the control group, this seemed to be no simple effect. Instead, there appeared to be an interaction effect of the experimental group's difference from the control group as a function of the type of IQ considered and the track position of the children. Thus, among the children of the medium track, those who started at a higher pretest level of verbal IQ gained less in verbal IQ if they were in the control group, but gained more in verbal IQ if they were in the experimental group. No such difference was observed in the children of the medium track when the pretest level and gains in reasoning IQ were considered.

Among the children of the slow track, those who started at a higher pretest level of verbal IQ gained relatively less in verbal IQ if they were in the experimental rather than the control group. In this same track, there was no relationship for the children of the experimental group between their pretest level of reasoning IQ and their subsequent gain in reasoning IQ, whereas for the children of the control group, the relationship was very large and negative ($r = -.74$). More detailed examination of Table A-31 shows only more such hard-to-explain interactions when individual grade levels are considered. To summarize, there appears to be no way in which the relatively greater gains of the experimental children can be accounted for on the basis of the correlations between initial level of IQ and magnitude of gain in IQ.

There is a probably more satisfactory method for examining the effects on IQ gains of initial IQ levels. That method involves finding for each child in the special group a child from the control group in the same classroom with exactly the same pretest IQ.[3] That method was employed though it was not always possible to find an exact match on pretest IQ. When no exact match was found, children from the experimental group were combined into small clusters of children for whom a cluster of control-group children could be found that showed a very nearly identical pretest IQ. Table 10-1 shows the magnitudes of expectancy advantage in total IQ after one year based on special children when matched for pretest IQ and when not matched for pretest IQ. Even when there was no prematching, magnitude of expectancy advantage was not related to the excess of pretest IQ shown by children of the experimental group. Thus the two grade levels showing greatest expectancy advantages included the grade levels in which the experimental group showed the most and least pretest IQ advantages.

| Table 10-1 | | | Comparison of Expectancy Advantage in Total IQ after One Year Shown on the Basis of Matched and Unmatched Pretest IQs | | |
|---|---|---|---|---|---|
| GRADE | EXPECTANCY ADVANTAGE | | | PRETEST IQ DIFFERENCE[a] | |
| | UNMATCHED | | MATCHED | | |
| | UNMATCHED | | MATCHED | UNMATCHED | MATCHED |
| | $N^b$ | Mean | $N^c$ | Mean | Mean | Mean |
| 1 | 7 | +15.4 | 7 | +14.5 | −2.07 | 0.00 |
| 2 | 12 | + 9.5 | 6 | + 7.5 | +7.94 | +0.49 |
| 3 | 14 | − 0.0 | 13 | 0.0 | +0.93 | +0.12 |
| 4 | 12 | + 3.4 | 10 | + 1.8 | +2.21 | 0.00 |
| 5 | 9 | − 0.0 | 6 | + 2.0 | −0.35 | −0.25 |
| 6 | 11 | − 0.7 | 10 | + 0.5 | +4.67 | +0.20 |
| TOTAL | 65 | + 3.80 | 52 | + 3.48 | +2.687 | +0.096 |

[a] Excess of experimental over control-group pretest IQ.
[b] N of all special children.
[c] N of matched pairs of special and control-group children.

Matching for initial IQ level did not affect the over-all magnitude of expectancy advantage to any significant degree. In three grade levels prematching decreased the obtained expectancy advantage, while in the remaining three grade levels prematching increased the obtained expectancy advantage. These analyses suggest that the over-all sig-

nificant effects of teachers' favorable expectations cannot be attributed
to differences between the experimental- and control-group children
in pretest IQ.

## TESTING PROCESS

A very reasonable "theory" to explain the results of our experiment
proposes that children's IQs were affected only because teachers treated
the special children differently during the actual period of test taking.
A number of factors serve to weaken the plausibility of this explanation
though there is no way whatever in which it can be disproved.[4]

### Intermeasure Patterning

Children who were expected to bloom intellectually showed gains in
our nonverbal IQ test measure but also showed gains in achievement
test measures and in report-card grades. Since classroom teachers administered all tests, IQ, achievement, and classroom quizzes, the theory
is not weakened by showing measures of intellectual gain to be in
agreement with one another. It is the patterning of expectancy advantages that weakens the theory of the effects of differential testing
procedures. In general, we would not expect the somewhat subjective
process of assigning classroom grades to be more resistant to the effects
of teacher expectation than the more objectively administered tests
of intelligence and achievement. But, it will be recalled, the effects
of teacher expectation were greater in the case of standardized, objective tests of IQ and achievement than they were in the considerably
less standardized and less objective assignment of classroom report-
card grades.

### Intrameasure Patterning

It was only during the basic year of the experiment that the retests had
been administered by the classroom teachers who had been given
special expectations about the intellectual development of some of their
pupils. At the end of that year most of the expectancy advantage had
been found to occur in the reasoning rather than the verbal subtest
of our IQ measure. But it was the verbal subtest that permitted more
teacher-pupil interaction to occur. The verbal items are untimed and
are read aloud to the children, and the teacher is required to make
frequent trips up and down the aisles to see that the children are
following directions properly. Reasoning items, on the other hand, are
timed and self-administered. There seems, then, to be less opportunity

for differential teacher-pupil interaction on that subtest which showed the greater effects of teacher expectation after one year.

To our knowledge, there is only one experiment to show that the expectation of the examiner can affect the IQ scores earned by children (Larrabee and Kleinsasser, 1967). In their study, however, only the verbal subtest scores of the WISC were affected significantly by the expectation of the examiner. These subtests all require subjects to interact individually and verbally with the examiner. On the performance subtests, which also require individual interaction but much less verbal interaction, there were no significant effects of examiner expectation. The results of that study suggest that if differential teacher behavior during the course of retesting had occurred, the effects of teacher expectations should have shown themselves more on the verbal than on the reasoning IQ subtest.

### Blind Retesting

So that it could be determined whether expectancy advantages were dependent on the teachers' behavior during the administration of the post-tests, three classrooms were retested by a "blind" examiner. A few weeks after the one-year post-test had been administered, a school administrator, not attached to Oak School, retested in three classrooms without knowing which of the children were in the experimental group. The three classrooms for this retest were chosen to include (1) that classroom showing the least expectancy advantage of any class after the four-month retest, (2) that classroom in the lower three grades showing the greatest expectancy advantage after the four-month retest, and (3) that classroom in the upper three grades showing the greatest expectancy advantage after the four-month retest. In one of these classrooms only the verbal IQ post-test had been administered by the classroom teacher so that to maintain comparability only the verbal IQs were computed when the testing was by the blind examiner.

Table 10-2 shows the results of the testing by the three classroom teachers and by the blind examiner for exactly the same children. The results of the retesting by the blind examiner were very close to those obtained a few weeks earlier by the classroom teachers in both total IQ and verbal IQ. In reasoning IQ, however, the blind examiner obtained an expectancy advantage nine points greater (NS) than that obtained by the three classroom teachers. It does not seem that a teacher's differential behavior toward children for whom greater expectations are held is necessary to obtain expectancy advantages as measured by IQ tests.

**Table 10-2**            Post-test IQs after One Year
                          Obtained by Classroom Teachers and
                          Blind Examiner in Three Classrooms

|  | CLASSROOM TEACHERS | | | | |
|  | CONTROL | | EXPERIMENTAL | | DIFFERENCE |
|  | N | IQ | N | IQ |  |
| Total IQ | 48 | 98.0 | 4 | 109.8 | +11.8 |
| Verbal IQ | 67 | 104.5 | 7 | 102.9 | − 1.6 |
| Reasoning IQ | 48 | 92.8 | 4 | 106.0 | +13.2 |

|  | BLIND EXAMINER | | | | |
|  | CONTROL | | EXPERIMENTAL | | DIFFERENCE |
|  | N | IQ | N | IQ |  |
| Total IQ | 48 | 100.1 | 4 | 113.3 | +13.2 |
| Verbal IQ | 67 | 105.9 | 7 | 103.0 | − 2.9 |
| Reasoning IQ | 48 | 96.9 | 4 | 119.3 | +22.4 |

**Accuracy of Recall**

Though by itself not a strong source of evidence bearing on the tenability of testing process theories of the mediation of expectancy advantages, it is relevant to report the results of postexperimental interviews with the classroom teachers. In June of 1966, two years after the administration of the IQ pretest, and several weeks after the follow-up IQ testing, all teachers were interviewed individually after the actual nature of the experiment had been explained to all teachers in a group meeting. There were sixteen teachers to be interviewed, two teachers of the original eighteen having left the school after the basic year of the experiment.

Each teacher was asked informally her reaction to the original list of "magic" children she had been given nearly two years earlier. These reactions were startling. While all teachers recalled glancing at their lists, most felt they paid little or no attention to them. Many teachers threw their lists away after glancing at them. Many of the teachers felt that there were so many memos coming from the office that first week of school that the list of names was just another list and got no special attention. (Had we known how casually our list of names would be treated, we might have thought twice about the likelihood of obtaining any IQ gains as a function of teachers' expectations.)

Part of the interview involved a somewhat more formal assessment of teachers' recollections of which of their children had, the year before, been in the special group. The sixteen teachers recalled the names of a total of eighteen of the seventy-two children who had originally been designated as special. Another eighteen names were recalled as having been on the original list when, in fact, they had been control-group children. Those teachers who recalled more of the names of the special children assigned to their class might have been expected to show greater expectancy effects. Such was not the case; the correlation between expectancy advantage per classroom with the number of names accurately recalled as special children was —.27 (NS). The correlation between (1) expectancy advantage per classroom and (2) the number of accurately recalled names divided by the sum of accurately and inaccurately recalled names was +.09 (NS). The worst recall occurred among teachers of the second-grade children. Of the twelve children originally alleged to be potential spurters who remained in the school for the entire year of the experiment, not a single one was recalled as a potential spurter by any second-grade teacher. Yet, it will be recalled, effects of teachers' expectations were prominent in the second grade.

The recall of names is a more demanding test of memory than the ability to recognize names. A test of recognition was also included in the interviews held. Each teacher was presented with a list of four names, two boys and two girls, and asked to indicate which of the four children had been designated as her special children at the beginning of the preceding academic year. These lists of four names were made up of two special children, one boy and one girl, and two control-group children, one boy and one girl. The names of the special children were drawn at random but the names of the control-group children were selected so that their pretest IQs would be equal to or nearly equal to the pretest IQs of the special children. A teacher's score on the recognition test was the number of magic children identified minus the number of control-group children incorrectly identified as special. Scores, then, could range from +2 to —2. The mean recognition score was only +0.44 (greater than zero at $p < .04$, one-tail, $t = 1.96$). Just as was the case for the recall test, teachers' recognition test scores were not significantly related to the magnitude of expectancy advantage their special children had enjoyed ($r = +.21$, NS).

## The Curve of Blooming

We should not be too surprised that there was no relationship between magnitude of expectancy effects and teachers' recollection of which children were in the special group. If we expected teachers with better recall of children's experimental group status to show greater expectancy effects we might also have thought that expectancy advantages would be greater earlier in the academic year of the basic experiment since recall is known to decay over time. Yet, we noted in the last chapter that expectancy effects increased rather than decreased during the course of the basic year of the experiment.

The final point in the curve of blooming came some two years after the administration of the IQ pretest. This follow-up testing was again conducted by the classroom teacher, but this classroom teacher had not been given any special expectation about the performance of any of her pupils. If the expectancy advantages obtained during the first year of the experiment had been due only to the teacher's differential treatment of special- and control-group children during the testing process we would have expected no expectancy advantage at all at the end of the follow-up year. But, as we saw in the last chapter, while there was some decrease in expectancy advantage after the follow-up year, the final magnitude of expectancy advantage was greater than that obtained after one semester by the teachers who had been given the expectations for some of the children's intellectual growth.

## WAS PETER ROBBED?

It seemed reasonable to think that the children for whom unusual intellectual growth had been predicted would be more attended to by their teachers. If teachers were more attentive to the children earmarked for growth, we might expect that teachers might be robbing Peter to see Paul grow. With a finite amount of time to spend with each child, if a teacher gave more time to the children of the experimental group she would have less time to spend with the children of the control group. If the teacher's spending more time with a child led to greater gains, we could test the "robbing Peter" hypothesis by comparing the gains made by children of the experimental group with gains made by children of the control group in each class. The robbing-Peter hypothesis predicts a negative correlation. The greater the gains made by the children of the experimental group (with the implication of more time spent on them) the less should be the gains made by the children of the control group (with the implication of less time spent on them). In fact, however, the correlation was positive, large, and statistically significant ($r = +.58$, $p = .02$, two-tail). The greater the gain made by the children of whom gain was expected, the greater the gain made in the same classroom by the children from whom no special gain was expected.[5] This evidence, though indirect, suggests that perhaps Peter was not robbed.

Another indirect check on the robbing-Peter theory was possible.

On intuitive grounds it seemed that where there were fewer Peters (forgetting about Pauls for the moment) there would be more time for each one. In addition, where there were fewer Peters it should be easier to keep in mind which of the children had been earmarked for intellectual growth. Indirect support for the theory would come from a finding that greater expectancy advantages occurred in those class- rooms in which there were fewer "magic" children. Although it was not significant statistically, such a relationship was in fact found. The correlation between number of special children per classroom and the average expectancy advantage of that classroom was found to be —.36. It is of interest to note that this relationship could not be attributed to better recall or recognition of the names of the special children by teachers who had fewer Peters to keep in mind. The cor- relation of the number of special children designated for each class with the number of such children accurately recalled after the fol- low-up test was only +.18, and with scores on the recognition test it was only —.11.

The indirect evidence bearing on the robbing-Peter theory, then, is a little equivocal. Where Peter gains more, Paul also does. But where there are fewer Peters each one does a little better than where there are more Peters, though this finding was at most a tendency. More direct evidence bearing on the theory was available, however.

Some ten months after the one-year post-test had been administered, each of the teachers was asked to estimate how much time, relatively, she had devoted to each of four children. All four of these children had been in her classroom the preceding academic year, the year of the basic experiment. Two children had been in the control group and two had been in the experimental group. There was one boy and one girl in each of these two subgroups. The boys of each group were matched on their pretest IQ as were the girls. The mean difference in IQ was less than one-half point in favor of the children of the experimental group ($t = .71$). The specific question asked of the teacher was: given a unit of time available to spend on these four children (100 percent), how much of that unit was spent with each child? For each matched pair of boys and girls the percentage of time allocated to the control-group child was subtracted from the percentage of time allo- cated to the experimental-group child. A positive difference score, then, meant that the experimental-group child was given more time by the teacher according to her own assessment. Table 10-3 shows the mean and median difference scores for the entire school, for boys and girls, for each of the three tracks, and for each of the six grades. None of the obtained mean differences was significantly different from

zero. In fact, there was a slight tendency for the children of the experimental group to be given less time than the children of the control
group ($t < .66$).

| Table 10-3 | Differences in Time Spent with Children of the Experimental and Control Groups | | |
| --- | --- | --- | --- |
| | MEAN DIFFERENCE | MEDIAN DIFFERENCE | $N$ OF PAIRS[a] |
| *Children* | | | |
| All children | − 2.6% | 0.0% | 31 |
| Boys | + 0.3% | + 5.0% | 15 |
| Girls | − 5.3% | 0.0% | 16 |
| *Track* | | | |
| Fast track | − 2.4% | 0.0% | 12 |
| Medium track | − 5.0% | 0.0% | 8 |
| Slow track | − 1.1% | 0.0% | 11 |
| *Grade* | | | |
| Grade 1 | + 5.0% | 0.0% | 6 |
| Grade 2 | − 8.8% | 0.0% | 5 |
| Grade 3 | +10.0% | +10.0% | 4 |
| Grade 4 | − 3.3% | 0.0% | 6 |
| Grade 5 | − 2.5% | − 2.5% | 4 |
| Grade 6 | −12.8% | 0.0% | 6 |

[a] No data were available from the two teachers who had left the school.

Although the special children were not favored with a greater over-
all investment of teacher time, it was still possible that among the
special children those who were given more teacher time would show
greater expectancy advantages during the year of the basic experiment.
Table 10-4 shows the correlations between the relative time different
teachers invested in their special boys and girls and the mean expectancy advantage found in their classrooms. Considering total IQ there
was no relationship between the amount of time teachers spent with
the special children and the magnitude of expectancy advantage obtained. The rest of Table 10-4 shows that (1) when more time was
spent with the special boys there were greater expectancy advantages in
reasoning IQ relative to verbal IQ, and (2) when more time was spent
with the special girls there were greater expectancy advantages in verbal
IQ relative to reasoning IQ. In view of the reservations we must make
about the accuracy of teachers' recall of time spent with various children, these findings can serve at most as a basis for speculation. Per-

haps teachers feel that time spent with boys should go into helping them with more nonverbal skills while time spent with girls should go into helping them with more verbal skills so that boys and girls might each improve in those areas generally regarded as the culturally proper areas of strength. To weaken this speculation somewhat we should recall, however, that in Oak School the boys excelled in pretest verbal IQ while the girls excelled in pretest reasoning IQ.

| Table 10-4 | Correlations between Expectancy Advantages and Time Spent with Special Children ($N = 16$ for all $rs$) | | | |
|---|---|---|---|---|
| PUPIL SEX | MEASURE OF EXPECTANCY ADVANTAGE | | | |
| | TOTAL IQ | VERBAL IQ | REASONING IQ | VERBAL MINUS REASONING IQ |
| Boys | −.01 | −.16 | +.55[b] | −.41 } $p$ of difference |
| Girls | +.35 | +.36 | −.29 | +.43[a] } = .02, two-tail |

[a] $p = .10$, two-tail.
[b] $p < .04$, two-tail.

Despite the fact that certain expectancy advantages were related to teachers' recollections of their relative time investments in the special children, we should not lose sight of the fact that over-all, no more time seemed to be spent on the special- than on the control-group children. That was a surprising finding which bears some discussion.

The pattern of the expectancy advantage shown by the special children during the basic year of the experiment serves to make the finding a little less surprising. If, for example, teachers had talked more to the special children we might have expected greater gains in verbal IQ, but, we recall, the greater gains were found not in verbal but in reasoning IQ. It may be, of course, that the teachers were inaccurate in their estimates of time spent with each of the children. Possibly direct observation of the teacher-pupil interactions would have given different results, but that method was not possible in the present study. Even direct observation by judges who could agree with one another might not have revealed a difference in the amounts of teacher time invested in each of the two groups of children. It seems plausible to think that it was not a difference in amount of time spent with the children of the two groups which led to the difference in their rates of intellectual development. It may have been more a matter of the type of interaction which took place between the teachers and their pupils which served as the determinant of the expected intellectual gains.

## INTERACTION QUALITY

Under the interaction quality theory we must ask how teachers may have behaved differently toward those special children who were expected to bloom intellectually. So far there is only a poor beginning to the development of a psychology of unintentional influence or communication and, so far, none of it is based on a study of teachers subtly influencing the intellectual behavior of their pupils.

Perhaps hints as to where to look can come from research on the unintentional influence of behavioral researchers on their subjects. When experimenters had believed their animal subjects to be brighter, the animals became brighter and they were seen by their experimenters as brighter and as better "adjusted," just as pupils expected to become brighter became brighter and were seen by their teachers as brighter and better adjusted. The experimenters working with animal subjects felt they treated their subjects in a more pleasant, friendly, enthusiastic fashion when they expected superior performance from them. Perhaps teachers also treated their pupils in a more pleasant, friendly, and enthusiastic fashion when they had more favorable expectations for their intellectual development.

It may not be too far-fetched to seek our clues to covert communication between teacher and pupil from clues to covert communication between experimenter and animal subject. That is suggested by data reported earlier (Chapter 4) in which examiners who believed their human subjects to be brighter treated them in a more friendly, likeable, interested, expressive, and encouraging manner. In that particular experiment (Wartenberg-Ekren, 1962) such favorable treatment during the administration of a nonverbal IQ test did not result in an increase in IQ, but one wonders whether such favorable treatment administered day after day for many months might not have resulted in improved performance. Indeed, there are a number of studies to show that warmer behavior on the part of the examiner often leads to intellectually more competent behavior on the part of the subject even when examiner and subject meet and interact only once (Rosenthal, 1966).

There may be another hint available to us from research on experimenters' expectations as a determinant of the learning ability of animal subjects. Animals believed by their experimenters to be brighter were watched more intently by their experimenters. More careful observation of an organism's behavior permits (1) a more rapid judgment of the correctness of its behavior and (2) the more rapid rewarding of correct or desired behavior. The experimenter who observes more carefully may, therefore, be the more effective teacher. In the Oak School Experiment the special children were called to the teachers' attention and it seems reasonable to think that they, therefore, attended more closely to the behavior of these children. Correct responding on the part of these children may have been more rapidly reinforced by teachers because they were watching more closely and expecting to see more correct responses to be reinforced. More rapid reinforcement may have led to greater learning.

In addition to the increased rapidity of reinforcement, teachers' expectations for superior performance may have led to an increase in the appropriateness of reinforcement. In most classrooms some proportion of pupils' responses are discursive and regarded as "on the wrong track" by the teacher when, in fact, the track is right but indirect. Given an expectation that a pupil will be getting brighter, his teacher may permit greater opportunity for discursive reflective responses to show themselves to be correct. If that were the case, there would be more occasions for the appropriate reinforcement of correct responses. The "special" pupil may, therefore, be in a better position to learn not only when he is correct but also that he will be rewarded for inputs into the intellectual give and take of the classroom. By giving more opportunity and time for the special children to show the competence that is expected of them, a more reflective cognitive style may have been encouraged (Kagan, 1966). That such changes in cognitive style can be brought about within just one school year by classroom teachers has been clearly shown by Yando and Kagan (1966). The nature of the nonverbal IQ test employed in the Oak School Experiment was such that a more reflective attitude on the part of the special children might well have contributed to their advantage over the other children in IQ gains.

Chapter 3 described some findings relevant to the unintentional communication of interpersonal expectations. Those experimenters who were seen to be of higher status, who behaved in a more professional and more competent manner, and who were more likeable and more relaxed, were more successful in exerting unintentional influence upon their subjects. Perhaps, when the relevant experiments are carried out they will show that successful unintentional communication in the classroom also depends on certain characteristics of the communicator. Chapter 3 also reported that the communication of interpersonal expectations could occur in the auditory channel alone (that is, by tone of voice), but that visual channel cues might also be effective. Both channels of influence require investigation in the class-room and, especially in the lower grades, physical contact should be added as an additional channel requiring investigation.

There is some evidence from the Crest School Experiment to suggest that successful unintentional communication in the classroom may also depend heavily on certain characteristics of the children themselves (Conn, Edwards, Rosenthal, and Crowne, 1967). A crude measure was developed to determine how well the emotional component of an adult female's voice could be judged by each of the children. Those children who were better able to judge the tone of voice of an adult female speaker profited significantly more ($p < .04$) from favorable teacher expectations than did those children who were less successful judges of tone of voice. Such evidence serves as a basis for speculating that much of the unintentional communication of interpersonal expectations may occur through the auditory channel.

The speculative nature of the interaction processes suggested to account for teachers' expectancy effects must be emphasized. We do not know how a teacher's expectation for a pupil's intellectual growth is communicated to the pupil. Indeed, very little is known of the interaction processes by which any teacher influences any pupil whether that influence be intentional or unintentional, overt or covert, helpful or harmful (Biddle, 1964; K. B. Clark, 1963). One reason for this ignorance is that, although much has been written about teacher influence, very few investigators have systematically observed the processes by which teachers influence (Biddle, 1964; Biddle and Adams, 1967).

~§

[1] The analyses to be presented here are internal to the Oak School Experiment. When we consider evidence external to this experiment the "accident" theories become implausible. The three replications briefly mentioned earlier all showed significant effects of teacher expectations and all showed them to be most significant in the case of reasoning IQ. Of the total of four experiments, two showed the predicted main effect of teacher expectancy but two showed the effect of teachers' expectancy only in interaction with either characteristics of the pupils or situational variables. While the results of all four studies taken together make it difficult to doubt the effectiveness of changes in teachers' expectations they also serve to emphasize the probable complexity of the operation of teacher expectancy effects. Such complexity, which should not surprise us in any area of the behavioral sciences, has been

demonstrated in a related research area investigating the effects on the behavior of research subjects of the expectation of the experimenter (Rosenthal, 1966).

[2] Table A-30 of the Appendix shows the retest reliabilities for total, verbal, and reasoning IQ from the pretest to the post-test one year later. Reliabilities are tabulated separately for experimental and control groups for each grade, for each track, and for all of Oak School. The over-all mean reliability of the verbal and total IQs was +.75, while the over-all reliability of the reasoning IQ was +.49. The average reliability of the IQ scores was not different among the experimental and the control groups, suggesting that among children of the experimental group, where intellectual gains did occur, the gains did not disturb the ranking of the children within their own experimental condition.

[3] We thank Jerome Kagan for suggesting this analysis.

[4] There is an experiment by Theye and Wright (1967) that shows how difficult it is to increase IQ scores even by intentional coaching and even in the protracted face-to-face relationship of an individually administered test of intelligence.

[5] When the analogous rank correlations were computed separately within each grade level the median rho was found to be +.75. We thank N. L. Gage for suggesting this within-grade analysis.

# 11

# Some
# Methodological
# Considerations

We have already examined briefly the proposition that, in the healing professions, newer treatments seem more effective than older treatments (Chapter 2). "Treat as many patients as possible with the new drugs," suggests the wise healer, "while they still have the power to heal" (Shapiro, 1960, p. 114). Such statements are recognitions of the power of nonspecific factors in the application of healing skills, and may be loosely referred to as "placebo effects." The behavioral scientist or social engineer might rephrase the old physician's adage. "Solve as many social problems as possible with the new programs of social change while they still have the power to change." In the behavioral sciences, we refer not to "placebo effects" but to "Hawthorne effects."

## HAWTHORNE EFFECTS

In the mid-1920s the Hawthorne Works of the Western Electric Company, located in the Chicago area, was the largest supply unit for the telephone companies of the Bell System. The Hawthorne Works was the scene of a very intensive series of experiments investigating the effects of a variety of working conditions on workers' performance (Roethlisberger and Dickson, 1939).

One variable to receive early attention was the level of illumination under which work was conducted. In the first study of the effects of illumination, it was learned that as illumination level was changed so was the efficiency of production; but efficiency seemed as much related to the fact of change as to the direction of changes in lighting. In this first study the effects of changes were compared only to the workers' pre-experimental level of efficiency so that it seemed desirable to institute a "no-change" control group for the second study.

In the second study the control group was given a fairly constant level of illumination ranging from sixteen to twenty-eight foot-candles. The experimental group worked under three different conditions of illumination. One of these was at about the same level as the control group, a second was at about twice the level of the control group, and the third was at about three times the level of the control group. Compared to the pretest level of efficiency, both the experimental and control groups achieved remarkable and virtually identical gains in efficiency of production.

In a third experiment two groups were again employed. The control group was given a constant illumination level of ten foot-candles. The experimental group was given ten foot-candles to begin with, but that level was systematically decreased one foot-candle at a time until a level of three foot-candles was reached. Results of this experiment showed that up to the final level of three foot-candles, both the experimental and the control groups showed slowly and steadily increasing levels of efficiency. That was not the sort of finding an illumination engineer would have predicted.

The final and most dramatic study employed only two workers. The illumination level was reduced to 0.06 foot-candle, the amount of light obtained from moonlight. Efficiency remained unimpaired, eyestrain was denied, and the advantages of avoiding the glare of bright lights were pointed out by the workers.

After this series of studies, conducted by C. E. Snow, it seemed clear that the introduction of any change might lead to behavioral effects greater than the effects that might be predicted from a knowledge of the specific effects of any particular manipulation of the workers' environment. In order to verify this conclusion further, an additional series of illumination changes was introduced. On each of a series of days a new and brighter light bulb was installed and the workers reported a preference for each new higher level of illumination.

Then, Snow introduced what must have been one of the earliest forms of "placebo control." As before, an electrician installed new light bulbs, but this time they were not brighter bulbs. The workers, however, responded to these light bulb changes just as they had responded to actual increases in illumination. Level of illumination was then decreased day by day, a series of changes which the workers did not like so well. They continued to like it less well even when the decrease was a pseudodecrease made plausible by the electrician's changing the light bulb (but for one of just the same brightness). In this series of illumination changes, though the workers' preference for higher levels or pseudohigher levels was clear, the level of productivity did not change appreciably.

Though the research from which Hawthorne effects take their name was conducted four decades ago, the implications for research in medicine (Honigfeld, 1964) and in industry (Rosen and Sales, 1966) are currently receiving close attention.

## HAWTHORNE, PLACEBO, AND EXPECTANCY EFFECTS

For all the popularity of the concept, Hawthorne effects are only poorly understood. It is not only that we do not know how these effects operate but also that we do not know quite what we mean when we use the term. Sometimes we use it to mean that in any program of intervention (for example, medical, industrial, or educational) there are variables helping to bring about changes that were not originally considered as effective agents of change. Sometimes when we use the term we mean it to emphasize the introduction of anything new that in itself leads to changes following the institution of a treatment or change procedure. Since many programs of medical, industrial, or educational change arise in a context of scientific inquiry, the term Hawthorne (or placebo) effects is sometimes used to refer to the effects of scientific prestige suggestion that may serve to increase the effectiveness of many programs of planned change or treatment.

One concept that may underlie the various usages of the term is the concept of expectancy. When programs of change or treatment are instituted, expectations for their effectiveness are very likely to be involved, and they seem to be of two kinds. First, there is the expectation of those whose behavior or well-being is to be affected by the institution of the new program. These are the workers, the patients, the pupils, the research subjects, who, by knowing that a new procedure is being tried out, "know" that the procedure may well have some effect on them, else why would it be worth anyone's time or effort to try it out? Secondly, there is the expectation of those who institute the program of change or treatment. This expectation can affect the response of those whose behavior is under investigation, and it is the expectation in which we have been most interested in this book. It is a more interpersonal type of expectancy effect; not the effect of one person's expectation of his own behavior on that behavior, but the effect of one person's expectation for another person's behavior on that other person's behavior.

The results of the Oak School Experiment suggest that the interpersonal expectancy effect can operate in a "real-life" educational setting. Those children from whom their teachers were led to expect greater intellectual gains showed greater intellectual gains than did the children for whom teachers were given no special expectations. In addition to this specific effect of interpersonal expectation, however, there may also have been a more general Hawthorne-like effect in operation throughout all of Oak School. The basis for this possibility is the large gain in IQ during the basic year of the experiment shown by the children of the control group (see Table 7-1). For comparison purposes we cite the results of a "total-push" educational program. K. B. Clark (1963) reported that after three years a ten-point IQ gain was shown by 38 percent of the children. Table 7-2 shows that among first and second graders of our control group 49 percent showed a ten-point IQ gain after only one year, and these two grades were not those to show the greatest gains among the control-group children. Clark reported further that 12 percent of the children showed a twenty-point IQ gain. Among the first and second graders of our control group 19 percent gained twenty or more IQ points. The gains in IQ of our control-group children appear to be large enough to have been the result of some program of educational innovation.

The gains in IQ of our control-group children could have been due solely to the effects of practice since all children were tested three times with the same form of the IQ test employed. In the Oak School Experiment, there was unfortunately no way to rule out the effects of practice. In order to do so it would have been necessary to select a large number of schools in some of which no experimental manipulation would have been introduced. These control schools might, in addition, have received varying numbers of testings ranging from all three testings to post-test only.

Although we cannot rule out the effects of test-taking practice, there are some considerations that weaken the adequacy of that interpretation of the dramatic IQ gains of the control-group children. One such consideration is the fact that on a retest one year later a child must be able to perform considerably better than he did originally in order only to hold his own in terms of IQ score. The older a child, the better he must perform to earn a given IQ score.

A stronger consideration serving to weaken the adequacy of the practice-effect interpretation comes also from the fact that over time a child must perform much better in order only to maintain the same IQ level. Because of this, it seems likely that a retest administered after only a short interval would lead to the greatest practice effect. The child has an opportunity to practice items on the pretest, and if the retest comes soon thereafter, the child can increase his IQ score by performing only a little better than on the pretest. His chronological age has not increased enough to demand a great increase in performance for him to maintain his IQ level. Just a brief interval retest had been employed when, at the end of the basic year of the experiment, three classrooms were retested just a few weeks after the entire school had taken the post-test. This brief interval retest had been administered by a school administrator, and Table 10-2 shows that the control group children gained only two IQ points that might be attributed to practice effects.

These considerations suggest the possibility that in part, at least, the gains in IQ of the control group may have been due to the operation of Hawthorne effects. Just what elements in the study of Oak School might have been responsible we cannot say. Perhaps the very fact that university researchers, supported by federal funds, were so interested in Oak School may have elevated the already good level of morale and of teaching technique shown by the teachers of Oak School.

## HAWTHORNE, PLACEBO, AND EXPECTANCY CONTROLS

Whether the context be medical, industrial, or educational when the effects of an innovation are to be assessed, it is not enough to show that patients, workers, or pupils are better off after the innovation's introduction than before it. It is always possible that, had the innovation not been introduced, the benefits to patients, workers, and pupils would have been greater still. At the very least, we want to know whether the introduction of the new procedure is better than its omission, and that calls for a control condition in which the new procedure is not introduced. But in the light of what we have learned about Hawthorne and placebo effects, such a "no-treatment" control group may not be sufficient.

### Hawthorne Controls
When a new treatment procedure is under consideration, there are usually theoretical reasons for expecting it to be effective in a fairly specific way. If the new treatment procedure turns out to be better than the no-treatment procedure, we cannot attribute its success to the theoretically postulated specific effects of the new treatment. Confounded with these specific effects there are the nonspecific placebo or Hawthorne effects. These nonspecific effects can be evaluated by means of "Hawthorne controls."

Unlike the no-treatment controls, Hawthorne controls do require the introduction of a new procedure, but one which cannot be thought to have the specific effects of the new treatment procedure whose effectiveness we want to evaluate. If our new procedure is more effective than the Hawthorne-control procedure we can have a little more confidence that our innovation is responsible for something more than Hawthorne or placebo effects. If a no-treatment control has been employed as well as a Hawthorne control we can assess how much of the over-all improvement associated with the new procedure is attributable to Hawthorne effects.

| Table 11-1 | Hypothetical Results of a Hawthorne-Controlled Experiment | |
|---|---|---|
| GROUPS | | PERCENTAGE BENEFITING |
| 1. No-treatment control | | 20% |
| 2. Hawthorne control | | 30% |
| 3. Experimental procedure | | 40% |

Table 11-1 shows the results of an hypothetical experiment in which children (or classrooms or schools) have been assigned at random to one of three conditions or groups. Group 1 is the no-treatment control group; no changes have been introduced into the curriculum. Group 2 is the Hawthorne-control group; changes have been introduced into the curriculum that do not include the specific changes that are hypothesized to affect the children's learning. Group 3 is the experimental-procedure group that involves changes specifically hypothesized to affect the children's learning. For each group the hypothetical percentage of children showing a clear gain in learning ability is given.

Children of the experimental group were twice as likely to show benefits at the end of the experiment as were children of the no-treatment control group. However, half the advantage of the experimental-group children could be attributed to the effects of a pseudo-experimental procedure or to Hawthorne effects.

Whenever it is practical to do so, and it often is, it seems wisest to employ both the no-treatment and the Hawthorne-control groups. If, for logistic reasons, only one control group can be employed, the Hawthorne control is preferable if we wish to make inferences about specific effects of innovations. The use of only the no-treatment control is preferable, however, if we want only to compare the new procedure to the old and are willing to leave Hawthorne and specific procedural effects confounded.

In the educational context the more basic difficulty seems to have been that most educational innovations are not systematically evaluated at all (Nichols, 1966) much less are they evaluated with methodological rigor (Dyer, 1965). There are indications, however, that increasing attention is being given not only to the careful assessment of educational innovations, but also to the important role of Hawthorne effects in increasing the apparent effectiveness of the specific variables postulated to be useful in bringing about beneficial changes (Bruner, 1965; Cook, 1966; Entwisle, 1961; Riessman, 1962).

## Expectancy Controls

In educational change research, the agent of change is often the teacher, and Hawthorne effects may operate directly upon the children and/or indirectly by way of affecting the teacher. While there is much we do not yet know about various components of educational Hawthorne effects, one such component may well be the expectation of the teacher. However the teacher's expectation may affect her pupils, the results of the research described in this book suggest that her expectations can have a major effect on the intellectual performance of her pupils.

There are elaborate and expensive ways of changing teachers' expectancies, but the method employed in our research was quite simple and quite inexpensive. If such a simple and direct method is effective, then a more elaborate method employing curriculum changes of major proportion may be more effective. Of that we cannot be sure, but it does seem necessary to suggest that future studies of educational innovation introduce controls not only for the nonspecific Hawthorne effect but also for the more specific effect of teacher expectations.

When educational innovations are introduced into operating educational systems, it seems very likely that the administrators whose permission is required and the teachers whose cooperation is required will expect the innovation to be effective. If they did not, they would be unlikely to give the required permission and cooperation. The experimental innovation, then, will likely be confounded with favorable expectations regarding their efficacy.

When educational innovations are introduced into newly created educational systems with specially selected and specially trained teachers and administrators, the problems are similar. Those teachers and those administrators who elect to go and are selected to serve are likely to have expectations favorable to the efficacy of the new program. In this situation, as that in which changes are introduced into pre-existing systems, teachers' and administrators' expectations are likely to be confounded with the educational innovations. All this argues for the systematic employment of the "expectancy control group" (Rosenthal, 1966).

In expectancy-control designs applied to a simple experiment in educational innovation in which only an experimental and control group are employed, the experiment is subdivided into a total of four conditions, two of them involving the experimental treatment and two of them involving the control "treatment." In one experimental-treatment subcondition, teachers are given reason to believe that the experimental innovation will be successful. In the other experimental subcondition teachers are led to believe that the treatment is "only a control condition." In one of the control-group subconditions, teachers are led to believe that their condition is "only a control condition" which, in fact, it is. In the other control-group subcondition, teachers are given reason to believe that the "treatment" is actually an experimental innovation which should give good results.

The data from such an expectancy controlled experiment can be analyzed by a simple two-way analysis of variance. Such an analysis permits us to make inferences about the magnitudes of the effects of the educational innovation, the teachers' expectations, and the interaction between these two sources of variance. There may be experiments in which the magnitude of the effects of the innovation will be large relative to the effects of the teachers' expectations. But there may also be experiments in which the effects of teachers' expectations turn out to be more important sources of variation than the educational innovation under investigation. Without the use of expectancy-control groups, however, it is impossible to tell whether the results of experiments in educational practices are due to the practices themselves or to the correlated expectations of the teachers who are to try out the educational reforms.

### Combined Controls

Because it is not known to what extent Hawthorne effects in educational procedures are associated with or due to teacher-expectation effects, it may be desirable to employ both Hawthorne and expectancy controls. Table 11-2 shows the experimental design employing both kinds of controls. All teachers in the three conditions in the cells A, C, E have been led to expect that there would be educational benefits. All the teachers in the cells B, D, F have been led to expect that there would be no special educational benefits. The three groups found within each of the two conditions of teacher expectation are those that were described earlier and shown in Table 11-1.

In the most typical educational experiment in which a control group is employed it is likely to be a no-treatment control rather than a Hawthorne control. Teachers involved in the no-treatment control condition ordinarily do not have any expectation of benefit to their pupils. That situation is the case of cell B. Teachers involved in an experimental program are likely to expect some benefit for their pupils. That situation is depicted in cell E. If, in an educational experiment, children in cell E benefit more than those in cell B, we cannot say whether the advantage comes from the new procedure itself, the fact of any novelty introduced into the situation, or the favorable expectations of the teacher. To disentangle these three possibilities will require the addition of the other four cells A, C, D, and F.

| Table 11-2 | Experimental Design with Controls for Hawthorne and Expectancy Effects | |
| --- | --- | --- |
| GROUPS | TEACHER EXPECTATION | |
| | FOR BENEFIT | FOR NO BENEFIT |
| 1. No-treatment control | A | B |
| 2. Hawthorne control | C | D |
| 3. Experimental procedure | E | F |

PARTIAL CONTROLS

Sometimes the logistics of the research situation will dictate that fewer than six cells be employed. In those cases where we have no need of Hawthorne controls (in fact, these cases should be rare) we can drop cells C and D. In those cases where we have no need for a no-treatment control (these cases seem less rare) cells A and B can be omitted. Suppose that we feel it necessary to include both control groups but have resources for the employment of only three cells. That situation seems best handled by employing either cells A, C, E or cells B, D, F. In either case we control for teacher expectation by having all teachers of the experiment share the same expectation; either that the children will benefit, or that they will not. We lose thereby the possibility of evaluating the effects of teacher expectation but will not have the problem of having teacher expectations confounded with the experimental and control groups' conditions. Such confounding would occur if we selected our three groups such that in one of them teachers had expectations different from the expectations held by teachers of the other two groups.

If only two cells can be employed, either group A or C should be dropped from the set A, C, E; or B or D should be dropped from the set B, D, F. Which group is dropped depends, of course, on whether we feel the no-treatment control or the Hawthorne control to be the more important to the purpose at hand.

If we feel it necessary to include both control groups, and four cells can be employed, and we decide to include set A, C, E, we might add cell B since that is the cell that would be employed if we were not controlling for teacher expectancy. The experiment would then include the two cells most likely to be employed by other investigators not controlling for expectancy. Similarly, if we were using as our basic set cells B, D, F we might want to include cell E as our fourth cell. If we could afford five groups we would probably want to drop either cell C or cell D but ordinarily, if we can afford five cells, we can afford six.[1]

## Ethical Considerations

When Hawthorne controls are employed and when a teacher is led to believe that a new procedure is or is not effective, the teacher has been more or less deceived. Such deception raises ethical questions. Perhaps the most important of these questions is whether the distasteful though necessary deception is warranted by the importance of achieving accurate information on how school children can benefit from various educational procedures.

In medical research employing placebo controls, in behavioral research investigating the effects of experimenter expectancies on the results of their research, and, now, in the education experiment described in this book, deception has of necessity been employed. We know of no untoward effects of these deceptions. Most to the point is the deception of the teachers of Oak School. After the experiment and the follow-up were concluded, all teachers were told of the results of the experiment, and each was invited to react individually to the fact of having been deceived. There was no resentment expressed, and, even on a purely intellectual level, none of the teachers felt the deception to have been unethical. There was, instead, a sense of excitement on the part of most of the teachers of having played a part in what they regarded as important research. It would seem that when teachers are satisfied that the motives for deception are impersonal and rational rather than personal and irrational they react with appreciation of the necessity for their having been deceived.

 

[1] A more complete discussion of the logic, implementation, and statistical analysis of the type of experimental design described here can be found in an earlier publication (Rosenthal, 1966) in which the ethical issues raised next are also dealt with in more detail.

# 12

# Summary
# and
# Implications

The central idea of this book has been that one person's expectation for another's behavior could come to serve as a self-fulfilling prophecy. This is not a new idea, and anecdotes and theories can be found that support its tenability. Much of the experimental evidence for the operation of interpersonal self-fulfilling prophecies comes from a research program in which prophecies or expectancies were experimentally generated in psychological experimenters in order to learn whether these prophecies would become self-fulfilling.

The general plan of past studies has been to establish two groups of "data collectors" and give to the experimenters of each group a different hypothesis as to the data their research subjects would give them. In many such experiments, though not in all, experimenters obtained data from their subjects in accordance with the expectancy they held regarding their subjects' responses. Quite naturally, some of the experiments involved expectations held by the experimenters of the intellectual performance of their subjects.

In addition to those experiments in which the subjects were humans, there were studies in which the subjects were animals. When experimenters were led to believe that their animal subjects were genetically inferior, these animals performed more poorly. When experimenters were led to believe that their animal subjects were more favorably endowed genetically, their animals' performance was superior. In reality, of course, there were no genetic differences between the animals that had been alleged to be dull or bright.

If animal subjects believed to be brighter by their trainers actually became brighter because of their trainers' beliefs, then it might also be true that school children believed by their teachers to be brighter would become brighter because of their teachers' beliefs. Oak School became the laboratory in which an experimental test of that proposition was carried out.

Oak School is a public elementary school in a lower-class community of a medium-size city. The school has a minority group of Mexican children who comprise about one-sixth of the school's population. Every year about 200 of its 650 children leave Oak School, and every year about 200 new children are enrolled.

Oak School follows an ability-tracking plan whereby each of the six grades is divided into one fast, one medium, and one slow classroom. Reading ability is the primary basis for assignment to track. The Mexican children are heavily over-represented in the slow track.

On theoretical grounds it would have been desirable to learn whether teachers' favorable or unfavorable expectations could result in a corresponding increase or decrease in pupils' intellectual competence. On ethical grounds, however, it was decided to test only the proposition that favorable expectations by teachers could lead to an increase in intellectual competence.

All of the children of Oak School were pretested with a standard nonverbal test of intelligence. This test was represented to the teachers as one that would predict intellectual "blooming" or "spurting." The IQ test employed yielded three IQ scores: total IQ, verbal IQ, and reasoning IQ. The "verbal" items required the child to match pictured items with verbal descriptions given by the teacher. The reasoning items required the child to indicate which of five designs differed from the remaining four. Total IQ was based on the sum of verbal and reasoning items.

At the very beginning of the school year following the schoolwide pretesting, each of the eighteen teachers of grades one through six was given the names of those children in her classroom who, in the academic year ahead, would show dramatic intellectual growth. These predictions were allegedly made on the basis of these special children's scores on the test of academic blooming. About 20 percent of Oak School's children were alleged to be potential spurters. For each classroom the names of the special children had actually been chosen by means of a table of random numbers. The difference between the special children and the ordinary children, then, was only in the mind of the teacher.

All the children of Oak School were retested with the same IQ test after one semester, after a full academic year, and after two full academic years. For the first two retests, children were in the classroom of the teacher who had been given favorable expectations for the intellectual growth of some of her pupils. For the final retesting all children had been promoted to the classes of teachers who had not been given any special expectations for the intellectual growth of any of the children. That follow-up testing had been included so that we could learn whether any expectancy advantages that might be found would be dependent on a continuing contact with the teacher who held the especially favorable expectation.

For the children of the experimental group and for the children of the control group, gains in IQ from pretest to retest were computed. Expectancy advantage was defined by the degree to which IQ gains by the "special" children exceeded gains by the control-group children. After the first year of the experiment a significant expectancy advantage was found, and it was especially great among children of the first and second grades. The advantage of having been expected to bloom was evident for these younger children in total IQ, verbal IQ, and reasoning IQ. The control-group children of these grades gained well in IQ, 19 percent of them gaining twenty or more total IQ points. The "special" children, however, showed 47 percent of their number gaining twenty or more total IQ points.

During the subsequent follow-up year the younger children of the first two years lost their expectancy advantage. The children of the upper grades, however, showed an increasing expectancy advantage during the follow-up year. ⊲The younger children who seemed easier to influence may have required more continued contact with their influencer in order to maintain their behavior change. The older children, who were harder to influence initially, may have been better able to maintain their behavior change autonomously once it had occurred.⊳

Differences between boys and girls in the extent to which they were helped by favorable expectations were not dramatic when gains in total IQ were considered. After one year, and after two years as well, boys who were expected to bloom intellectually bloomed more in verbal IQ; girls who were expected to bloom intellectually bloomed more in reasoning IQ. Favorable teacher expectations seemed to help each sex more in that sphere of intellectual functioning in which they had excelled on the pretest. At Oak School boys normally show the higher verbal IQ while girls show the higher reasoning IQ.

It will be recalled that Oak School was organized into a fast, a medium, and a slow track system. We had thought that favorable expectations on the part of teachers would be of greatest benefit to the children of the slow track. That was not the case. After one year, it was the children of the medium track who showed the greatest expectancy advantage, though children of the other tracks were close behind. After two years, however, the children of the medium track very clearly showed the greatest benefits from having had favorable expectations held of their intellectual performance. It seems surprising that it should be the more average child of a lower-class school who stands to benefit more from his teacher's improved expectation.

After the first year of the experiment and also after the second year, the Mexican children showed greater expectancy advantages than did the non-Mexican children, though the difference was not significant statistically. One interesting minority-group effect did reach significance, however, even with just a small sample size. For each of the Mexican children, magnitude of expectancy advantage was computed by subtracting from his or her gain in IQ from pretest to retest, the IQ gain made by the children of the control group in his or her classroom. These magnitudes of expectancy advantage were then correlated with the "Mexican-ness" of the children's faces. After one year, and after two years, those boys who looked more Mexican benefited more from their teachers' positive prophecies. Teachers' pre-experimental expectancies for these boys' intellectual performance were probably lowest of all. Their turning up on a list of probable bloomers must have surprised their teachers. Interest may have followed surprise and, in some way, increased watching for signs of increased brightness may have led to increased brightness.

In addition to the comparison of the "special" and the ordinary children on their gains in IQ it was possible to compare their gains after the first year of the experiment on school achievement as defined by report-card grades. Only for the school subject of reading was there a significant difference in gains in report-card grades. The children expected to bloom intellectually were judged by their teachers to show greater advances in their reading ability. Just as in the case of IQ gains, it was the younger children who showed the greater expectancy advantage in reading scores. The more a given grade level had benefited in over-all IQ gains, the more that same grade level benefited in reading scores.

It was the children of the medium track who showed the greatest expectancy advantage in terms of reading ability just as they had been the children to benefit most in terms of IQ from their teachers' favorable expectations.

Report-card reading grades were assigned by teachers, and teachers' judgments of reading performance may have been affected by their expectations. It is possible, therefore, that there was no real benefit to the earmarked children of having been expected to bloom. The effect could very well have been in the mind of the teacher rather than in the reading performance of the child. Some evidence was available to suggest that such halo effects did not occur. For a number of grade levels, objective achievement tests had been administered. Greater expectancy advantages were found when the assessment was by these objective tests than when it was by the more subjective evaluation made by the teacher. If anything, teachers' grading seemed to show a negative halo effect. It seemed that the special children were graded more severely by the teachers than were the ordinary children. It is even possible that it is just this sort of standard-setting behavior that is responsible in part for the effects of favorable expectations.

The fear has often been expressed that the disadvantaged child is further disadvantaged by his teacher's setting standards that are inappropriately low (Hillson and Myers, 1963; Rivlin, undated). Wilson (1963) has presented compelling evidence that teachers do, in fact, hold up lower standards of achievement for children of more deprived areas. It is a possibility to be further investigated that when a teacher's expectation for a pupil's intellectual performance is raised, she may set higher standards for him to meet (that is, grade him tougher). There may be here the makings of a benign cycle. Teachers may not only get more when they expect more; they may also come to expect more when they get more.

All teachers had been asked to rate each of their pupils on variables related to intellectual curiosity, personal and social adjustment, and need for social approval. In general, children who had been expected to bloom intellectually were rated as more intellectually curious, as happier, and, especially in the lower grades, as less in need of social approval. Just as had been the case with IQ and reading ability, it was the younger children who showed the greater expectancy advantage in terms of their teachers' perceptions of their classroom behavior. Once again, children of the medium track were most advantaged by having been expected to bloom, this time in terms of their perceived greater intellectual curiosity and lessened need for social approval.

When we consider expectancy advantages in terms of perceived intellectual curiosity, we find that the Mexican children did not share in the advantages of having been expected to bloom. Teachers did not see the Mexican children as more intellectually curious when they had been expected to bloom. There was even a slight tendency, stronger for Mexican boys, to see the special Mexican children as less curious intellectually. That seems surprising, particularly since the Mexican children showed the greatest expectancy advantages in IQ, in reading scores, and for Mexican boys, in over-all school achievement. It seemed almost as though, for these minority-group children, intellectual competence may have been easier for teachers to bring about than to believe.

Children's gains in IQ during the basic year of the experiment were correlated with teachers' perceptions of their classroom behavior. This was done separately for the upper- and lower-track children of the experimental and control groups. The more the upper-track children of the experimental group gained in IQ, the more favorably they were rated by their teachers. The more the lower-track children of the control group gained in IQ, the more unfavorably they were viewed by their teachers. No special expectation had been created about these children, and their slow-track status made it unlikely in their teachers' eyes that they would behave in an intellectually competent manner. The more intellectually competent these children became, the more negatively they were viewed by their teachers. Future research should address itself to the possibility that there may be hazards to "unwarranted," unpredicted intellectual growth. Teachers may require a certain amount of preparation to be able to accept the unexpected classroom behavior of the intellectually upwardly mobile child.

There are a number of alternative "theories" available to account for our general findings. One such class of theories, the "accident" theories, maintain that artifacts are responsible for the results obtained, that there is really nothing to explain. The problems of test unreliability and of pretest IQ differences were discussed and found wanting as explanations of our results. The possibility that teachers treated the special children differently only during the retesting process itself was considered. The patterning of results, the fact that a "blind" examiner obtained even more dramatic expectancy effects than did the teachers, teachers' poor recall of the names of their "special" children, and the fact that the results did not disappear one year after the children left the teachers who had been given the expectations, all weaken the plausibility of that argument. Most important to the tenability of the hypothesis that teachers' expectations can significantly affect their pupils' performance are the preliminary results of three replications all of which show significant effects of teacher expectations. These replications also suggest, however, that the effects of teacher expectations may be quite complicated and affected both as to magnitude and direction by a variety of pupil characteristics and by situational variables in the life of the child.[1]

It might reasonably be thought that the improved intellectual competence of the special children was bought at the expense of the ordinary children. Perhaps teachers gave more time to those who were expected to bloom. But teachers appeared to give slightly less time to their special children. Furthermore, those classrooms in which the special children showed the greatest gains in IQ were also the classrooms in which the ordinary children gained the most IQ. The robbing-Peter theory would predict that ordinary children gain less IQ where special children gain more IQ.

On the basis of other experiments on interpersonal self-fulfilling prophecies, we can only speculate as to how teachers brought about intellectual competence simply by expecting it. Teachers may have treated their children in a more pleasant, friendly, and encouraging fashion when they expected greater intellectual gains of them. Such behavior has been shown to improve intellectual performance, probably by its favorable effect on pupil motivation.

Teachers probably watched their special children more closely, and this greater attentiveness may have led to more rapid reinforcement of correct responses with a consequent increase in pupils' learning. Teachers may also have become more reflective in their evaluation of the special children's intellectual performance. Such an increase in teachers' reflectiveness may have led to an increase in their special pupils' reflectiveness, and such a change in cognitive style would be helpful to the performance of the nonverbal skills required by the IQ test employed.

To summarize our speculations, we may say that by what she said, by how and when she said it, but her facial expressions, postures, and perhaps by her touch, the teacher may have communicated to the children of the experimental group that she expected improved intellectual performance. Such communications together with possible changes in teaching techniques may have helped the child learn by changing his self concept, his expectations of his own behavior, and his motivation, as well as his cognitive style and skills.

It is self-evident that further research is needed to narrow down the range of possible mechanisms whereby a teacher's expectations become translated into a pupil's intellectual growth. It would be valuable, for example, to have sound films of teachers interacting with their pupils. We might then look for differences in the way teachers interact with those children from whom they expect intellectual growth compared to those from whom they expect less. On the basis of films of psychological experimenters interacting with subjects from whom different responses are expected, we know that even in such highly standardized situations, unintentional communications can be incredibly subtle and complex (Rosenthal, 1966). Much more subtle and much more complex may be the communications between children and their teachers, teachers not constrained by the demands of the experimental laboratory to treat everyone equally to the extent that it is possible to do so.

The implications of the research described herein are of several kinds. There are methodological implications for the conduct of educational research, and these were discussed in the last chapter. There are implications for the further investigation of unintentional influence processes especially when these processes result in interpersonally self-fulfilling prophecies, and some of these have been discussed. Finally, there are some possible implications for the educational enterprise, and some of these will be suggested briefly.

Over time, our educational policy question has changed from "who ought to be educated?" to "who is capable of being educated?" The ethical question has been traded in for the scientific question. For those children whose educability is in doubt there is a label. They are the educationally, or culturally, or socioeconomically, deprived children and, as things stand now, they appear not to be able to learn as do those who are more advantaged. The advantaged and the disadvantaged differ in parental income, in parental values, in scores on various tests of achievement and ability, and often in skin color and other phenotypic expressions of genetic heritage. Quite inseparable from these differences between the advantaged and the disadvantaged are the differences in their teachers' expectations for what they can achieve in school. There are no experiments to show that a change in pupils' skin color will lead to improved intellectual performance. There is, however, the experiment described in this book to show that change in teacher expectation can lead to improved intellectual performance.

Nothing was done directly for the disadvantaged child at Oak School. There was no crash program to improve his reading ability, no special lesson plan, no extra time for tutoring, no trips to museums or art galleries. There was only the belief that the children bore watching, that they had intellectual competencies that would in due course be revealed. What was done in our program of educational change was done directly for the teacher, only indirectly for her pupils. Perhaps, then, it is the teacher to whom we should direct more of our research attention. If we could learn how she is able to effect dramatic improvement in her pupils' competence without formal changes in her teaching methods, then we could teach other teachers to do the same. If further research shows that it is possible to select teachers whose untrained interactional style does for most of her pupils what our teachers did for the special children, it may be possible to combine sophisticated teacher selection and placement with teacher training to optimize the learning of all pupils.

As teacher-training institutions begin to teach the possibility that teachers' expectations of their pupils' performance may serve as self-fulfilling prophecies, there may be a new expectancy created. The new expectancy may be that children can learn more than had been believed possible, an expectation held by many educational theorists, though for quite different reasons (for example, Bruner, 1960). The new expectancy, at the very least, will make it more difficult when they encounter the educationally disadvantaged for teachers to think, "Well, after all, what can you expect?" The man on the street may be permitted his opinions and prophecies of the unkempt children loitering in a dreary schoolyard. The teacher in the schoolroom may need to learn that those same prophecies within her may be fulfilled; she is no casual passer-by. Perhaps Pygmalion in the classroom is more her role.

ᴥ§

[1] As this book went to press we learned of an additional experiment showing the effects on pupil performance of teacher expectation (Beez, 1967). This time the pupils were sixty preschoolers from a summer Headstart program. Each child was taught the meaning of a series of symbols by one teacher. Half the sixty teachers had been led to expect good symbol learning and half had been led to expect poor symbol learning. Most (77 percent) of the children alleged to have better intellectual prospects learned five or more symbols but only 13 percent of the children alleged to have poorer intellectual prospects learned five or more symbols ($p < 2$ in one million). In this study the children's actual performance was assessed by an experimenter who did not know what the child's teacher had been told about the child's intellectual prospects. Teachers who had been given favorable expectations about their pupil tried to teach more symbols to their pupil than did the teachers given unfavorable expectations about their pupil. The difference in teaching effort was dramatic. Eight or more symbols were taught by 87 percent of the teachers expecting better performance, but only 13 percent of the teachers expecting poorer performance tried to teach that many symbols to their pupil ($p < 1$ in ten million). Surprisingly, however, even when these differences in teaching benefit were controlled, the children expected to be superior showed superior performance ($p < .005$, one-tail), though the magnitude of the effect was diminished by nearly half. We are very grateful to W. Victor Beez for making his data available to us.

# Shaw's Summary

... You see, really and truly, apart from
the things anyone can pick up (the dressing
and the proper way of speaking, and so
on), the difference between a lady and a
flower girl is not how she behaves, but how
she's treated. I shall always be a flower girl
to Professor Higgins, because he always
treats me as a flower girl, and always will;
but I know I can be a lady to you, because
you always treat me as a lady, and always
will.

G. B. Shaw, *Pygmalion*

# APPENDIX

**Table A-1**      Means and Standard Deviations of
Pretest Total IQs in Two Conditions
within Eighteen Classrooms

| CLASS | CONTROL | | | EXPERIMENTAL | | | DIFFERENCE BETWEEN MEANS | $p^a < .10$ |
|---|---|---|---|---|---|---|---|---|
| | N | MEAN | SD | N | MEAN | SD | | |
| 1A | 19 | 105.90 | 12.17 | 3 | 95.00 | 2.45 | −10.90 | |
| 1B | 16 | 87.69 | 18.65 | 4 | 97.00 | 12.45 | + 9.31 | |
| 1C | 15 | 76.90 | 15.41 | 2 | 60.50 | 0.50 | −16.40 | |
| 2A | 19 | 105.74 | 11.38 | 6 | 113.33 | 11.10 | + 7.60 | |
| 2B | 16 | 89.13 | 11.42 | 3 | 102.67 | 9.74 | +13.54 | |
| 2C | 14 | 79.86 | 9.38 | 5 | 84.80 | 8.18 | + 4.94 | |
| 3A | 14 | 98.36 | 14.89 | 9 | 102.78 | 11.59 | + 4.42 | |
| 3B | 17 | 102.18 | 11.89 | 1 | 88.00 | 0.00 | −14.18 | |
| 3C | 16 | 100.31 | 13.84 | 5 | 101.40 | 10.67 | + 1.09 | |
| 4A | 22 | 121.86 | 15.67 | 5 | 133.00 | 15.84 | +11.14 | |
| 4B | 17 | 103.94 | 12.45 | 3 | 97.33 | 7.13 | − 6.61 | |
| 4C | 18 | 92.11 | 13.98 | 4 | 88.75 | 1.64 | − 3.36 | |
| 5A | 20 | 107.65 | 12.17 | 6 | 122.00 | 12.83 | +14.35 | .04 |
| 5B | 15 | 104.47 | 13.82 | 4 | 81.00 | 13.64 | −23.47 | .004 |
| 5C | 12 | 83.33 | 12.09 | 4 | 86.25 | 5.40 | + 2.92 | |
| 6A | 21 | 106.10 | 17.73 | 6 | 112.83 | 11.80 | + 6.74 | |
| 6B | 15 | 99.27 | 11.35 | 4 | 97.25 | 25.17 | − 2.02 | |
| 6C | 15 | 82.60 | 15.72 | 3 | 86.00 | 7.87 | + 3.40 | |

[a] Two-tail, based on mean square within.

**Table A-2**    Means and Standard Deviations of
Pretest Verbal IQs in Two Conditions
within Eighteen Classrooms

| CLASS | CONTROL | | | EXPERIMENTAL | | | DIFFERENCE BETWEEN MEANS | $p^a < .10$ |
|---|---|---|---|---|---|---|---|---|
| | $N$ | MEAN | SD | $N$ | MEAN | SD | | |
| 1A | 19 | 119.47 | 20.53 | 3 | 102.00 | 2.16 | −17.47 | |
| 1B | 16 | 104.25 | 19.97 | 4 | 116.25 | 12.87 | +12.00 | |
| 1C | 19 | 95.68 | 15.22 | 2 | 67.50 | 2.50 | −28.18 | .05 |
| 2A | 19 | 111.53 | 12.07 | 6 | 114.33 | 9.57 | + 2.81 | |
| 2B | 16 | 96.50 | 10.36 | 3 | 103.67 | 4.78 | + 7.17 | |
| 2C | 14 | 82.21 | 11.76 | 5 | 90.20 | 8.68 | + 7.99 | |
| 3A | 14 | 98.86 | 18.37 | 9 | 105.89 | 15.70 | + 7.03 | |
| 3B | 17 | 107.71 | 18.07 | 1 | 95.00 | 0.00 | −12.71 | |
| 3C | 16 | 109.06 | 17.65 | 5 | 117.40 | 13.31 | + 8.34 | |
| 4A | 22 | 129.23 | 16.63 | 5 | 149.40 | 22.79 | +20.17 | .04 |
| 4B | 17 | 106.24 | 16.89 | 3 | 99.33 | 6.65 | − 6.90 | |
| 4C | 18 | 96.06 | 20.00 | 4 | 87.50 | 8.53 | − 8.56 | |
| 5A | 20 | 111.85 | 24.04 | 6 | 130.00 | 18.32 | +18.15 | .05 |
| 5B | 15 | 107.73 | 19.94 | 4 | 90.50 | 17.39 | −17.23 | |
| 5C | 12 | 84.17 | 15.88 | 4 | 85.25 | 9.09 | + 1.08 | |
| 6A | 21 | 109.57 | 21.48 | 6 | 119.00 | 16.27 | + 9.43 | |
| 6B | 15 | 101.20 | 18.26 | 4 | 93.75 | 31.99 | − 7.45 | |
| 6C | 15 | 86.40 | 22.87 | 3 | 93.00 | 24.91 | + 6.60 | |

ª Two-tail, based on mean square within.

**Table A-3**  Means and Standard Deviations of Pretest Reasoning IQs in Two Conditions within Eighteen Classrooms

| CLASS | CONTROL | | | EXPERIMENTAL | | | DIFFERENCE BETWEEN MEANS | $p^a < .10$ |
|---|---|---|---|---|---|---|---|---|
| | $N$ | MEAN | SD | $N$ | MEAN | SD | | |
| 1A | 19 | 91.32 | 16.52 | 3 | 84.67 | 8.99 | − 6.65 | |
| 1B | 16 | 47.19 | 37.74 | 4 | 54.00 | 37.25 | + 6.81 | |
| 1C | 19 | 30.79 | 25.63 | 2 | 53.50 | 4.50 | +22.71 | |
| 2A | 19 | 100.95 | 15.16 | 6 | 112.50 | 15.97 | +11.55 | |
| 2B | 16 | 80.56 | 18.95 | 3 | 102.33 | 14.43 | +21.77 | .08 |
| 2C | 14 | 73.93 | 18.65 | 5 | 77.40 | 12.64 | + 3.47 | |
| 3A | 14 | 98.07 | 17.33 | 9 | 100.44 | 15.75 | + 2.37 | |
| 3B | 17 | 96.53 | 12.11 | 1 | 78.00 | 0.00 | −18.53 | |
| 3C | 16 | 90.19 | 17.20 | 5 | 83.40 | 11.36 | − 6.79 | |
| 4A | 22 | 117.59 | 23.67 | 5 | 120.40 | 16.43 | + 2.81 | |
| 4B | 17 | 102.06 | 11.66 | 3 | 96.67 | 12.37 | − 5.39 | |
| 4C | 18 | 88.78 | 13.20 | 4 | 91.25 | 11.10 | + 2.47 | |
| 5A | 20 | 107.05 | 16.52 | 6 | 117.00 | 20.27 | + 9.95 | |
| 5B | 15 | 100.20 | 15.19 | 4 | 69.75 | 13.66 | −30.45 | .006 |
| 5C | 12 | 79.00 | 13.03 | 4 | 84.00 | 13.25 | + 5.00 | |
| 6A | 21 | 104.14 | 20.50 | 6 | 108.83 | 16.72 | + 4.69 | |
| 6B | 15 | 98.93 | 11.77 | 4 | 101.50 | 17.15 | + 2.57 | |
| 6C | 15 | 79.47 | 13.63 | 3 | 82.00 | 9.20 | + 2.53 | |

[a] Two-tail, based on mean square within.

**Table A-4**          Means and Standard Deviations of
                       Post-test Total IQs in Two
                       Conditions within Eighteen Classrooms

| CLASS | CONTROL | | | EXPERIMENTAL | | | DIFFERENCE BETWEEN MEANS | $p^a < .05$ |
|---|---|---|---|---|---|---|---|---|
| | $N$ | MEAN | SD | $N$ | MEAN | SD | | |
| 1A | 17 | 111.35 | 14.23 | 1 | 113.00 | 0.00 | + 1.65 | |
| 1B | 15 | 100.27 | 12.24 | 4 | 120.00 | 12.90 | +19.73 | .02 |
| 1C | 16 | 92.19 | 13.41 | 2 | 101.50 | 4.50 | + 9.31 | |
| 2A | 19 | 110.00 | 11.63 | 6 | 135.83 | 30.26 | +25.83 | .0004 |
| 2B | 14 | 98.93 | 14.05 | 3 | 109.67 | 17.25 | +10.74 | |
| 2C | 14 | 87.71 | 9.26 | 3 | 92.67 | 6.24 | + 4.95 | |
| 3A | 12 | 116.75 | 17.04 | 8 | 110.25 | 13.04 | − 6.50 | |
| 3B | 15 | 102.47 | 14.99 | 1 | 97.00 | 0.00 | − 5.47 | |
| 3C | 13 | 98.54 | 11.78 | 5 | 97.60 | 10.25 | − 0.94 | |
| 4A | 18 | 129.22 | 16.17 | 5 | 140.20 | 16.77 | +10.98 | |
| 4B | 16 | 102.38 | 9.35 | 3 | 97.00 | 14.97 | − 5.38 | |
| 4C | 15 | 90.27 | 17.19 | 4 | 96.75 | 6.83 | + 6.48 | |
| 5A | 16 | 126.38 | 17.77 | 5 | 137.00 | 25.07 | +10.63 | |
| 5B | 0[b] | —— | —— | 0[b] | —— | —— | ——[b] | |
| 5C | 10 | 98.40 | 14.58 | 4 | 102.50 | 11.93 | + 4.10 | |
| 6A | 20 | 121.90 | 17.15 | 4 | 129.25 | 8.56 | + 7.35 | |
| 6B | 13 | 106.69 | 14.92 | 4 | 106.75 | 30.73 | + 0.06 | |
| 6C | 12 | 89.42 | 16.17 | 3 | 92.33 | 7.85 | + 2.92 | |

[a] One-tail, based on mean square within.
[b] Through examiner error only the verbal subtest was administered.

**Table A-5**  Means and Standard Deviations
of Post-test Verbal IQs in Two
Conditions within Eighteen Classrooms

| CLASS | CONTROL | | | EXPERIMENTAL | | | DIFFERENCE BETWEEN MEANS | $p^a < .05$ |
|-------|---|------|------|---|--------|-------|-------------------------|-------------|
| | N | MEAN | SD | N | MEAN | SD | | |
| 1A | 17 | 119.00 | 28.48 | 1 | 108.00 | 0.00 | −11.00 | |
| 1B | 15 | 108.67 | 12.12 | 4 | 123.75 | 15.66 | +15.08 | |
| 1C | 16 | 96.13 | 12.84 | 2 | 104.50 | 1.50 | + 8.38 | |
| 2A | 19 | 113.42 | 15.11 | 6 | 131.83 | 31.65 | +18.41 | |
| 2B | 14 | 105.43 | 16.39 | 3 | 114.33 | 18.26 | + 8.90 | |
| 2C | 14 | 95.07 | 13.68 | 3 | 94.67 | 12.39 | − 0.40 | |
| 3A | 12 | 132.00 | 53.82 | 8 | 114.13 | 15.35 | −17.88 | |
| 3B | 15 | 111.53 | 19.10 | 1 | 104.00 | 0.00 | − 7.53 | |
| 3C | 13 | 102.31 | 18.64 | 5 | 100.80 | 17.70 | − 1.51 | |
| 4A | 18 | 137.94 | 18.71 | 5 | 163.40 | 55.61 | +25.46 | .03 |
| 4B | 16 | 112.19 | 15.62 | 3 | 91.00 | 13.14 | −21.19 | |
| 4C | 15 | 98.87 | 20.94 | 4 | 99.00 | 6.52 | + 0.13 | |
| 5A | 17 | 133.82 | 33.63 | 5 | 141.20 | 28.22 | + 7.38 | |
| 5B | 13 | 105.69 | 18.89 | 3 | 88.00 | 14.45 | −17.69 | |
| 5C | 10 | 98.20 | 22.26 | 4 | 102.50 | 12.38 | + 4.30 | |
| 6A | 20 | 122.90 | 23.15 | 4 | 127.75 | 16.62 | + 4.85 | |
| 6B | 13 | 106.54 | 27.91 | 4 | 115.00 | 59.61 | + 8.46 | |
| 6C | 12 | 91.17 | 19.71 | 3 | 100.67 | 23.44 | + 9.50 | |

a One-tail, based on mean square within.

**Table A-6**          Means and Standard Deviations of
Post-test Reasoning IQs in Two
Conditions within Eighteen Classrooms

| CLASS | CONTROL | | | EXPERIMENTAL | | | DIFFERENCE BETWEEN MEANS | $p^a < .05$ |
|---|---|---|---|---|---|---|---|---|
|  | $N$ | MEAN | SD | $N$ | MEAN | SD |  |  |
| 1A | 17 | 111.12 | 19.76 | 1 | 120.00 | 0.00 | + 8.88 |  |
| 1B | 15 | 90.60 | 17.48 | 4 | 116.25 | 9.18 | +25.65 | .04 |
| 1C | 16 | 87.75 | 22.95 | 2 | 98.50 | 8.50 | +10.75 |  |
| 2A | 19 | 114.32 | 29.11 | 6 | 150.17 | 40.71 | +35.85 | .002 |
| 2B | 14 | 94.36 | 16.17 | 3 | 128.67 | 56.10 | +34.31 | .02 |
| 2C | 14 | 82.93 | 15.74 | 3 | 94.67 | 14.71 | +11.74 |  |
| 3A | 12 | 114.08 | 21.81 | 8 | 107.75 | 21.16 | − 6.33 |  |
| 3B | 15 | 94.33 | 20.21 | 1 | 90.00 | 0.00 | − 4.33 |  |
| 3C | 13 | 95.62 | 8.04 | 5 | 95.60 | 4.41 | − 0.02 |  |
| 4A | 18 | 131.33 | 39.33 | 5 | 134.60 | 5.68 | + 3.27 |  |
| 4B | 16 | 94.38 | 12.83 | 3 | 108.33 | 23.04 | +13.96 |  |
| 4C | 15 | 80.40 | 27.03 | 4 | 95.25 | 13.08 | +14.85 |  |
| 5A | 16 | 125.38 | 22.78 | 5 | 133.00 | 24.70 | + 7.63 |  |
| 5B | 0[b] | —— | —— | 0[b] | —— | —— | ——[b] |  |
| 5C | 10 | 103.20 | 20.13 | 4 | 131.25 | 70.27 | +28.05 | .04 |
| 6A | 20 | 125.70 | 21.75 | 4 | 138.50 | 22.39 | +12.80 |  |
| 6B | 13 | 115.77 | 25.02 | 4 | 111.50 | 18.77 | − 4.27 |  |
| 6C | 12 | 89.83 | 17.63 | 3 | 93.00 | 13.14 | + 3.17 |  |

[a] One-tail, based on mean square within.
[b] Through examiner error only the verbal subtest was administered.

**Table A-7**     Means and Standard Deviations of Gains in Total IQs in Two Conditions within Eighteen Classrooms

| CLASS | CONTROL | | | EXPERIMENTAL | | | DIFFERENCE BETWEEN MEANS | $p^a < .05$ |
|-------|---------|---------|------|--------------|---------|------|-----------------|--------|
| | $N$ | MEAN | SD | $N$ | MEAN | SD | | |
| 1A | 17 | + 6.77 | 13.66 | 1 | +18.00 | 0.00 | +11.24 | |
| 1B | 15 | +13.40 | 17.97 | 4 | +23.00 | 11.38 | + 9.60 | |
| 1C | 16 | +16.25 | 16.62 | 2 | +41.00 | 4.00 | +24.75 | .006 |
| 2A | 19 | + 4.26 | 10.59 | 6 | +22.50 | 22.91 | +18.24 | .002 |
| 2B | 14 | + 9.86 | 9.23 | 3 | + 7.00 | 12.19 | − 2.86 | |
| 2C | 14 | + 7.86 | 8.81 | 3 | +14.00 | 3.56 | + 6.14 | |
| 3A | 12 | +14.25 | 10.95 | 8 | +10.00 | 7.11 | − 4.25 | |
| 3B | 15 | − 0.13 | 10.65 | 1 | + 9.00 | 0.00 | + 9.13 | |
| 3C | 13 | + 2.46 | 8.89 | 5 | − 3.80 | 6.24 | − 6.26 | |
| 4A | 18 | + 7.17 | 15.20 | 5 | + 7.20 | 12.78 | + 0.03 | |
| 4B | 16 | − 0.50 | 11.58 | 3 | − 0.33 | 10.08 | + 0.17 | |
| 4C | 15 | − 1.00 | 10.85 | 4 | + 8.00 | 7.07 | + 9.00 | |
| 5A | 16 | +18.94 | 12.97 | 5 | +18.40 | 21.18 | − 0.54 | |
| 5B | 0ᵇ | —— | —— | 0ᵇ | —— | —— | ——ᵇ | |
| 5C | 10 | +15.10 | 12.83 | 4 | +16.25 | 12.07 | + 1.15 | |
| 6A | 20 | +14.55 | 11.36 | 4 | +13.25 | 3.63 | − 1.30 | |
| 6B | 13 | + 8.31 | 7.82 | 4 | + 9.50 | 8.85 | + 1.19 | |
| 6C | 12 | + 6.83 | 6.69 | 3 | + 6.33 | 1.70 | − 0.50 | |

ᵃ One-tail, based on mean square within.
ᵇ Through examiner error only the verbal subtest was administered.

**Table A-8**        Means and Standard Deviations of
Gains in Verbal IQs in Two
Conditions within Eighteen Classrooms

| CLASS | | CONTROL | | | EXPERIMENTAL | | DIFFERENCE BETWEEN MEANS | $p^a < .05$ |
|---|---|---|---|---|---|---|---|---|
| | $N$ | MEAN | SD | $N$ | MEAN | SD | | |
| 1A | 17 | + 0.29 | 14.90 | 1 | + 8.00 | 0.00 | + 7.71 | |
| 1B | 15 | + 4.87 | 15.59 | 4 | + 7.50 | 9.86 | + 2.63 | |
| 1C | 16 | + 1.69 | 16.90 | 2 | +37.00 | 4.00 | +35.31 | .005 |
| 2A | 19 | + 1.90 | 10.98 | 6 | +17.50 | 24.16 | +15.61 | .04 |
| 2B | 14 | + 7.57 | 9.04 | 3 | +10.67 | 13.57 | + 3.10 | |
| 2C | 14 | +12.86 | 15.17 | 3 | + 9.00 | 7.48 | − 3.86 | |
| 3A | 12 | +29.08 | 40.49 | 8 | + 9.38 | 4.95 | −19.71 | .02[b] |
| 3B | 15 | + 5.07 | 9.93 | 1 | + 9.00 | 0.00 | + 3.93 | |
| 3C | 13 | − 1.62 | 11.50 | 5 | −16.60 | 12.13 | −14.99 | |
| 4A | 18 | + 8.67 | 17.78 | 5 | +14.00 | 47.24 | + 5.33 | |
| 4B | 16 | + 6.88 | 12.95 | 3 | − 8.33 | 10.53 | −15.21 | |
| 4C | 15 | + 4.07 | 9.62 | 4 | +11.50 | 6.34 | + 7.43 | |
| 5A | 17 | +21.77 | 24.07 | 5 | +16.00 | 25.42 | − 5.77 | |
| 5B | 13 | + 1.23 | 7.75 | 3 | + 3.33 | 3.30 | + 2.10 | |
| 5C | 10 | +14.60 | 12.22 | 4 | +17.25 | 9.65 | + 2.65 | |
| 6A | 20 | +11.80 | 12.26 | 4 | + 8.75 | 8.35 | − 3.05 | |
| 6B | 13 | + 7.15 | 15.99 | 4 | +21.25 | 29.94 | +14.10 | |
| 6C | 12 | + 6.42 | 6.38 | 3 | + 7.67 | 10.08 | + 1.25 | |

[a] One-tail, based on mean square within.
[b] Two-tail.

**Table A-9**      Means and Standard Deviations of
Gains in Reasoning IQs in Two
Conditions within Eighteen Classrooms

| CLASS | N | CONTROL MEAN | SD | N | EXPERIMENTAL MEAN | SD | DIFFERENCE BETWEEN MEANS | $p^a < .05$ |
|---|---|---|---|---|---|---|---|---|
| 1A | 17 | +21.65 | 23.64 | 1 | +30.00 | 0.00 | + 8.35 | |
| 1B | 15 | +45.87 | 34.58 | 4 | +62.25 | 36.47 | +16.38 | |
| 1C | 16 | +56.88 | 32.58 | 2 | +45.00 | 4.00 | −11.88 | |
| 2A | 19 | +13.37 | 28.56 | 6 | +37.67 | 35.63 | +24.30 | .03 |
| 2B | 14 | +15.43 | 16.91 | 3 | +26.33[c] | 51.86 | +10.90 | |
| 2C | 14 | + 9.00 | 14.56 | 3 | +26.33[c] | 14.61 | +17.33 | |
| 3A | 12 | +11.25 | 18.75 | 8 | +11.50 | 13.95 | + 0.25 | |
| 3B | 15 | − 4.53 | 21.36 | 1 | +12.00 | 0.00 | +16.53 | |
| 3C | 13 | + 8.92 | 12.53 | 5 | +12.20 | 12.69 | + 3.28 | |
| 4A | 18 | +13.78 | 36.05 | 5 | +14.20 | 17.15 | + 0.42 | |
| 4B | 16 | − 6.38 | 15.22 | 3 | +11.67 | 16.82 | +18.04 | |
| 4C | 15 | − 8.27 | 21.53 | 4 | + 4.00 | 9.46 | +12.27 | |
| 5A | 16 | +16.94 | 22.63 | 5 | +18.00 | 30.28 | + 1.06 | |
| 5B | 0[b] | — | — | 0[b] | — | — | —[b] | |
| 5C | 10 | +23.60 | 24.57 | 4 | +47.25 | 60.87 | +23.65 | |
| 6A | 20 | +20.45 | 18.58 | 4 | +23.50 | 17.78 | + 3.05 | |
| 6B | 13 | +16.69 | 19.31 | 4 | +10.00 | 7.45 | − 6.69 | |
| 6C | 12 | + 9.25 | 11.14 | 3 | +11.00 | 7.48 | + 1.75 | |

[a] One-tail, based on mean square within.
[b] Through examiner error only the verbal subtest was administered.
[c] This is not a typographical error, simply an unusual coincidence.

**Table A-10**          Mean Gains in Achievement Test Scores
and School Grades Shortly after
Instituting the Experimental Program
among Fifth- and Sixth-Grade Children

|  | READING | | LANGUAGE | | ARITHMETIC | |
|---|---|---|---|---|---|---|
|  | ITBS[a] | GRADES[b] | ITBS[a] | GRADES[b] | ITBS[a] | GRADES[b] |
| Experimental | +0.93 | +.13 | −7.56 | −.17 | −6.70 | −.22 |
| Control | −0.37 | +.01 | −4.03 | −.23 | −9.31 | −.09 |
| Difference | +1.30 | +.12 | −3.53 | +.06 | +2.61 | −.13 |
| $t$ | +0.37 | +.82 | −1.07 | +.37 | +0.72 | −.73 |
| One-tail $p < .10$ | —— | —— | —— | —— | —— | —— |
| $N$ Experimental | 27 | 23 | 27 | 23 | 27 | 23 |
| $N$ Control | 91 | 88 | 91 | 88 | 91 | 88 |

[a] Percentile unit gains from Spring 1964 to November 1964.
[b] Grade-point gains from Spring 1964 to January 1965.

**Table A-11**  Mean Gains in Achievement Test Scores
and School Grades after One Year
by Experimental and Control
Fourth- and Fifth-Grade Children

|  | READING | | LANGUAGE | | ARITHMETIC | |
|---|---|---|---|---|---|---|
|  | ITBS[a] | GRADES[b] | ITBS[a] | GRADES[b] | ITBS[a] | GRADES[b] |
| Experimental | +2.27 | −.20 | +5.82 | + .39 | +6.57 | .00 |
| Control | −1.05 | −.11 | +1.07 | + .19 | +0.83 | +.16 |
| Difference | +3.32 | −.09 | +4.75 | + .20 | +5.74 | −.16 |
| $t$ | + .91 | −.69 | +1.53 | +1.49 | +1.41 | −.96 |
| One-tail $p < .10$ | —— | —— | .07 | .08 | .09 | —— |
| $N$ Experimental | 22 | 25 | 22 | 23 | 21 | 23 |
| $N$ Control | 78 | 89 | 85 | 89 | 86 | 89 |

[a] Percentile unit gains from November 1964 to October 1965.
[b] Grade-point gains from June 1964 to June 1965.

**Table A-12**        Intercorrelations among Classroom
Behaviors Rated by Teachers

| | CLUSTER I | | | CLUSTER II | | | | |
| | [a]CURIOUS | [a]INTERESTING | [a]FUTURE SUCCESS | [b]ADJUSTED | [b]APPEALING | [b]HAPPY | [b]AFFECTIONATE | [b]NONHOSTILE |
|---|---|---|---|---|---|---|---|---|
| [a]Interesting | +.64 [a] | | | | | | | |
| [a]Future success | +.63 | +.60 | | | | | | |
| [b]Adjusted | +.32 | +.45 | +.61 | | | | | |
| [b]Appealing | +.36 | +.55 | +.58 | +.66 | [b] | [b] | | |
| [b]Happy | +.35 | +.44 | +.48 | +.69 | +.59 | | | |
| [b]Affectionate | +.28 | +.37 | +.23 | +.39 | +.40 | +.51 | | |
| [b]Nonhostile | +.02 | +.09 | +.22 | +.50 | +.46 | +.41 | +.27 | |
| [c]Needs approval | −.03 | +.02 | −.20 | −.29 | −.04 | −.20 | +.05 | −.15 |

[a] Cluster I intercorrelations.
[b] Cluster II intercorrelations.
[c] Cluster III (single variable), minimum $N = 347$.

**Table A-13**  Correlations between Classroom Behavior and Total IQ Gains after One Year in Slow and Upper Tracks

| | CONTROL | | | | EXPERIMENTAL | | | |
| | UPPER | | SLOW | | UPPER | | SLOW | |
| | df | r | df | r | df | r | df | r |
|---|---|---|---|---|---|---|---|---|
| *Cluster I* | | | | | | | | |
| Curious | 167 | −.01 | 76 | −.10 | 37 | +.20 | 18 | −.26 |
| Interesting | 166 | −.12 | 74 | −.19[a] | 38 | +.38[b] | 18 | −.21 |
| Future success | 165 | −.05 | 75 | −.06 | 37 | +.31[a] | 18 | +.11 |
| MEAN | | −.06 | | −.12 | | +.30[a] | | −.12 |
| | | | | | | | | |
| *Cluster II* | | | | | | | | |
| Adjusted | 167 | −.11 | 76 | −.11 | 38 | +.37[b] | 17 | +.02 |
| Appealing | 167 | −.02 | 76 | −.10 | 38 | +.32[b] | 18 | −.05 |
| Happy | 167 | −.10 | 75 | −.13 | 38 | +.25 | 18 | +.07 |
| Affectionate | 167 | −.08 | 76 | −.12 | 38 | +.30[a] | 18 | −.47[b] |
| Nonhostile | 166 | +.04 | 76 | +.03 | 38 | +.15 | 17 | +.19 |
| MEAN | | −.05 | | −.09 | | +.28[a] | | −.05 |
| | | | | | | | | |
| *Cluster III* | | | | | | | | |
| Needs approval | 166 | +.09 | 76 | −.12 | 38 | −.04 | 18 | −.59[c] |

[a] $p < .10$, two-tail.
[b] $p < .05$, two-tail.
[c] $p < .01$, two-tail.

**Table A-14**     Correlations between Classroom Behavior and Verbal IQ Gains after One Year in Slow and Upper Tracks

| | CONTROL | | | | EXPERIMENTAL | | | |
| | UPPER | | SLOW | | UPPER | | SLOW | |
| | df | r | df | r | df | r | df | r |
|---|---|---|---|---|---|---|---|---|
| *Cluster I* | | | | | | | | |
| Curious | 181 | +.00 | 76 | +.03 | 40 | +.17 | 18 | −.24 |
| Interesting | 180 | −.07 | 74 | +.00 | 41 | +.28ª | 18 | −.15 |
| Future success | 179 | −.04 | 75 | +.02 | 40 | +.30ᵇ | 18 | +.03 |
| MEAN | | −.04 | | +.02 | | +.25 | | −.12 |
| *Cluster II* | | | | | | | | |
| Adjusted | 181 | −.20ᶜ | 76 | +.05 | 41 | −.03 | 17 | −.00 |
| Appealing | 181 | −.06 | 76 | +.01 | 41 | +.11 | 18 | +.07 |
| Happy | 181 | −.20ᶜ | 75 | +.15 | 41 | +.22 | 18 | +.23 |
| Affectionate | 181 | −.12ª | 76 | +.12 | 41 | −.15 | 18 | −.49ᵇ |
| Nonhostile | 180 | −.04 | 76 | +.03 | 41 | +.07 | 17 | +.25 |
| MEAN | | −.12ª | | +.07 | | +.04 | | +.01 |
| *Cluster III* | | | | | | | | |
| Needs approval | 180 | +.04 | 76 | −.20ª | 41 | +.04 | 18 | −.32 |

ª $p < .10$, two-tail.
ᵇ $p < .05$, two-tail.
ᶜ $p < .01$, two-tail.

## Table A-15    Correlations between Classroom Behavior and Reasoning IQ Gains after One Year in Slow and Upper Tracks

| | CONTROL | | | | EXPERIMENTAL | | | |
| | UPPER | | SLOW | | UPPER | | SLOW | |
| | df | r | df | r | df | r | df | r |
|---|---|---|---|---|---|---|---|---|
| *Cluster I* | | | | | | | | |
| Curious | 167 | −.03 | 76 | −.21[a] | 37 | +.17 | 18 | −.03 |
| Interesting | 166 | −.06 | 74 | −.32[c] | 38 | +.29[a] | 18 | −.05 |
| Future success | 165 | +.01 | 75 | −.16 | 37 | +.22 | 18 | +.27 |
| MEAN | | −.03 | | −.23[b] | | +.23 | | +.06 |
| *Cluster II* | | | | | | | | |
| Adjusted | 167 | +.08 | 76 | −.20[a] | 38 | +.43[c] | 17 | +.19 |
| Appealing | 167 | +.03 | 76 | −.19[a] | 38 | +.15 | 18 | +.07 |
| Happy | 167 | −.00 | 75 | −.29[c] | 38 | +.23 | 18 | +.09 |
| Affectionate | 167 | −.05 | 76 | −.28[b] | 38 | +.35[b] | 18 | +.05 |
| Nonhostile | 166 | +.14[a] | 76 | +.01 | 38 | +.03 | 17 | +.26 |
| MEAN | | +.04 | | −.19[a] | | +.24 | | +.13 |
| *Cluster III* | | | | | | | | |
| Needs approval | 166 | +.07 | 76 | −.05 | 38 | −.09 | 18 | −.55[b] |

[a] $p < .10$, two-tail.
[b] $p < .05$, two-tail.
[c] $p < .01$, two-tail.

**Table A-16**   Means and Standard Deviations of
Total IQs after One Semester in Two
Conditions within Eighteen Classrooms

| CLASS | CONTROL | | | EXPERIMENTAL | | | DIFFERENCE BETWEEN MEANS | $p^{a} < .05$ |
|---|---|---|---|---|---|---|---|---|
| | $N$ | MEAN | SD | $N$ | MEAN | SD | | |
| 1A | 18 | 114.67 | 18.07 | 3 | 106.67 | 14.38 | − 8.00 | |
| 1B | 15 | 102.87 | 9.11 | 4 | 100.75 | 12.99 | − 2.12 | |
| 1C | 18 | 84.39 | 13.45 | 2 | 102.00 | 8.00 | +17.61 | |
| 2A | 18 | 106.89 | 12.39 | 6 | 117.50 | 12.15 | +10.61 | |
| 2B | 16 | 90.75 | 15.67 | 3 | 93.33 | 1.89 | + 2.58 | |
| 2C | 14 | 83.07 | 8.84 | 5 | 87.20 | 4.40 | + 4.13 | |
| 3A | 14 | 106.43 | 9.38 | 9 | 108.67 | 10.78 | + 2.24 | |
| 3B | 17 | 102.35 | 14.25 | 1 | 120.00 | 0.00 | +17.65 | |
| 3C | 16 | 94.69 | 12.12 | 4 | 93.50 | 9.12 | − 1.19 | |
| 4A | 22 | 110.73 | 9.33 | 5 | 122.80 | 17.37 | +12.07 | |
| 4B | 17 | 102.00 | 11.87 | 3 | 97.00 | 20.07 | − 5.00 | |
| 4C | 16 | 93.81 | 12.80 | 4 | 90.25 | 7.08 | − 3.56 | |
| 5A | 18 | 116.72 | 19.23 | 6 | 127.83 | 22.21 | +11.11 | |
| 5B | 14 | 105.21 | 20.21 | 4 | 98.25 | 17.80 | − 6.96 | |
| 5C | 12 | 93.58 | 12.27 | 4 | 100.75 | 8.90 | + 7.17 | |
| 6A | 20 | 115.10 | 17.96 | 6 | 122.33 | 9.39 | + 7.23 | |
| 6B | 15 | 101.73 | 15.40 | 4 | 102.50 | 28.06 | + 0.77 | |
| 6C | 14 | 83.64 | 16.40 | 3 | 87.67 | 4.71 | + 4.03 | |

[a] One-tail, based on mean square within.

**Table A-17**   Means and Standard Deviations of Verbal IQs after One Semester in Two Conditions within Eighteen Classrooms

| CLASS | CONTROL | | | EXPERIMENTAL | | | DIFFERENCE BETWEEN MEANS | $p^a < .05$ |
|---|---|---|---|---|---|---|---|---|
| | $N$ | MEAN | SD | $N$ | MEAN | SD | | |
| 1A | 18 | 118.50 | 19.24 | 3 | 103.00 | 10.68 | −15.50 | |
| 1B | 15 | 111.53 | 9.28 | 4 | 107.25 | 1.64 | − 4.28 | |
| 1C | 18 | 92.22 | 12.22 | 2 | 102.00 | 2.00 | + 9.78 | |
| 2A | 18 | 116.89 | 13.16 | 6 | 121.67 | 14.85 | + 4.78 | |
| 2B | 16 | 99.44 | 15.80 | 3 | 101.67 | 9.57 | + 2.23 | |
| 2C | 14 | 86.00 | 11.00 | 5 | 89.80 | 6.01 | + 3.80 | |
| 3A | 14 | 116.21 | 24.11 | 9 | 114.33 | 13.65 | − 1.88 | |
| 3B | 17 | 111.59 | 19.73 | 1 | 122.00 | 0.00 | +10.41 | |
| 3C | 16 | 99.00 | 16.30 | 4 | 95.50 | 11.69 | − 3.50 | |
| 4A | 22 | 118.27 | 17.45 | 5 | 157.40 | 70.56 | +39.13 | .0002 |
| 4B | 17 | 113.29 | 19.88 | 3 | 93.00 | 22.64 | −20.29 | |
| 4C | 16 | 105.06 | 24.14 | 4 | 88.00 | 8.52 | −17.06 | |
| 5A | 18 | 122.89 | 25.91 | 6 | 127.83 | 23.41 | + 4.94 | |
| 5B | 14 | 109.14 | 24.15 | 4 | 94.75 | 19.40 | −14.39 | |
| 5C | 12 | 94.92 | 18.09 | 4 | 99.00 | 12.35 | + 4.08 | |
| 6A | 20 | 117.60 | 20.11 | 6 | 125.33 | 14.20 | + 7.73 | |
| 6B | 15 | 102.47 | 18.33 | 4 | 104.75 | 40.10 | + 2.28 | |
| 6C | 14 | 85.79 | 22.52 | 3 | 91.67 | 19.36 | + 5.88 | |

a One-tail, based on mean square within.

**Table A-18**  Means and Standard Deviations of Reasoning IQs after One Semester in Two Conditions within Eighteen Classrooms

| CLASS | CONTROL | | | EXPERIMENTAL | | | DIFFERENCE BETWEEN MEANS | $p^a < .05$ |
|---|---|---|---|---|---|---|---|---|
| | $N$ | MEAN | SD | $N$ | MEAN | SD | | |
| 1A | 18 | 113.00 | 23.62 | 3 | 111.00 | 20.70 | − 2.00 | |
| 1B | 15 | 94.73 | 16.48 | 4 | 91.50 | 38.73 | − 3.23 | |
| 1C | 18 | 71.39 | 24.60 | 2 | 103.00 | 21.00 | +31.61 | .03 |
| 2A | 18 | 99.94 | 17.99 | 6 | 113.83 | 14.05 | +13.89 | |
| 2B | 16 | 79.81 | 25.96 | 3 | 87.00 | 4.32 | + 7.19 | |
| 2C | 14 | 83.36 | 19.58 | 5 | 86.00 | 9.78 | + 2.64 | |
| 3A | 14 | 99.36 | 13.64 | 9 | 103.33 | 12.30 | + 3.97 | |
| 3B | 17 | 93.71 | 16.69 | 1 | 117.00 | 0.00 | +23.29 | |
| 3C | 16 | 90.00 | 14.47 | 4 | 93.25 | 14.58 | + 3.25 | |
| 4A | 22 | 107.41 | 18.38 | 5 | 115.00 | 12.71 | + 7.59 | |
| 4B | 17 | 92.77 | 13.64 | 3 | 102.33 | 17.99 | + 9.56 | |
| 4C | 16 | 85.75 | 14.15 | 4 | 94.00 | 15.33 | + 8.25 | |
| 5A | 18 | 115.11 | 27.33 | 6 | 127.50 | 21.16 | +12.39 | |
| 5B | 14 | 100.36 | 24.49 | 4 | 98.75 | 19.52 | − 1.61 | |
| 5C | 12 | 88.58 | 12.86 | 4 | 101.50 | 22.38 | +12.92 | |
| 6A | 20 | 115.80 | 26.64 | 6 | 120.33 | 9.88 | + 4.53 | |
| 6B | 15 | 103.47 | 19.12 | 4 | 104.75 | 21.15 | + 1.28 | |
| 6C | 14 | 82.21 | 13.69 | 3 | 88.67 | 11.09 | + 6.46 | |

a One-tail, based on mean square within.

**Table A-19**  Means and Standard Deviations of Gains in Total IQs after One Semester in Two Conditions within Eighteen Classrooms

| CLASS | CONTROL | | | EXPERIMENTAL | | | DIFFERENCES BETWEEN MEANS | $p^a < .05$ |
|---|---|---|---|---|---|---|---|---|
| | $N$ | MEAN | SD | $N$ | MEAN | SD | | |
| 1A | 18 | + 8.78 | 17.03 | 3 | +11.67 | 16.52 | + 2.89 | |
| 1B | 15 | +15.00 | 19.28 | 4 | + 3.75 | 18.90 | −11.25 | |
| 1C | 18 | + 6.94 | 15.07 | 2 | +41.50 | 7.50 | +34.56 | .0002 |
| 2A | 18 | + 0.06 | 9.70 | 6 | + 4.17 | 8.51 | + 4.11 | |
| 2B | 16 | + 1.63 | 9.63 | 3 | − 9.33 | 8.73 | −10.96 | |
| 2C | 14 | + 3.21 | 7.88 | 5 | + 2.40 | 6.47 | − 0.81 | |
| 3A | 14 | + 8.07 | 8.74 | 9 | + 5.89 | 5.57 | − 2.18 | |
| 3B | 17 | + 0.18 | 9.61 | 1 | +32.00 | 0.00 | +31.82 | .008 |
| 3C | 16 | − 5.63 | 12.53 | 4 | − 5.75 | 5.76 | − 0.12 | |
| 4A | 22 | −11.14 | 13.66 | 5 | −10.20 | 12.06 | + 0.94 | |
| 4B | 17 | − 1.94 | 12.44 | 3 | − 0.33 | 14.01 | + 1.61 | |
| 4C | 16 | + 1.00 | 7.73 | 4 | + 1.50 | 8.20 | + 0.50 | |
| 5A | 18 | + 9.61 | 12.93 | 6 | + 5.83 | 18.43 | − 3.78 | |
| 5B | 14 | + 1.29 | 12.23 | 4 | +17.25 | 6.76 | +15.96 | .02 |
| 5C | 12 | +10.25 | 13.97 | 4 | +14.50 | 12.38 | + 4.25 | |
| 6A | 20 | + 8.60 | 9.25 | 6 | + 9.50 | 4.35 | + 0.90 | |
| 6B | 15 | + 2.47 | 11.24 | 4 | + 5.25 | 8.84 | + 2.78 | |
| 6C | 14 | + 1.36 | 7.25 | 3 | + 1.67 | 3.30 | + 0.31 | |

a One-tail, based on mean square within.

**Table A-20**     Means and Standard Deviations of Gains
in Verbal IQs after One Semester in Two
Conditions within Eighteen Classrooms

| CLASS | CONTROL | | | EXPERIMENTAL | | | DIFFERENCE BETWEEN MEANS | $p^a < .05$ |
|---|---|---|---|---|---|---|---|---|
| | $N$ | MEAN | SD | $N$ | MEAN | SD | | |
| 1A | 18 | − 1.39 | 15.67 | 3 | + 1.00 | 8.64 | + 2.39 | |
| 1B | 15 | + 7.47 | 22.94 | 4 | − 9.00 | 13.36 | −16.47 | |
| 1C | 18 | − 3.83 | 14.40 | 2 | +34.50 | 0.50 | +38.33 | .001 |
| 2A | 18 | + 4.11 | 7.13 | 6 | + 7.33 | 10.45 | + 3.22 | |
| 2B | 16 | + 2.94 | 12.25 | 3 | − 2.00 | 6.68 | − 4.94 | |
| 2C | 14 | + 3.79 | 10.97 | 5 | − 0.40 | 8.31 | − 4.19 | |
| 3A | 14 | +17.36 | 13.03 | 9 | + 8.44 | 11.23 | − 8.92 | |
| 3B | 17 | + 3.88 | 10.98 | 1 | +27.00 | 0.00 | +23.12 | |
| 3C | 16 | −10.06 | 19.04 | 4 | −18.00 | 12.47 | − 7.94 | |
| 4A | 22 | −10.96 | 20.93 | 5 | + 8.00 | 61.47 | +18.96 | .01 |
| 4B | 17 | + 7.06 | 15.14 | 3 | − 6.33 | 20.73 | −13.39 | |
| 4C | 16 | + 8.06 | 7.75 | 4 | + 0.50 | 3.91 | − 7.56 | |
| 5A | 18 | +12.56 | 15.56 | 6 | − 2.17 | 20.68 | −14.73 | |
| 5B | 14 | + 1.00 | 8.61 | 4 | + 4.25 | 6.42 | + 3.25 | |
| 5C | 12 | +10.75 | 11.47 | 4 | +13.75 | 10.89 | + 3.00 | |
| 6A | 20 | + 7.75 | 11.53 | 6 | + 6.33 | 5.94 | − 1.42 | |
| 6B | 15 | + 1.27 | 10.23 | 4 | +11.00 | 12.06 | + 9.73 | |
| 6C | 14 | − 1.36 | 9.26 | 3 | − 1.33 | 19.60 | + 0.03 | |

a One-tail, based on mean square within.

**Table A-21**  Means and Standard Deviations of Gains in Reasoning IQs after One Semester in Two Conditions within Eighteen Classrooms

| CLASS | N | CONTROL MEAN | SD | N | EXPERIMENTAL MEAN | SD | DIFFERENCE BETWEEN MEANS | $p^a < .05$ |
|-------|---|------|-----|---|------|-----|---------|-----|
| 1A | 18 | +21.94 | 25.86 | 3 | +26.33 | 29.53 | + 4.39 | |
| 1B | 15 | +45.47 | 32.84 | 4 | +37.50 | 55.45 | − 7.97 | |
| 1C | 18 | +38.89 | 30.49 | 2 | +49.50 | 16.50 | +10.61 | |
| 2A | 18 | − 2.00 | 14.84 | 6 | + 1.33 | 13.92 | + 3.33 | |
| 2B | 16 | − 0.75 | 21.49 | 3 | −15.33 | 17.78 | −14.58 | |
| 2C | 14 | + 9.43 | 18.60 | 5 | + 8.60 | 12.50 | − 0.83 | |
| 3A | 14 | + 1.29 | 13.43 | 9 | + 2.89 | 13.02 | + 1.60 | |
| 3B | 17 | − 2.82 | 19.32 | 1 | +39.00 | 0.00 | +41.82 | .03 |
| 3C | 16 | − 0.19 | 16.11 | 4 | +10.75 | 19.68 | +10.94 | |
| 4A | 22 | −10.18 | 16.77 | 5 | − 5.40 | 10.89 | + 4.78 | |
| 4B | 17 | − 9.29 | 14.92 | 3 | + 5.67 | 7.54 | +14.96 | |
| 4C | 16 | − 3.75 | 15.17 | 4 | + 2.75 | 15.12 | + 6.50 | |
| 5A | 18 | + 7.61 | 18.53 | 6 | +10.50 | 22.49 | + 2.89 | |
| 5B | 14 | + 1.86 | 18.87 | 4 | +29.00 | 8.86 | +27.14 | .02 |
| 5C | 12 | + 9.58 | 20.23 | 4 | +17.50 | 15.98 | + 7.92 | |
| 6A | 20 | +11.10 | 16.21 | 6 | +11.50 | 8.85 | + 0.40 | |
| 6B | 15 | + 4.53 | 16.06 | 4 | + 3.25 | 11.01 | − 1.28 | |
| 6C | 14 | + 4.43 | 8.44 | 3 | + 6.67 | 10.21 | + 2.24 | |

a One-tail, based on mean square within.

**Table A-22**  Mean Gains in Vocabulary Test Scores[a] Shortly after Instituting the Experimental Program among Fifth- and Sixth-Grade Children

| CLASS | CONTROL | | EXPERIMENTAL | | EXPECTANCY ADVANTAGE | |
|---|---|---|---|---|---|---|
| | $N$ | GAIN | $N$ | GAIN | DIFFERENCE | ONE-TAIL $p < .10$[b] |
| 5A | 19 | −4.1 | 6 | −1.5 | + 2.6 | |
| 5B | 14 | −9.9 | 4 | +3.0 | +12.9 | .07 |
| 5C | 9 | +5.4 | 4 | +7.3 | + 1.9 | |
| 6A | 20 | −4.3 | 6 | +0.5 | + 4.8 | |
| 6B | 15 | −5.5 | 4 | +3.3 | + 8.8 | |
| 6C | 14 | +0.1 | 3 | −7.3 | − 7.4 | |
| TOTAL | 91 | −3.68 | 27 | +0.96 | + 4.64[c] | .08 |

[a] Percentile unit gains.
[b] Mean square within = 197.92.
[c] One year later, for fifth graders, this value was +2.92, NS.

Table A-23    Mean Gains in Work-Study Skills
Test Scores[a] Shortly after Instituting
the Experimental Program
among Fifth- and Sixth-Grade Children

| CLASS | CONTROL | | EXPERIMENTAL | | EXPECTANCY ADVANTAGE | |
| | N | GAIN | N | GAIN | DIFFERENCE | ONE-TAIL $p < .10$[b] |
|---|---|---|---|---|---|---|
| 5A | 19 | −3.4 | 6 | + 2.2 | + 5.6 | |
| 5B | 14 | +7.0 | 4 | +27.5 | +20.5 | .03 |
| 5C | 9 | +8.1 | 4 | +18.5 | +10.4 | |
| 6A | 20 | −3.4 | 6 | − 4.2 | − 0.8 | |
| 6B | 15 | +0.3 | 4 | +17.0 | +16.7 | .05 |
| 6C | 14 | −7.0 | 3 | + 7.3 | +14.3 | .10 |
| TOTAL | 91 | −0.60 | 27 | + 9.70 | +10.30[c] | .003 |

[a] Percentile unit gains.
[b] Mean square within = 265.51.
[c] One year later, for fifth graders, this value was +12.36, $p < .05$.

**Table A-24**        Means and Standard Deviations
of Total IQs after Two Years
in Two Conditions
within Fifteen Classrooms

| CLASS | CONTROL | | | EXPERIMENTAL | | | DIFFERENCE BETWEEN MEANS | $p^a < .05$ |
|---|---|---|---|---|---|---|---|---|
| | $N$ | MEAN | SD | $N$ | MEAN | SD | | |
| 1A | 14 | 117.21 | 20.70 | 1 | 97.00 | 0.00 | −20.21 | |
| 1B | 9 | 102.67 | 7.10 | 3 | 111.67 | 12.37 | + 9.00 | |
| 1C | 13 | 83.77 | 8.61 | 2 | 96.50 | 7.50 | +12.73 | |
| 2A | 16 | 117.44 | 16.53 | 4 | 128.50 | 4.92 | +11.06 | |
| 2B | 11 | 94.82 | 17.59 | 3 | 111.00 | 10.23 | +16.18 | |
| 2C | 12 | 85.50 | 8.09 | 2 | 81.00 | 3.00 | − 4.50 | |
| 3A | 9 | 108.67 | 16.17 | 6 | 104.50 | 16.72 | − 4.17 | |
| 3B | 13 | 107.08 | 23.73 | 1 | 97.00 | 0.00 | −10.08 | |
| 3C | 14 | 89.36 | 8.49 | 3 | 84.67 | 4.19 | − 4.69 | |
| 4A | 17 | 116.71 | 14.52 | 5 | 125.40 | 20.16 | + 8.69 | |
| 4B | 15 | 94.93 | 12.12 | 2 | 101.50 | 13.50 | + 6.57 | |
| 4C | 15 | 90.80 | 15.96 | 4 | 90.50 | 6.27 | − 0.30 | |
| 5A | 16 | 118.94 | 14.78 | 4 | 138.25 | 28.22 | +19.31 | .02 |
| 5B | 12 | 109.00 | 21.15 | 3 | 99.67 | 18.01 | − 9.33 | |
| 5C | 10 | 91.90 | 13.50 | 4 | 102.25 | 6.30 | +10.35 | |

$^a$ One-tail, based on mean square within.

Table A-25        Means and Standard Deviations of Verbal IQs after Two Years in Two Conditions within Fifteen Classrooms

| CLASS | CONTROL | | | EXPERIMENTAL | | | DIFFERENCE BETWEEN MEANS | $p^a < .05$ |
|-------|---|---|---|---|---|---|---|---|
| | $N$ | MEAN | SD | $N$ | MEAN | SD | | |
| 1A | 14 | 121.07 | 21.06 | 1 | 103.00 | 0.00 | −18.07 | |
| 1B | 9 | 90.11 | 13.21 | 3 | 114.00 | 16.97 | +23.89 | .05 |
| 1C | 13 | 83.85 | 6.67 | 2 | 90.00 | 10.00 | + 6.15 | |
| 2A | 16 | 120.63 | 21.02 | 4 | 130.25 | 12.05 | + 9.62 | |
| 2B | 11 | 94.00 | 22.46 | 3 | 107.00 | 17.28 | +13.00 | |
| 2C | 12 | 87.25 | 11.99 | 2 | 72.50 | 2.50 | −14.75 | |
| 3A | 9 | 105.44 | 14.69 | 6 | 109.17 | 16.28 | + 3.73 | |
| 3B | 13 | 110.31 | 25.20 | 1 | 104.00 | 0.00 | − 6.31 | |
| 3C | 14 | 86.71 | 14.32 | 3 | 81.67 | 10.66 | − 5.04 | |
| 4A | 17 | 115.00 | 15.42 | 5 | 125.60 | 22.68 | +10.60 | |
| 4B | 15 | 95.73 | 16.84 | 2 | 89.50 | 9.50 | − 6.23 | |
| 4C | 15 | 88.53 | 15.56 | 4 | 88.25 | 11.05 | − 0.28 | |
| 5A | 16 | 126.31 | 29.78 | 4 | 158.75 | 42.51 | +32.44 | .003 |
| 5B | 12 | 114.50 | 20.93 | 3 | 104.33 | 25.90 | −10.17 | |
| 5C | 10 | 92.20 | 22.60 | 4 | 100.50 | 9.07 | + 8.30 | |

a One-tail, based on mean square within.

**Table A-26**    Means and Standard Deviations of
Reasoning IQs after Two Years in Two
Conditions within Fifteen Classrooms

| CLASS | CONTROL | | | EXPERIMENTAL | | | DIFFERENCE BETWEEN MEANS | $p^a < .05$ |
|---|---|---|---|---|---|---|---|---|
| | $N$ | MEAN | SD | $N$ | MEAN | SD | | |
| 1A | 14 | 114.64 | 27.86 | 1 | 90.00 | 0.00 | −24.64 | |
| 1B | 9 | 121.22 | 13.05 | 3 | 111.00 | 10.23 | −10.22 | |
| 1C | 13 | 84.08 | 16.21 | 2 | 104.50 | 6.50 | +20.42 | |
| 2A | 16 | 117.19 | 19.43 | 4 | 136.75 | 28.03 | +19.56 | |
| 2B | 11 | 96.18 | 13.81 | 3 | 116.67 | 7.93 | +20.49 | |
| 2C | 12 | 84.50 | 18.77 | 2 | 91.00 | 11.00 | + 6.50 | |
| 3A | 9 | 114.11 | 24.94 | 6 | 100.83 | 24.63 | −13.28 | |
| 3B | 13 | 106.23 | 31.31 | 1 | 88.00 | 0.00 | −18.23 | |
| 3C | 14 | 92.93 | 13.76 | 3 | 88.00 | 3.74 | − 4.93 | |
| 4A | 17 | 123.06 | 26.23 | 5 | 125.00 | 18.60 | + 1.94 | |
| 4B | 15 | 94.87 | 11.73 | 2 | 121.50 | 22.50 | +26.63 | |
| 4C | 15 | 96.87 | 29.14 | 4 | 98.25 | 19.69 | + 1.38 | |
| 5A | 16 | 116.75 | 16.69 | 4 | 128.75 | 27.20 | +12.00 | |
| 5B | 12 | 105.42 | 26.44 | 3 | 94.67 | 10.34 | −10.75 | |
| 5C | 10 | 96.80 | 19.75 | 4 | 110.75 | 24.28 | +13.95 | |

ᵃ One-tail, based on mean square within.

Table A-27     Means and Standard Deviations of Gains
in Total IQs after Two Years in Two
Conditions within Fifteen Classrooms

| CLASS | $N$ | CONTROL MEAN | SD | $N$ | EXPERIMENTAL MEAN | SD | DIFFERENCE BETWEEN MEANS | $p^a < .05$ |
|---|---|---|---|---|---|---|---|---|
| 1A | 14 | +12.00 | 15.42 | 1 | + 2.00 | 0.00 | −10.00 | |
| 1B | 9 | +19.78 | 19.89 | 3 | +15.67 | 3.77 | − 4.11 | |
| 1C | 13 | +11.00 | 13.73 | 2 | +36.00 | 7.00 | +25.00 | .01 |
| 2A | 16 | +10.56 | 13.47 | 4 | +11.00 | 7.78 | + 0.44 | |
| 2B | 11 | + 8.00 | 11.54 | 3 | + 8.33 | 5.74 | + 0.33 | |
| 2C | 12 | + 5.58 | 7.33 | 2 | −13.00 | 0.00 | −18.58 | |
| 3A | 9 | +14.33 | 9.35 | 6 | + 2.50 | 9.57 | −11.83 | |
| 3B | 13 | + 4.00 | 16.53 | 1 | + 9.00 | 0.00 | + 5.00 | |
| 3C | 14 | − 9.86 | 10.70 | 3 | − 9.33 | 10.50 | + 0.53 | |
| 4A | 17 | − 5.77 | 12.58 | 5 | − 7.60 | 16.56 | − 1.83 | |
| 4B | 15 | − 8.40 | 12.19 | 2 | + 3.00 | 5.00 | +11.40 | |
| 4C | 15 | − 1.27 | 16.20 | 4 | + 1.75 | 7.40 | + 3.02 | |
| 5A | 16 | +10.88 | 14.22 | 4 | +17.50 | 22.68 | + 6.62 | |
| 5B | 12 | + 2.83 | 12.60 | 3 | +24.67 | 10.34 | +21.84 | .01 |
| 5C | 10 | + 8.70 | 11.77 | 4 | +16.00 | 9.22 | + 7.30 | |

[a] One-tail, based on mean square within.

**Table A-28**    Means and Standard Deviations of Gains in Verbal IQs after Two Years in Two Conditions within Fifteen Classrooms

| CLASS | | CONTROL | | | EXPERIMENTAL | | DIFFERENCE BETWEEN MEANS | $p^a < .05$ |
|---|---|---|---|---|---|---|---|---|
| | $N$ | MEAN | SD | $N$ | MEAN | SD | | |
| 1A | 14 | + 0.86 | 11.80 | 1 | + 3.00 | 0.00 | + 2.14 | |
| 1B | 9 | − 6.78 | 19.19 | 3 | − 3.33 | 2.87 | + 3.45 | |
| 1C | 13 | − 8.00 | 13.00 | 2 | +22.50 | 12.50 | +30.50 | .01 |
| 2A | 16 | + 8.25 | 16.79 | 4 | +12.25 | 19.02 | + 4.00 | |
| 2B | 11 | − 0.55 | 16.75 | 3 | + 3.33 | 12.92 | + 3.88 | |
| 2C | 12 | + 6.25 | 14.81 | 2 | −24.50 | 0.50 | −30.75 | .02$^b$ |
| 3A | 9 | +11.33 | 10.92 | 6 | + 4.17 | 4.06 | − 7.16 | |
| 3B | 13 | + 2.23 | 14.13 | 1 | + 9.00 | 0.00 | + 6.77 | |
| 3C | 14 | −22.64 | 16.63 | 3 | −27.67 | 21.00 | − 5.03 | |
| 4A | 17 | −12.29 | 16.70 | 5 | −23.80 | 23.78 | −11.51 | |
| 4B | 15 | −10.00 | 11.93 | 2 | − 7.00 | 3.00 | + 3.00 | |
| 4C | 15 | − 8.20 | 12.30 | 4 | + 0.75 | 6.30 | + 8.95 | |
| 5A | 16 | +12.44 | 26.42 | 4 | +31.25 | 27.40 | +18.81 | .03 |
| 5B | 12 | + 2.92 | 10.17 | 3 | +19.67 | 9.74 | +16.75 | |
| 5C | 10 | + 9.30 | 14.64 | 4 | +15.25 | 9.23 | + 5.95 | |

[a] One-tail, based on mean square within.
[b] Two-tail.

**Table A-29**      Means and Standard Deviations of Gains in Reasoning IQs after Two Years in Two Conditions within Fifteen Classrooms

| CLASS | N | CONTROL MEAN | SD | N | EXPERIMENTAL MEAN | SD | DIFFERENCE BETWEEN MEANS | $p^a < .05$ |
|---|---|---|---|---|---|---|---|---|
| 1A | 14 | +25.29 | 30.69 | 1 | 0.00 | 0.00 | −25.29 | |
| 1B | 9 | +70.00 | 45.01 | 3 | +65.67 | 31.48 | − 4.33 | |
| 1C | 13 | +58.92 | 29.77 | 2 | +51.00 | 2.00 | − 7.92 | |
| 2A | 16 | +15.06 | 19.73 | 4 | +18.75 | 16.33 | + 3.69 | |
| 2B | 11 | +19.18 | 14.26 | 3 | +14.33 | 18.37 | − 4.85 | |
| 2C | 12 | + 8.00 | 16.10 | 2 | 0.00 | 2.00 | − 8.00 | |
| 3A | 9 | +19.56 | 17.21 | 6 | + 1.33 | 18.44 | −18.23 | |
| 3B | 13 | + 8.46 | 29.75 | 1 | +10.00 | 0.00 | + 1.54 | |
| 3C | 14 | + 5.71 | 15.53 | 3 | +11.67 | 9.84 | + 5.96 | |
| 4A | 17 | + 3.29 | 20.68 | 5 | + 4.60 | 24.03 | + 1.31 | |
| 4B | 15 | − 6.47 | 16.43 | 2 | +19.50 | 10.50 | +25.97 | |
| 4C | 15 | + 8.80 | 29.61 | 4 | + 7.00 | 15.02 | − 1.80 | |
| 5A | 16 | +10.19 | 18.00 | 4 | +10.50 | 26.37 | + 0.31 | |
| 5B | 12 | + 5.33 | 20.56 | 3 | +32.00 | 13.37 | +26.67 | .05 |
| 5C | 10 | +16.20 | 25.33 | 4 | +26.75 | 17.14 | +10.55 | |

[a] One-tail, based on mean square within.

**Table A-30**              Retest Reliabilities
                           after One Year

| | TOTAL IQ | | VERBAL IQ | | REASONING IQ | |
|---|---|---|---|---|---|---|
| | CONTROL | EXPERI-MENTAL | CONTROL | EXPERI-MENTAL | CONTROL | EXPERI-MENTAL |
| *Grades* | | | | | | |
| 1 | +.59 | +.75 | +.74 | +.77 | +.46 | +.26 |
| 2 | .79 | .82 | .71 | .83 | .58 | .62 |
| 3 | .70 | .72 | .68 | .60 | .41 | .67 |
| 4 | .80 | .90 | .83 | .77 | .63 | .73 |
| 5 | .79 | .75 | .78 | .81 | .46 | .31 |
| 6 | .88 | .97 | .89 | .88 | .74 | .87 |
| *Tracks* | | | | | | |
| Fast | .66 | .73 | .67 | .71 | .46 | .51 |
| Medium | .58 | .80 | .77 | .87 | .36 | .24 |
| Slow | .61 | .25 | .72 | .49 | .25 | .37 |
| TOTAL | .74 | .78 | .75 | .76 | .50 | .47 |
| *N* | 255 | 65 | 269 | 68 | 255 | 65 |

### Table A-31     Intellectual Performance Gain after One Year as a Function of Pretest IQ

| | TOTAL IQ | | VERBAL IQ | | REASONING IQ | |
|---|---|---|---|---|---|---|
| | CONTROL | EXPERI-MENTAL | CONTROL | EXPERI-MENTAL | CONTROL | EXPERI-MENTAL |
| *Grades* | | | | | | |
| 1 | —.65[a] | —.73[c] | —.36[c] | —.78[c] | —.80[a] | —.93[b] |
| 2 | —.37[b] | +.39 | —.37[b] | +.52[c] | —.28[c] | +.17 |
| 3 | —.07 | —.09 | +.26[c] | —.41 | —.37[c] | —.08 |
| 4 | —.14 | —.01 | —.19 | +.17 | +.04 | —.18 |
| 5 | —.02 | +.07 | —.01 | +.03 | —.40[c] | —.18 |
| 6 | +.05 | +.49 | +.11 | +.34 | +.01 | +.35 |
| *Tracks* | | | | | | |
| Fast | —.29[b] | +.05 | —.01 | +.09 | —.29[b] | —.10 |
| Medium | —.57[a] | +.11 | —.27[c] | +.46[c] | —.77[a] | —.62[c] |
| Slow | —.48[a] | —.76[a] | —.39[a] | —.70[a] | —.74[a] | —.06 |
| TOTAL | —.30[a] | —.05 | —.08 | +.04 | —.54[a] | —.28[c] |
| N | 255 | 65 | 269 | 68 | 255 | 65 |

[a] $p < .001$, two-tail.
[b] $p < .01$, two-tail.
[c] $p < .10$, two-tail.

# References

Adair, J. G., and Joyce Epstein.    Verbal cues in the mediation of experimenter bias. Paper read at Midwestern Psychological Association, Chicago, May 1967.

Allport, G. W.    The role of expectancy. In H. Cantril (Ed.) *Tensions that cause wars*. Urbana, Ill.: University of Illinois, 1950. Pp. 43–78.

Allport, G. W.    Mental health: a generic attitude. *Journal of Religion and Health*, 1964, *4*, 7–21.

Anderson, Margaret, and Rhea White.    A survey of work on ESP and teacher-pupil attitudes. *Journal of Parapsychology*, 1958, *22*, 246–268.

Asbell, B.    Not like other children. *Redbook*, October 1963, *121*, 65, 114–118, 120.

Aronson, E., and J. M. Carlsmith.    Performance expectancy as a determinant of actual performance. *Journal of Abnormal and Social Psychology*, 1962, *65*, 178–182.

Aronson, E., J. M. Carlsmith, and J. M. Darley.    The effects of expectancy on volunteering for an unpleasant experience. *Journal of Abnormal and Social Psychology*, 1963, *66*, 220–224.

Barber, T. X., and D. S. Calverley.    Toward a theory of hypnotic behavior: effects on suggestibility of defining the situation as hypnosis and defining response to suggestions as easy. *Journal of Abnormal and Social Psychology*, 1964, *68*, 585–593.

Bavelas, A.    Personal communication, December 6, 1965.

Becker, H. S.    Social class variations in the teacher-pupil relationship. *Journal of Educational Sociology*, 1952, *25*, 451–465.

Beecher, H. K.    The powerful placebo. *Journal of the American Medical Association*, 1955, *159*, 1602–1606.

Beecher, H. K.    Surgery as placebo. *Journal of the American Medical Association*, 1961, *176*, 1102–1107.

Beecher, H. K.    Nonspecific forces surrounding disease and the treatment of disease. *Journal of the American Medical Association*, 1962, *179*, 437–440.

Beecher, H. K.    Pain: one mystery solved. *Science*, 1966, *151*, 840–841.

Beez, W. V.    Influence of biased psychological reports on teacher behavior. Unpublished manuscript, Indiana University, 1967.

Bernstein, B.    Language and social class. *British Journal of Psychology*, 1960, *11*, 271–276.

Biddle, B. J.    The integration of teacher effectiveness research. In B. J. Biddle and W. J. Ellena (Eds.) *Contemporary research on teacher effectiveness.* New York: Holt, Rinehart and Winston, 1964. Pp. 1–40.

Biddle, B. J., and R. S. Adams.    *An analysis of classroom activities.* Center for Research in Social Behavior, University of Missouri, 1967.

Boring, E. G.    Perspective: artifact and control. In R. Rosenthal and R. L. Rosnow (Eds.) *Artifact in social research* (tentative title). New York: Academic Press, in press.

Brookover, W. B., E. Erickson, D. Hamachek, L. Joiner, Jean LePere, Ann Patterson, and S. Thomas.    Self-concept of ability and school achievement. Paper read at International Sociological Association, Evian, France, September 1966.

Bruner, J. S.    *The process of education.* Cambridge, Mass.: Harvard University Press, 1960.

Bruner, J. S.    The growth of mind. *American Psychologist*, 1965, *20*, 1007–1017.

Burnham, R.    Experimenter bias and lesion labeling. Unpublished paper, Purdue University, 1966.

Bushard, B. L.    The U.S. Army's Mental Hygiene Consultation Service. In *Symposium on preventive and social psychiatry.* Washington, D.C.: Walter Reed Army Institute of Research, 1957. Pp. 431–443.

Cahen, L. S.    Experimental manipulation of bias in teachers' scoring of subjective tests. Paper read at American Psychological Association, New York, September 1966.

Carlsmith, J. M., and E. Aronson.    Some hedonic consequences of the confirmation and disconfirmation of expectancies. *Journal of Abnormal and Social Psychology*, 1963, *66*, 151–156.

Chapman, L. J., and Jean P. Chapman.    Genesis of popular but erroneous psycho-diagnostic observations. *Journal of Abnormal Psychology*, 1967, *72*, 193–204.

Charters, W. W., Jr.    The social background of teaching. In N. L. Gage (Ed.) *Handbook of research on teaching.* Skokie, Ill.: Rand McNally, 1963. Pp. 715–813.

Clark, B. R.    *Educating the expert society.* San Francisco, Calif.: Chandler Publishing Company, 1962.

Clark, K. B.    Educational stimulation of racially disadvantaged children. In A. H. Passow (Ed.) *Education in depressed areas.* New

York: Bureau of Publications, Teachers College, Columbia University, 1963. Pp. 142–162.

Cloward, R. A., and J. A. Jones. Social class: educational attitudes and participation. In A. H. Passow (Ed.) *Education in depressed areas.* New York: Bureau of Publications, Teachers College, Columbia University, 1963. Pp. 190–216.

Coffey, H. S., R. M. Dorcus, E. M. Glaser, T. C. Greening, J. B. Marks, and I. G. Sarason. *Learning to work.* Los Angeles, Calif.: Human Interaction Research Institute, 1964.

Coffin, T. E. Some conditions of suggestion and suggestibility. *Psychological Monographs,* 1941, *53*, No. 4 (Whole No. 241).

Conn, L. K., C. N. Edwards, R. Rosenthal, and D. P. Crowne. Emotion perception and response to teacher expectancy in elementary school children. Unpublished paper, Harvard University, 1967.

Cook, D. L. The Hawthorne effect: fact or artifact. Paper read at American Educational Research Association, Chicago, February 1966.

Cordaro, L., and J. R. Ison. Observer bias in classical conditioning of the planarian. *Psychological Reports,* 1963, *13*, 787–789.

Crow, Linda. Public attitudes and expectations as a disturbing variable in experimentation and therapy. Unpublished paper, Harvard University, 1964.

Crowne, D. P., and D. Marlowe. *The approval motive.* New York: Wiley, 1964.

Davis, A., and J. Dollard. *Children of bondage.* Washington, D.C.: American Council on Education, 1940.

Deutsch, M. The disadvantaged child and the learning process. In A. H. Passow (Ed.) *Education in depressed areas.* New York: Bureau of Publications, Teachers College, Columbia University, 1963. Pp. 163–179.

Deutsch, M., J. A. Fishman, L. Kogan, R. North, and M. Whiteman. Guidelines for testing minority group children. *Journal of Social Issues,* 1964, *20*, 129–145.

Drayer, C. S. (Chairman). *Disaster fatigue.* Washington, D.C.: Committee on Civil Defense, American Psychiatric Association, 1956.

Dyer, H. S. Signals for innovation. Paper read at Ohio Conference on Educational Leadership, Columbus, October 1965.

Entwisle, Doris R. Attensity: factors of specific set in school learning. *Harvard Educational Review,* 1961, *31*, 84–101.

Festinger, L. *A theory of cognitive dissonance.* New York: Harper & Row, 1957.

Fisher, S., J. O. Cole, K. Rickels, and E. H. Uhlenhuth. Drug-set interaction: the effect of expectations on drug response in out-patients. In P. B. Bradley, F. Flügel, and P. Hoch (Eds.)  *Neuro-psychopharmacology*, Vol. 3. New York: Elsevier, 1964. Pp. 149–156.

Flanagan, J. C.  *Test of general ability: technical report*. Chicago: Science Research Associates, 1960.

Flowers, C. E.  Effects of an arbitrary accelerated group placement on the tested academic achievement of educationally disadvantaged students. Unpublished doctoral dissertation, Teachers College, Columbia University, 1966.

Fode, K. L.  The effect of non-visual and non-verbal interaction on experimenter bias. Unpublished master's thesis, University of North Dakota, 1960.

Frank, J.  Discussion of Eysenck's "The effects of psychotherapy." *International Journal of Psychiatry*, 1965, *1*, 150–152.

Friedman, Pearl.  A second experiment on interviewer bias. *Sociometry*, 1942, *5*, 378–379.

Fromm-Reichmann, Frieda.  *Principles of intensive psychotherapy*. Chicago: University of Chicago Press, 1950.

Getter, H., R. C. Mulry, C. Holland, and Patricia Walker.  Experimenter bias and the WAIS. Unpublished data, University of Connecticut, 1967.

Gibson, G.  Aptitude tests. *Science*, 1965, *149*, 583.

Goffman, E.  *Asylums*. Garden City, N.Y.: Anchor-Doubleday, 1961.

Goldstein, A. P.  Therapist and client expectation of personality change in psychotherapy. *Journal of Counseling Psychology*, 1960, *7*, 180–184.

Goldstein, A. P.  *Therapist-patient expectancies in psychotherapy*. New York: Pergamon, 1962.

Gordon, L. V., and M. A. Durea.  The effect of discouragement on the revised Stanford Binet Scale. *Journal of Genetic Psychology*, 1948, *73*, 201–207.

Goslin, D. A.  The social impact of testing in guidance. Unpublished paper, Russell Sage Foundation, 1966.

Greenblatt, M.  Controls in clinical research. Unpublished paper, Tufts University School of Medicine, 1964.

Gruenberg, B. C.  *The story of evolution*. Princeton, N.J.: Van Nostrand, 1929.

Guthrie, E. R.  *The psychology of human conflict*. New York: Harper & Row, 1938.

Halsey, A. H., Jean Floud, and C. A. Anderson (Eds.).  *Education, economy, and society*. New York: Free Press, 1961.

Hanson, R. H., and E. S. Marks.  Influence of the interviewer on the accuracy of survey results. *Journal of the American Statistical Association*, 1958, *53*, 635–655.

Harlem Youth Opportunities Unlimited, Inc.  *Youth in the ghetto*. New York: HARYOU, 1964.

Harvey, O. J., and W. F. Clapp.  Hope, expectancy, and reactions to the unexpected. *Journal of Personality and Social Psychology*, 1965, *2*, 45–52.

Harvey, S. M.  Preliminary investigation of the interview. *British Journal of Psychology*, 1938, *28*, 263–287.

Havighurst, R. J.  Education for the great society. *The Instructor*, September 1965, *75*, 31, 62, 65–66.

Heine, R. W., and H. Trosman.  Initial expectations of the doctor-patient interaction as a factor in continuance in psychotherapy. *Psychiatry*, 1960, *23*, 275–278.

Heller, K., and A. P. Goldstein.  Client dependency and therapist expectancy as relationship maintaining variables in psychotherapy. *Journal of Consulting Psyschology*, 1961, *25*, 371–375.

Hillson, H. T., and Florence C. Myers.  *The demonstration guidance project: 1957–1962*. New York: New York City Board of Education, 1963.

Honigfeld, G.  Non-specific factors in treatment. *Diseases of the Nervous System*, 1964, *25*, 145–156, 225–239.

Hurwitz, Susan, and Virginia Jenkins.  Effects of experimenter expectancy on performance of simple learning tasks. Unpublished paper, Harvard University, 1966.

Hyman, H. H., W. J. Cobb, J. J. Feldman, C. W. Hart, and C. H. Stember.  *Interviewing in social research*. Chicago: University of Chicago Press, 1954.

Ingraham, L. H., and G. M. Harrington.  Psychology of the scientist: XVI. Experience of $E$ as a variable in reducing experimenter bias. *Psychological Reports*, 1966, *19*, 455–461.

Jacobson, Lenore.  Explorations of variations in educational achievement among Mexican children, grades one to six. Unpublished doctoral dissertation, University of California, Berkeley, 1966.

Jastrow, J.  *Fact and fable in psychology*. Boston: Houghton Mifflin, 1900.

Kagan, J.  Reflection-impulsivity: the generality and dynamics of conceptual tempo. *Journal of Abnormal Psychology*, 1966, *71*, 17–24.

Kahl, J. A.  "Common man" boys. In A. H. Halsey, Jean Floud, and C. A. Anderson (Eds.) *Education, economy, and society*. New York: Free Press, 1961. Pp. 348–366.

Katz, I.  Review of evidence relating to effects of desegregation on the intellectual performance of Negroes. *American Psychologist,* 1964, *19,* 381–399.

Katz, I., and M. Cohen.    The effects of training Negroes upon co-operative problem solving in biracial teams. *Journal of Abnormal and Social Psychology,* 1962, *64,* 319–325.

Kelly, G. A.    *The psychology of personal constructs.* New York: Norton, 1955.

Kennedy, J. L.    Experiments on "unconscious whispering." *Psychological Bulletin* (Abstract), 1938, *35,* 526.

Kluckhohn, Florence R.    Dominant and variant value orientations. In C. Kluckhohn and H. A. Murray (Eds.) *Personality in nature, society, and culture,* Second edition. New York: Knopf, 1953. Pp. 342–357.

Kobler, A. L., and E. Stotland.    *The end of hope: a social-clinical study of suicide.* New York: Free Press, 1964.

Kramer, E., and E. P. Brennan.    Hypnotic susceptibility of schizophrenic patients. *Journal of Abnormal and Social Psychology,* 1964, *69,* 657–659.

Kvaraceus, W. C.    Disadvantaged children and youth: programs of promise or pretense? *Proceedings of the 17th annual state conference on educational research,* California Advisory Council on Educational Research. Burlingame: California Teachers' Association, 1965. Mimeo.

Larrabee, L. L., and L. D. Kleinsasser.    The effect of experimenter bias on WISC performance. Unpublished paper. St. Louis, Mo.: Psychological Associates, 1967.

Lesse, S.    Placebo reactions and spontaneous rhythms in psychotherapy. *Archives of General Psychiatry,* 1964, *10,* 497–505.

Levitt, E. E., and J. P. Brady.    Expectation and performance in hypnotic phenomena. *Journal of Abnormal and Social Psychology,* 1964, *69,* 572–574.

Levy, L. H., and T. B. Orr.    The social psychology of Rorschach validity research. *Journal of Abnormal and Social Psychology,* 1959, *58,* 79–83.

Lindzey, G.    A note on interviewer bias. *Journal of Applied Psychology,* 1951, *35,* 182–184.

Loban, W. D.    Mastery of conventional usage and grammar. Unpublished report to the U.S. Office of Education, 1964.

*Look* Editorial Board.    Sweeney's miracle. *Look.* November 16, 1965, 117–118.

Loranger, A. W., C. T. Prout, and Mary A. White.    The placebo effect in psychiatric drug research. *Journal of the American Medical Association,* 1961, *176,* 920–925.

McClelland, D. C. *The achieving society.* Princeton, N.J.: Van Nostrand, 1961.

McGuire, W. J. Attitudes and opinions. *Annual Review of Psychology,* 1966, *17,* 475–514.

MacKinnon, D. W. The nature and nurture of creative talent. *American Psychologist,* 1962, *17,* 484–495.

Marwit, S. J., and J. E. Marcia. Tester-bias and response to projective instruments. *Journal of Consulting Psychology,* 1967, *31,* 253–258.

Masling, J. Differential indoctrination of examiners and Rorschach responses. *Journal of Consulting Psychology,* 1965, *29,* 198–201.

Menninger, K. Review of: J. S. Bockoven, *Moral treatment in American psychiatry* (New York: Springer, 1963). *Bulletin of the Menninger Clinic,* 1964, *28,* 274–275.

Merton, R. K. The self-fulfilling prophecy. *Antioch Review,* 1948, *8,* 193–210. Also in Merton, R. K. *Social theory and social structure.* New York: Free Press, 1957. Pp. 421–436.

Moll, A. *Hypnotism,* Fourth edition. New York: Scribner, 1898.

Mulry, R. C. Personal communication, 1966.

Nichols, R. C. Schools and the disadvantaged. *Science,* 1966, *154,* 1312–1314.

Orne, M. T. The nature of hypnosis: artifact and essence. *Journal of Abnormal and Social Psychology,* 1959, *58,* 277–299.

Orne, M. T. On the social psychology of the psychological experiment: with particular reference to demand characteristics and their implications. *American Psychologist,* 1962, *17,* 776–783.

Passow, A. H. (Ed.). *Education in depressed areas.* New York: Bureau of Publications, Teachers College, Columbia University, 1963.

Péquignot, H. L'equation personnelle du juge. *Semaine des Hopitaux,* 1966, *14,* (Mars 20), Supplement 11, 4–11.

Pfungst, O. *Clever Hans (the horse of Mr. Von Osten): a contribution to experimental, animal, and human psychology.* Translated by C. L. Rahn. New York: Holt, Rinehart and Winston, 1911, reissued in 1965.

Pincus, G. Control of conception by hormonal steroids. *Science,* 1966, *153,* 493–500.

Pitt, C. C. V. An experimental study of the effects of teachers' knowledge or incorrect knowledge of pupil IQ's on teachers' attitudes and practices and pupils' attitudes and achievement. Unpublished doctoral dissertation, Columbia University, 1956.

Polanyi, M. The unaccountable element in science. *Transactions of the Bose Research Institute,* 1961, *24,* 175–184.

Potter, V. R.    Society and science. *Science*, 1964, *146*, 1018–1022.

*Quarterly Journal of Studies on Alcohol* Editorial Staff.    Mortality in delirium tremens. *North Dakota Review of Alcoholism*, 1959, *4*, 3. Abstract of Gunne, L. M. Mortaliteten vid delirium tremens. *Nord. Med.*, 1958, *60*, 1021–1024.

Ratner, S.    Personal communication, 1967.

Reed, C. F., and P. N. Witt.    Factors contributing to unexpected reactions in two human drug-placebo experiments. *Confinia Psychiatrica*, 1965, *8*, 57–68.

Rice, S. A.    Contagious bias in the interview: a methodological note. *American Journal of Sociology*, 1929, *35*, 420–423.

Riessman, F.    *The culturally deprived child.* New York: Harper & Row, 1962.

Riessman, F.    Teachers of the poor: a five point plan. *Proceedings of the 17th annual state conference on educational research.* California Advisory Council on Educational Research. Burlingame: California Teachers' Association, 1965. Mimeo.

Rivlin, H. N.    *Teachers for our big city schools.* New York: Anti-Defamation League of B'Nai B'Rith, undated.

Roethlisberger, F. J., and W. J. Dickson.    *Management and the worker.* Cambridge, Mass.: Harvard University Press, 1939.

Rose, A.    *The Negro in America.* Boston: Beacon, 1956.

Rosen, B. C.    Race, ethnicity and the achievement syndrome. *American Sociological Review*, 1959, *24*, 47–60.

Rosen, N. A., and S. M. Sales.    Behavior in a nonexperiment: the effects of behavioral field research on the work performance of factory employees. *Journal of Applied Psychology*, 1966, *50*, 165–171.

Rosenthal, R.    The effect of the experimenter on the results of psychological research. In B. A. Maher (Ed.) *Progress in experimental personality research*, Vol. I. New York: Academic, 1964. Pp. 79–114.

Rosenthal, R.    Clever Hans: a case study of scientific method. Introduction to O. Pfungst, *Clever Hans: (the horse of Mr. Von Osten).* New York: Holt, Rinehart and Winston, 1965. Pp. ix–xlii.

Rosenthal, R.    *Experimenter effects in behavioral research.* New York: Appleton, 1966.

Rosenthal, R.    Experimenter effects. In R. L. Rosnow and R. Rosenthal (Eds.) *Artifact in social research* (tentative title). New York: Academic, in press.

Rosenthal, R., and K. L. Fode.    The effect of experimenter bias on the performance of the albino rat. *Behavioral Science*, 1963, *8*, 183–189.

Rosenthal, R., and E. S. Halas.    Experimenter effect in the study of invertebrate behavior. *Psychological Reports*, 1962, *11*, 251–256.

Rosenthal, R., and Lenore Jacobson.    Teachers' expectancies: determinants of pupils' IQ gains. *Psychological Reports*, 1966, *19*, 115–118.

Rosenthal, R., and Lenore Jacobson.    Self-fulfilling prophecies in the classroom: teachers' expectations as unintended determinants of pupils' intellectual competence. In M. Deutsch, I. Katz, and A. Jensen (Eds.) *Race, social class, and psychological development.* New York: Holt, Rinehart and Winston, in press.

Rosenthal, R., and R. Lawson.    A longitudinal study of the effects of experimenter bias on the operant learning of laboratory rats. *Journal of Psychiatric Research*, 1964, *2*, 61–72.

Rotter, J. B.    *Social learning and clinical psychology.* Englewood Cliffs, N.J.: Prentice-Hall, 1954.

Sacks, Eleanor L.    Intelligence scores as a function of experimentally established social relationships between child and examiner. *Journal of Abnormal and Social Psychology*, 1952, *47*, 354–358.

Sampson, E. E., and Linda B. Sibley.    A further examination of the confirmation or nonconfirmation of expectancies and desires. *Journal of Personality and Social Psychology*, 1965, *2*, 133–137.

Sattler, J. M., W. A. Hillix, and Linda A. Neher.    The halo effect in examiner scoring of intelligence test responses. Unpublished paper, San Diego State College, 1967.

Schmeidler, Gertrude, and R. A. McConnell.    *ESP and personality patterns.* New Haven, Conn.: Yale University Press, 1958.

Schofield, W.    *Psychotherapy: the purchase of friendship.* Englewood Cliffs, N.J.: Prentice-Hall, 1964.

Schwab, W. B.    Looking backward: an appraisal of two field trips. *Human Organization*, 1965, *24*, 373–380.

Scott, J. P.    Critical periods in behavioral development. *Science*, 1962, *138*, 949–958.

Sexton, Patricia C.    *Education and income.* New York: Viking, 1961.

Shapiro, A. K.    A contribution to a history of the placebo effect. *Behavioral Science*, 1960, *5*, 109–135.

Shapiro, A. K.    Factors contributing to the placebo effect. *American Journal of Psychotherapy*, 1964, *18*, 73–88.

Sheard, M. H.    The influence of doctor's attitude on the patient's response to antidepressant medication. *Journal of Nervous and Mental Diseases*, 1963, *136*, 555–560.

Shor, R. E.    Shared patterns of nonverbal normative expectations in automobile driving. *Journal of Social Psychology*, 1964, *62*, 155–163.

Sommer, R.   Rorschach M responses and intelligence. *Journal of Clinical Psychology*, 1958, *14*, 58–61.

Stanton, A. H., and M. S. Schwartz.   *The mental hospital.* New York: Basic Books, 1954.

Stanton, F.   Further contributions at the twentieth anniversary of the Psychological Corporation and to honor its founder, James McKeen Cattel. *Journal of Applied Psychology*, 1942, *26*, 16–17.

Stanton, F., and K. H. Baker.   Interviewer bias and the recall of incompletely learned materials. *Sociometry*, 1942, *5*, 123–134.

Stevenson, H. W.   Social reinforcement of children's behavior. In L. P. Lipsitt and C. C. Spiker (Eds.) *Advances in child development and behavior*, Vol. 2. New York: Academic, 1965. Pp. 97–126.

Strauss, M. E.   Examiner expectancy: effects on Rorschach performance. Unpublished doctoral dissertation, Harvard University, 1967.

Strodtbeck, F. L.   Family integration, values, and achievement. In A. H. Halsey, Jean Floud, and C. A. Anderson (Eds.) *Education, economy, and society*. New York: Free Press, 1961. Pp. 315–347.

Strupp, H. H., and L. Luborsky (Eds.).   *Research in psychotherapy*, Vol. 2. Washington, D.C.: American Psychological Association, 1962.

Taylor, Gretchen.   The effect of hospital staff expectations upon patients' disposition. Unpublished paper, Harvard University, 1966.

Theye, F. W., and P. H. Wright.   The effects of graduated cues on intelligence test performance. Paper read at Midwestern Psychological Association, Chicago, May 1967.

Thompson, R., and J. V. McConnell.   Classical conditioning in the planarian, *dugesia dorotocephala. Journal of Comparative and Physiological Psychology*, 1955, *48*, 65–68.

Thorndike, R. L.   Intellectual status and intellectual growth. *Journal of Educational Psychology*, 1966, *57*, 121–127.

Tolman, E. C.   *Purposive behavior in animals and men.* New York: Appleton, 1932.

U.S. Office of Education.   *Focus on Title I: better schooling for educationally deprived children*, OE #35077, U.S. Department of Health, Education, and Welfare, U.S. Government Printing Office, 0-791-494, 1965.

Walker, Helen M., and J. Lev.   *Statistical inference.* New York: Holt, Rinehart and Winston, 1953.

Ware, J. R., B. Kowal, and R. A. Baker, Jr.   The role of experimenter attitude and contingent reinforcement in a vigilance task.

Unpublished paper, U.S. Army Armor Human Research Unit, Fort Knox, Kentucky, 1963.

Warner, L., and Mildred Raible. Telepathy in the psychophysical laboratory. *Journal of Parapsychology*, 1937, *1*, 44–51.

Warner, W. L., R. J. Havighurst, and M. B. Loeb. *Who shall Be educated?* New York: Harper & Row, 1944.

Wartenberg-Ekren, Ursula. The effect of experimenter knowledge of a subject's scholastic standing on the performance of a reasoning task. Unpublished master's thesis, Marquette University, 1962.

Whyte, W. F. *Street corner society*. Chicago: University of Chicago Press, 1943.

Wilson, A. B. Social stratification and academic achievement. In A. H. Passow (Ed.) *Education in depressed areas*. New York: Bureau of Publications, Teachers College, Columbia University, 1963. Pp. 217–235.

Wrightstone, J. W., S. D. McClelland, Judith I. Krugman, H. Hoffman, N. Tieman, and Linda Young. *Assessment of the demonstration guidance project*. New York: Bureau of Educational Research, Board of Education of the City of New York, undated (circa 1964).

Wyatt, D. F., and D. T. Campbell. A study of interviewer bias as related to interviewers' expectations and own opinions. *International Journal of Opinion and Attitude Research*, 1950, *4*, 77–83.

Wysocki, B. A. Assessment of intelligence level by the Rorschach test as compared with objective tests. *Journal of Educational Psychology*, 1957, *48*, 113–117.

Yando, Regina M., and J. Kagan. The effect of teacher tempo on the child. Unpublished paper, Harvard University, 1966.

Zusman, J. Some explanations of the changing appearance of psychotic patients. *International Journal of Psychiatry*, 1967, *3*, 216–237.

# INDEXES ❧

# Index
# of Names

# Subject Index

Ability grouping, 58 63–64
Achievement, and "attention," 50
  and federal aid, 48, 50–51
  and language, 50
  and lower-class children, 48–49
  and Mexican appearance, 54–55
  motivation for, 49–51
  school marks, 99–105, 124–125, 128–129
  tests of, 55, 105–106, 125–126
  training for, 49
American appearance, 54–55
Appearance, and IQ gain, 82, 94, 127, 135–136
  ethnic, 54–55, 82, 127, 135–136

Bank failure, 3
"Betsy," 90–91

Clever Hans, 36–37
Common-man boys, 49
"Constantine," 89
Control groups, 168ff.
  ethical considerations, 173
Crest School Experiment, 138ff.
  communication of expectancy, 162

Disadvantaged children, 47ff.
Double-blind, 18–19
"Douglas," 92–93
Drugs, 14–19

ESP, 25
Ethical considerations, 173

Examiner behavior, and IQ scores, 33
Examiner expectancy, 32–35
Expectancy, and animal behavior, 35ff., 160–161
  and athletics, 5
  and behavioral research, 21ff.
  and Block Design test, 32–33
  and bowling, 4
  of clinical staffs, 19–20
  of clinician, 11ff.
  communication of, 4, 28–30, 160–162
  controls for effects of, 169ff.
  and delirium tremens, 13–14
  and disaster reactions, 5
  and drug efficacy, 15–17
  and economic phenomena, 3
  and ESP research, 25
  and experimental psychology, 23ff.
  of experimenter, 21ff.
  and healing, 11ff.
  and hospital discharge, 19–20
  and hypnosis, 11–12
  and industrial performance, 5–6
  and ink-blot tests, 23–24, 31–32
  and intellectual performance, 31ff.
    *See also* Teacher expectancy
  of interviewer, 22–23
  and learning in mazes, 37–38
  and learning in rats, 37–44
  and learning in Skinner boxes, 38–40
  and learning in worms, 40–41
  and mathematical reasoning experiments, 34–35
  and medical prognoses, 14–15
  and mental illness, 13
  and mental retardation, 19, 145–146

[ 237 ]

371.26
R81

# Date Due